REFLECTIONS

IN A

GLASS EYE

Essays in the Time of COVID

Kenneth Ring

Published by Wheatmark®
2030 East Speedway Boulevard, Suite 106
Tucson, Arizona 85719 USA
www.wheatmark.com

ISBN: 978-1-62787-909-5
LCCN: 2021918968

To Kevin Williams,
my indispensable webmaster who makes all things
possible for me, at least digitally speaking

Contents

Preface

A couple of years ago, after having written about twenty books over the last half of my life (I was a late bloomer when it came to writing) and reached the venerable age of 83, I decided to retire my figurative pen and devote myself to watching television and Netflix. Well, not entirely. My fingers were still itchy to write something, so I decided I might take up the blogging life. Which is how I became a blogger.

After a while, I had managed to write a fair number of blogs and found a small but appreciative audience for them. And that's how things stood until just recently when it occurred to me that if I were to consider these blogs *essays*, I might be able to cull some of my better offerings and collect them into a book. After all, the damn things were already written. How difficult would this be?

So I've selected about two dozen (actually 26) of these essays for what I hope will be your enjoyment and entertainment (I will not make a claim the third, "e" in this series, "edification," though I am fond of alliteration). The six sections of this compilation reflect something of the diversity of my interests, and I hope that at least some of them will coincide with your own.

Finally, a word about my title, "Reflections in a Glass Eye." I have no idea what it means. The other night while engaging in another deploringly frequent activity of my later years, sitting on my toilet while waiting, in vain, for something emerge from my rear, something else emerged from head: That phrase. From out of nowhere. Thus are titles born while waiting for other things to form.

NDEs, Drugs and
Other Adventures

Introduction

During the second half of my life, beginning in my early 40s, I began to study near-death experiences, eventually writing five books on the subject, and also began my exploration of and experimentation with psychedelic drugs. Those were heady times for me, and looking back on them now, I know they were the greatest and most important events of my life, apart from the birth of my children. "Those were the days, my friend." In this section, I recall some of these experiences and other adventures from that period of my life.

How It All Began

Greetings, friends, and welcome to the Ringdom. I wish I could promise you that you will find it the realm of magic enchantment, but I'm afraid it is likely to be only a source of occasional entertainment and distraction from our dysphoric Trumpian times, even if Trump himself is no longer in the White House. Still, I will do my best to keep you interested enough to linger a while in the Ringdom and hope you will come to enjoy our time together.

Now, as Tonio, the clown in Leoncavallo's *I Plagliacci*, who introduces the opera by saying (or, rather, singing) that he is the prologue, perhaps I should introduce myself, if in a less dramatic fashion. Some of you may already be familiar with me if you were a part of Raymond Moody's University of Heaven crowd since for some fifteen months or so until December 2019, my essays were posted on that site. Well, I call them essays, but of course no one writes essays any longer, they blog. I have always resisted the use of the term although these days it seems we are stuck with it. I shudder to think of old Montaigne writhing in his grave in posthumous despair over the fate of the form he invented, which had such a long and glorious life in the world of literature. But I suffer enough as it is from being what used to be called an "old fogy" (someone will have to tell me what old farts are called these days; the only suitable term I can think of is in Yiddish—alter cocker). I don't want to risk eliciting even more derision by using terms that are clearly *demodé* (oops, I seem to have done it again).

But as I have apparently drifted into a confessional mode, I had best own up to one of my most besetting flaws.

I am old.

Very old.

Let's not get too specific but if I tell you I was born in the year that Babe Ruth hit his last home run, it will give you some idea. Suffice it to say that if I were a piece of Chippendale furniture, I would be an antique. But since I live in Marin County, perhaps a better sobriquet for myself would be that I am an ancient mariner (bad joke, I know—I can hear the hoots from here—but I couldn't resist).

The thing about being old, in case you have never tried it, is that you are on a very short and uncertain leash toward the future, but have a very long tail extending into the distant past. And in my case, where I find myself in the present is really in the epilogue of my life. You see, I have had my life; it is over. This is my afterlife, and it is from my afterlife that I am looking back on my life. When I look into the mirror of my life, all I see is the past. So that's some of what I would like to recall for you here—who I was before I became a has-been.

Some of you will know that those essays I wrote for Raymond Moody's website were on the theme of "waiting to die." As you will shortly learn, I had spent a good part of my life researching what it is like to die (it's not bad, and is actually much better than you could ever imagine). But what I was writing about in those essays was what it was like for me *waiting to die* (which is about as much fun as listening to bagpipes, which at least is not interminable). Still, the thing is, in the end I was an abject failure at it; I just didn't seem to have the knack for it.

But I digress.

I was going to introduce myself to you, wasn't I?

Well, suppose I start by telling you how I first found myself spending a lot of time in the company of the once nearly dead. I was young then—in my early forties—and I was about to have the time of my life. Here's the story:

It all began with two little purple pills. But they weren't Nexium.

They were two LSD capsules, but I didn't know that then.

I had better back up and explain.

In the early 1970s, just after I had turned 35, I was a newly minted full professor of psychology with tenure at the University of Connecticut. And I was discontented. Not with my personal life, but with the field of social psychology in which I had been trained and hired to teach. I had recently published a critique of experimental social psychology, castigating it for the pursuit of merely clever and flashy research of the "can you top this" variety, which did not make me many friends. In any event, I was suffering from a sort of early career crisis, having become disenchanted with this domain of psychology.

In March of 1971, when my wife and I went off to the Berkshires to celebrate our anniversary, I happened to pick up a book that my wife was then reading—Carlos Castañeda's first book, *The Teachings of Don Juan*. It looked intriguing and after she had finished it, I read it.

I was then a typical Jewish professor—wedded to rational thought, committed to science and atheistic in my worldview. I had no interest in religion and very little knowledge of mysticism. But I was open to new experiences, and what had particularly excited me about Castañeda's book was his discussion of what he called "seeing the crack between the worlds," which he had apparently effected through the use of mescaline.

At the time, I had never considered using psychedelic drugs and my only familiarity with anything close was having smoked marijuana a few times. But since I had never been a smoker, even that was difficult for me, and my experiences with it, though of the usual kind, did not have any particular impact on my life.

Nevertheless, since there was a colleague in my department at the time who I knew was familiar with psychedelics, I approached him to tell him about my interest to take mescaline and why. He had read Castañeda's book and knew what I was after.

I came to the point. Could he provide me with some mescaline? He could.

By then it was early May. The semester was just about over. He told me not to read anything further on the subject and just come to his apartment on the following Saturday.

That day turned out to be a rare beautiful sun-splashed day with everything beginning to bloom. My colleague lived at the edge of a forest. He suggested that I take the mescaline in his apartment, wait just a bit and listen to music and then go outside and into the nearby woods.

And then he gave me two purple pills to ingest.

I did not know my colleague well, and as I was soon to find out, he was not only impish, but embodied the trickster archetype. While he gave me to believe I was taking mescaline, he had actually given me 300 micrograms of LSD.

I will not bore you with an account of the next twelve hours. Suffice it to say that all the pillars of my previous ontological categories soon began to crumble into dust. I had the undeniable feeling I was seeing the world with pristine eyes *as it really was* for the first time. At the time and afterward I realized that this was the most important and most transformative experience of my life— and nearly fifty years later, I still feel the same way. Nothing could ever be the same.

The one portion of the experience I will allude to here— because it eventually led me to the study of near-death experiences —- took place when I was sitting on a log near a stream in the woods. I don't know how long I was there, but at some point for a moment outside of time I—except there was no "I" any longer– experienced an inrushing of the most intense and overwhelming rapturous LOVE and knew instantly that this was the real world, that the universe, if I can put this way, was stitched in the fabric of this love, and that I was home. However, again I have to repeat: There was *only* this energy of love and "I" was an indissoluble part of it, not separate from it.

I spent the next three years trying to come to terms with what had happened to me.

Before this, I had been very active as a young professor—I had published a fair amount, I had been promoted pretty fast and I was the head of my division of social psychology and served on important departmental committees, etc.

Afterward, I didn't publish anything for three years. During that time, I was engaged in a spiritual search for understanding, and there were consequences.

My wife could no longer relate to who I was and to the kind of company I was keeping, which eventually led to a very painful and traumatic divorce. My departmental colleagues didn't know what to make of me either. A very distinguished clinical psychologist, who had always taken an avuncular interest in me, put his arm around me one day and said, "We're just waiting for you to come back to us, Ken."

I never did.

At that time, there was a graduate student in my department named Bob Hoffman who, I soon discovered, was engaged in a similar quest of his own—a search for a new identity since mine had effectively been sundered. It was Bob who introduced me to the work of the English Theosophical researcher, Robert Crookall, whose books discussed phenomena that were, as I would only later realize, cognate to what would come to be called near-death experiences. And in 1972, Bob drew my attention to an article by the psychiatrist, Russell Noyes, entitled "The Experience of Dying," which recounted several examples of near-death experiences, though again that term was not yet in use. I remember how much these accounts affected me—I think in part because I recognized that they were describing revelations similar to those that had come to me during my LSD trip.

Also in that same year, Bob told me about a conference that was to be held up in Amherst, Massachusetts, on something called "transpersonal psychology" of which I had never heard.

"I think we should go to this," said Bob. And since Bob was leading me by the nose in those days, I quickly assented.

It was then that everything started to come together for me. As my LSD experience had been pivotal for me, so this conference would be.

I don't remember all the speakers who gave presentations that day—I do recall Stan Grof and Joan Halifax, Jim Fadiman, and I think Ram Dass may have there as well, and maybe even Stan Krippner—but I do remember my feeling of joy at discovering all these eminent professionals had been through something similar to me (only of course in far greater depth and with a level of erudition that was so much beyond my ken—or Ken—that they were really intellectual heroes to me) and had built new professional lives for themselves which stemmed from their own psychedelic experiences. And more—that I was, without having known it, a transpersonal psychologist! I had contemplated leaving the academy and psychology altogether, but now I saw I could remain a psychologist after all. Except I would have to teach a new way, learn a new subject and somehow undertake research in this emerging field of transpersonal psychology.

I returned to the university on fire. I was starting over.

Fortunately, I had a fair degree of freedom to teach at least one course of my own design, so I put together a graduate course on transpersonal psychology and offered it the next academic year. It attracted an unusual assortment of students and even a couple of professors as well as a Catholic priest.

One of the students was a rather hard-bitten and standoffish lesbian. Unlike most the rest of the students, she rarely expressed any emotion in class but was, on the contrary, rather phlegmatic and stolid. During one class, toward the end of that semester, I was reading some accounts of people's experiences of dying from the article by Russell Noyes, and I looked up to find that this student was sobbing uncontrollably. I think that was the first time I realized how powerful these stories could be.

In any event, over the next few years, my involvement and investment in transpersonal psychology continued to grow, which did not please my colleagues, but since I now had tenure and was a full professor, there was little they could do but shrug their cold shoulders at me or look at me somewhat sourly as if I were guilty of having left "real psychology" behind as well as my senses. They were, of course, right about that.

During that period, I made several extended trips out to California, then the epicenter of the nascent transpersonal movement. It was then that I was able to meet and spend time with many of the luminaries of the field, including Tony Sutich, now no longer much remembered, but then venerated as one of the two progenitors of transpersonal psychology (along with Abraham Maslow). I can still vividly remember when Tony, who suffered from severe rheumatoid arthritis, was once brought on stage at a transpersonal conference, still lying supine on a gurney of sorts, and placed behind a speaker who was giving a lecture. It was during these years, the middle 70's, that I also met and in most cases was befriended by many others who played significant roles in the development of transpersonal psychology—Stan Grof, Joan Halifax, Charley Tart, Jim Fadiman, Jean Houston, Stan Krippner, and others too numerous to mention.

And naturally as a result of these contacts and conversations, and my continued study and personal explorations of what Charley Tart had famously labeled "altered states of consciousness," I began to publish some articles in The Journal of Transpersonal Psychology, speak at conferences, the usual....

I don't have the space here (and you won't have the patience to read it) to continue to provide an account of my "spiritual adventures," so to speak, and related professional pursuits over the next few years that eventually led me to the study of near-death experiences, so let me just fast-forward to the spring of 1976. I was sitting outside my house, just after the spring semester had ended, and was reading a little book that I had come to my attention through a journal review by a new friend of mine. The book had been brought out by a small publisher in Georgia and was entitled *Life After Life.*

Written by a psychiatrist named Raymond Moody, Jr., it was an anecdotal account of what Moody dubbed "near-death experiences."

By the next year, after it had been picked up by Bantam Books, it was an international bestseller and the term near-death experience had entered the language of ordinary discourse.

I am holding a copy of the book now and I see all the excited marginal notes, exclamation points and underlinings that I made at the time. What I remember thinking was:

"This is it!"

I knew that I wanted to find a way to do research that would help me understand what had happened to me during my LSD trip—and that my own spiritual explorations weren't sufficient for me. I had always enjoyed doing research and needed to find a way to satisfy that need of mine. I also knew that I was not cut out to be a "druggie," and that for a multitude of reasons psychedelic research was not an option for me. And from reading Moody's book, I could see, with increasing clarity, that his near-death experiencers had indeed encountered the same realm—and so much more—that had so shattered me. I could learn from them. They would be my teachers.

You see, I was never interested in death per se, much less with the question of life after death. What animated me and drew me to study near-death experiences was my desire to understand the *state of consciousness* and the transpersonal domains that I had begun to experience when I took LSD.

Even then, of course, I could understand that NDEs were a kind of transpersonal experience in their own right since, according to Moody's account of them, they clearly transcended space, time and ego. Thus, researching NDEs, I immediately saw, could marry my spiritual search with my work as a transpersonal psychologist.

Just after I started my own research into NDEs in 1977, something else happened that changed the course of my life.

One evening in November, 1977, I was in my kitchen stirring some cream sauce when the phone rang. Still stirring the pot with my left hand, I reached across for the phone and heard an unfamiliar voice on the line speaking with a southern accent.

"Hello, Ken? This is Raymond Moody."

"No shit?" I replied. [Yes, I actually said that.]

I stopped stirring my cream sauce.

Raymond wanted to invite me down to Charlottesville, Virginia, where he then lived, along with several other researchers whom he had heard were following up on his work, and someone had drawn his attention to me. That someone—a sociologist colleague of Moody's named John Audette—would soon be in touch about the arrangements, but meanwhile Raymond was hoping I could come down.

Could I!

At that time, I was living near the University of Connecticut, where I then taught, with a former student of mine, Sue Palmer, and my daughter, Kathryn. Sue was one of the persons who had been of inestimable help to me in carrying out my first NDE research project, which would eventuate in my book, *Life at Death*, which I published in 1980, and is now recognized as the first major scientific investigation of NDEs.

Sue also was keen to go, so in short order, we loaded up my car and headed down to Virginia where I would meet not only Raymond, but several other professionals who were to play key pioneering roles in the development of the field of near-death studies—in particular, Bruce Greyson, Michael Sabom, and John Audette, all of whom were to become close colleagues of mine. Everything of importance really began from that first meeting and ultimately led to the formation of The International Association for Near-Death Studies of which I became the co-founder and its first president. It is still going strong after 40 years.

The rest, as the risible cliché goes, is history—for me the personal history going on two score of years now of studying, researching, thinking and writing about NDEs. There's no need to recapitulate that long sojourn in NDEland here. All I really wanted to express was how an adventitious LSD experience was the critical turning point for me that led, seemingly inevitably, to my life's work as an NDE researcher, which indeed has been the blessing of my life. And for that reason alone, though to be sure not the only one, I will always feel supremely grateful for what I was able to see and understand on a certain day in May in the woods of Connecticut.

In the Beginning

Not long ago, when I was reorganizing some of my books and papers, I happened to come upon an old newsletter from forty years ago that had been edited by some then friends of mine. At the time they lived just a few miles from where I now reside, and seeing that newsletter brought back warm memories of our friendship.

But what struck me most forcibly was a little essay I had written for their publication, which was sent only to the people who were members of their organization, probably something like fifty and surely not more than a hundred. I had completely forgotten about this essay, and obviously only a relatively few people had read it at the time.

When I wrote it, I had just completed the research for my first book on NDEs, *Life at Death*. I was then deeply affected by the interviews I had conducted for the book, and in the essay I wrote about it in a very personal way. I could never, and never would, have written about my research this way in my book, but here I was still in the emotional throes of my interviews and how they had already changed my life.

I was also aware that my work had completely validated that of Raymond Moody, and for that reason, I had actually entitled my essay, *Researching "Life After Life": Some Personal Reflections."* Now in retrospect, I find something else I hadn't been so much aware of at the time — my indebtedness to Moody's book, *Life After Life*. What if I had never come across his book? How would my life have developed without that book?? Was there ever a book that was so crucial to my life's path? So, in a very definite way, if only in hindsight, I would like this essay to be read as a kind of homage to Dr. Moody and the critical role that he and his book have played in my life.

But here's what I wrote forty years ago, when I was just at the beginning of my own journey into the world of NDEs.

Beginning in May of 1977, I spent thirteen months tracking down and interviewing persons who had come close to death. In some cases, these were persons who appeared to have suffered clinical death where there is no heartbeat or respiration; in most cases, however, the individuals I talked with had "merely" edged toward the brink of death but did not quite slip over.

Since this work was part of a research project, I had trained a staff of interviewers in the necessary procedures so that I — the busy professor—would not have to conduct all the interviews myself. After I had talked with a couple of near-death survivors, though, I saw that my life would just have to get busier: this stuff was plainly too fascinating to get it secondhand. I wound up interviewing 74 of the 102 persons who eventually comprised our sample.

Although I had been familiar with near-death experiences for some years, my interest in doing research in the area had been kindled by Raymond Moody's book, *Life After Life*. I found that, although I didn't really question the basic paradigm that he described, I was left with a lot of questions after finishing the book. How frequent were these experiences? Did it make any difference *how* one (almost) died? For example, do suicide attempts that bring one close to death engender the typical near-death experience? What role does prior religiousness play in shaping the experience? Can the changes that allegedly follow from these experiences be documented systematically and quantitatively?

So I wrote a little grant proposal and got some funds in order to answer these questions.

And thereby uncovered a source of spiritual wealth that will always sustain me.

This was not exactly what I had bargained for. But I am happy to "share the wealth" with you. Not that it's mine or was given to me. Nor does it "belong" to those who survive near-death episodes. It's just there. It's simply that talking to these persons helped me to see it.

In this little article, I am not going to bother to summarize the results from this study except to say that our data fully uphold Moody's findings. Virtually every aspect of the near-death experience he delineated is to be found in our interview protocols. I have no doubt whatever that he has described an authentic phenomenon (though its interpretation is up for grabs). And others, since the publication of Moody's book, have also corroborated his findings. As far as I'm concerned, then, the basic outline of the core near-death experience, as sketched by Moody (and before him by Kübler-Ross) is now established fact.

What I want to relate to you is something of the experiential residue that has remained with me now that the interviews are finished. I doubt that much of this is going to find its way into the professional publications I shall be writing based on this research or that it will even find explicit expression in a book I am planning on near-death experiences. And yet, in some way, I feel that it represents the essential *finding* of my research: that it is "the real message" hidden within the welter of statistics and the seemingly endless interview excerpts which so far make up the bulk of the manuscript I am presently working on.

You don't forget their faces or their manner during the interview. I talked to one woman who had been close to death perhaps eight or nine times owing to an unusual respiratory problem. Once, when her life was in danger, she saw a ball of light and heard what she took to be the voice of the Lord. The voice said, "You will suffer, but the Kingdom of heaven will be yours." This woman insisted that these were the exact words, nor a paraphrase or "an impression." As with so many other incidents that were disclosed to me, this one seemed fully real. People will deny indignantly that what they experienced was a dream or an hallucination. But what I remember most vividly from this interview is how this woman *looked.* She radiated peace, serenity, acceptance. She knew she didn't have long to live—that the next time could be "it." She has had many personal difficulties to contend with in her life. She lives every day as a *gift.* This was not said as an empty religious platitude. I could see it. She never said so, but it became clear that her friends are deeply inspired by her example. (She herself makes light of it all.) I looked at her face as she continued talking. It seemed lit up—from the inside.

How do you think I felt when I left her house?

I remember another woman. She had had her near-death experience more than twenty years ago. (Most of those we interviewed had come close to death within the past two years.) Her doctor had botched up a routine tonsillectomy and a cardiac arrest had resulted. According to the information she gave me and from what I could glean from her medical records, it appears that she was clinically dead for nearly three minutes. I'll relate just a portion of what she told me:

> *...the thing I could never—absolutely <u>never</u>—forget is that <u>absolute</u> feeling of [struggling for words] peace... joy...or something. Because I remember the <u>feeling</u>. I just remember this <u>absolutely beautiful feeling</u>. Of peace. And happy! Oh, so happy! That's about the only way I can explain it. And I was above. And there was a presence. It's the only way I can explain it because I didn't <u>see</u> anything. But there was a <u>presence</u>, and it may not have been <u>talking</u> to me, but it was like I knew what was going on between our minds. I wanted to go that way [toward the presence]. <u>Something</u> was there. And I had no fear of it. And the <u>peace</u>, the release. The fear was all gone. There was no pain, there was nothing. It was <u>absolutely beautiful</u>! I could <u>never</u> explain it in a million years. It was a feeling that I think everyone <u>dreams</u> of someday having. Reaching a point of ABSOLUTE peace. And ever since then I've never been afraid of death.*

The woman who told me all this (and much more!) is now in her mid-fifties and had recently suffered a near-fatal heart attack. There was nothing about her manner that suggested she was denying the fear of death that Ernest Becker says each of us carries within us. I wish he could have met this woman! No reaction-formation here! I have seen her socially several times since. She is the same woman. Love of life and of others animates her. Well, maybe she was always like this, but she denies it. She traces this attitude to the time when she was "dead."

Suppose you had interviewed her. Suppose you had interviewed dozens of persons who described to you similar feelings, experiences and aftereffects. What impressions do you think you'd be left with as you drove back to the university?

Another person who made a deep impact on me was a husky-voiced, elegant woman in her late forties. At the time of my interview with her, she lived in a tasteful, well-appointed home in a well-to-do suburb of Hartford. The outward comfort of her life was in sharp contrast, however, to her years of severe physical suffering and psychological torment. Two years before I met her, she had lain, alone and comatose, in her home for three days before she was discovered and brought to a hospital. She had apparently suffered heart failure and lay close to death for a long time. This extended period during which she hovered between life and death enabled her to have a very deep experience, perhaps the deepest of any I heard recounted. She eventually found herself surrounded by a radiant light, feeling totally peaceful and ecstatic, reunited with her deceased parents, and in an environment which can only be described as representing a vista of what most people would call heaven. At the height of her joy, however, she felt herself being pulled back by the appeals of her children who stood around her bed, and at this point remembers experiencing an agonizingly painful wrenching sensation, as though, she said, "I was being pulled out of a *tremendous vacuum* and just being torn to bits."

Before her return to life she remembers thinking:

one very, very strong feeling was that if I could <u>only</u> make them (her doctors and others) understand how comfortable and how <u>painless</u> it is, how <u>natural</u> it is. And the feeling that I had when this was happening was not that I was becoming non-existent, but that I was becoming just another identity, another part of me was being born. I don't feel that it was an ending of my personality or my being. I just felt it was another beginning of my being. I felt <u>no</u> sadness. No longing. No fear.

Even when she was feeling the pain of being caught between the worlds, her resolve did not ebb:

I cannot tell you exactly <u>what</u> happened—whether I heard my daughter or my children speak to me, and when they said, "we need you!" (But) suddenly, the immensity of what I had experienced somehow made me realize that I <u>had</u> to, I <u>have</u> to make people understand. I have to make them realize that death is not a frightening or horrible end. <u>It is not</u>. I <u>know</u> it is not! It's just an extension or another beginning.

Since the time of this incident, this woman has been attempting to share her experiences with others. She has spoken to journalists, radio reporters, and was even in a documentary film that dealt with the experiences of dying. To live in accordance with what her near-death experience disclosed has become her life's aim. At the present writing, this woman is undertaking a program to counsel the dying and the sick. She has found her life's work and she found it through encountering her own death.

She is not the only person I talked with whose experiences have led to a mode of life devoted to helping others deal with their own deaths. Such persons who have had a near-death experience come to engage in this work not simply out of a desire to do something useful or kind, but from an inner conviction that their own experience, by virtue of its having been vouchsafed to them, is meant to be shared so as to provide comfort and reassurance to those who are about to take their own journeys into something that we call death. And there is something about such people I have noticed, some special quality they have that draws you to them. They seem to radiate in life the peace that they felt when they were close to death. And it does something to you.

I could mention many other persons I talked with who have this ability to make a gift of their presence, but I think I'll relate just one more vignette. Again, it is a woman (I think I should say that I found no sex differences in incidents of near-death experiences and many men gave me deeply affecting accounts of their episodes; it just happens that the memories that come first to mind in connection with this article all involve women), but this time it is a woman who had no conscious, Moody-type experience. In fact, though she never read Moody's books, what she had heard about such purported experiences had left her feeling skeptical in the extreme.

I had driven a long way through a dreary rain to get to her home and when I rang the doorbell, there was no response. I was about to ring again when the door finally opened. A middle-aged woman, her face showing the pain which still affected her body, silently invited me inside. I understood immediately on seeing her that she could only move slowly and with difficulty. That explained the long delay on her doorstep. She lived alone. Her husband had died some years before. Her daughters, whose photographs were displayed on the living room wall, lived in nearby towns. I noticed that her daughters were strikingly beautiful. Her house was small, but tastefully furnished. Charming knickknacks and lovely flower filled-vases gave the living room a homey and cozy quality.

She sank heavily into a chair. Speaking slowly and with a German accent, she told me that a year and a half earlier, she had been severely injured in an automobile accident of which she remembers nothing. They didn't think she would live. She showed me photographs taken at the time; they were not pretty. She spoke matter-of-factly, without any sense of self-pity. She was still recovering and she was still suffering physically, but somehow she exuded a quality of repose and serene pensiveness. She began to reflect on what her experiences had taught her:

> *In my opinion, there are two things in life which keep a person going, or, I should say, which are important. To me, they are the most important things. And that is <u>love</u> and <u>knowledge</u>. And what I experienced when I was in intensive care, not only once but several times, when I went out of my consciousness, was the closeness of another human being, the love I was treated with from everybody including the doctors and including the nurses and most of all, my family, my children. And I think a lot of people who are very religious or so will say they more or less experienced God, whatever God I believe in, right? And love was one of the things I felt (when) I was close to them. I got more of it than others. And I could <u>give</u> more of it, too. I felt very much loved and I felt that I loved everybody. I did not only tell one time that I loved my doctor and I still feel that way because they [she paused], they gave me life back again. I think that this is worthwhile, to love somebody, because life is the most precious thing. And I think you don't realize that before you actually almost die. (And) the more knowledge you have the better you will understand whenever anything happens to you. You will understand why certain things have to be this way and why.*
>
> *For example, a friend who was on a dying list, too, but he never believed in doctors, in nurses or anything like that. And he is <u>still</u> ill, and this is over a year now and he's still ill, very ill. Because he did not <u>trust</u> in the people, that they can help. And [she paused again] I think that's very important that you <u>know</u> that certain people love you and not only certain people, but <u>most</u> people love other people... There may be some people, and one hears about*

it, that they live in hatred, but I think they don't have the knowledge that it is <u>so important to love</u> and to understand what life is all about because I think that's the main thing... that's what it is all about.

I asked her if she had felt that way before her accident:

I did, but I did not feel as strong as I do now. The accident, as bad as it was and as much as I suffered and as much as I will probably never be exactly the same as I was before, but mentally I think I grew. I grew a lot. I learned the value of life more than I did before and I actually gained by this experience. It's very important to me. That itself makes life worthwhile for me to go on and do whatever is in store for me, you know, and live to the full extent.

She grew quiet then, for even talking was an effort, and I noticed the timeless stillness that had come upon us. The illumination in the room was dim, and but woman's face was again aglow with that inward light of peace and love that I had seen before in other near-death survivors. Everything in that room seemed hushed and still and suffused in beauty. Those of you who meditate or who have taken psychedelic trips will understand...and will understand how much words fail here. Everything—all meaning, all mystery, all holiness—was present in the specificity and precision and time-lessness of that moment.

With a sense of wrong-doing, I finally broke the spell by asking another question. The interview continued. At the end I tried to express my thanks to her, but lamely. She thought I was thanking her for the interview.

Afterward, still feeling immensely moved, I felt that I wanted to send her something that would better express my gratitude to her. Since she had mentioned that she enjoyed listening to music, I chose a recording of Beethoven's A minor string quartet. The third movement of this quartet is sub-titled, Heiliger Dankgesang eines

Genesenden an die Gottheit (Hymn of Thanksgiving to the Creator from a convalescent), and in view of her accident and ancestry, it seemed fitting. This quartet also had a special personal meaning for me since I had listened to it over and over at one point in my life when I had feared (mistakenly, as it turned out) that I might be seriously ill. I thought in listening to it, she would understand.

She replied by sending me a printed card of thanks with her signature. No more. Sometime later I wrote to her in order to see whether she might be interested in appearing in a documentary film on near-death experiences, but my inquiry went unanswered. I was somehow reluctant to call her. But I have never forgotten her or what she looked like when she spoke the words I quoted to you and what happened when she had finished speaking them.

I had begun this work during a time of sorrow and inward emptiness in my life. I remember feeling spiritually adrift, as if I had somehow lost my way. Suddenly, I found that I simply did not know what to *do*. Concealing my barrenness and distress, I took myself that summer to a nearby convalescent home and offered my services as "a volunteer." I was secretly hoping that some old wise person, contemplating his own imminent death, would somehow give me a clue as to *what* I was supposed to do. Mainly, I played cards with people in desperate physical straits and saw suffering all around. And our conversations were mostly about how well someone had played a hand of bridge or when the refreshments would be brought in. Philosophical ruminations on life were not in vogue.

It was while I was vainly seeking "the answer" at the convalescent home that I happened to read Moody's book.

During the thirteen months of interviewing near-death survivors, I received my answer. The professor had found his teacher at last. They were ordinary people who described, in a consistent way, an extraordinary patterning of experiences which occurs at the point of death. The effect of personally seeing this pattern gradually reveal itself over the course of these interviews is something I shall probably never adequately be able to convey. But this effect, combined with that quality of luminous serenity which many near-death survivors manifest, made me feel that I myself was undergoing an extended religious awakening.

Quite a few of my interviewees claimed or believed that during their experiences they encountered God directly or sensed His presence intuitively. It was really astonishing how often this was asserted by persons of all sorts of religious persuasions including non-believers. What to make of such statements is, of course, another matter. Professional interpreters can debate the question. As for me, I can only say that I have no doubt I saw Him, too. He left His mark on those I talked to. And they left their mark on me.

Ketamine Days

My adventures with ketamine actually began with a fateful phone call more than thirty years ago.

In August of 1984, I was in California on a lecture tour and to see some professional colleagues in connection with my work and my recently published book on near-death experiences, *Heading Toward Omega*. The last of my talks on that visit was to a medical society in the Bay Area that had been arranged by my cousin Cliff, a cardiologist. That evening, while I was still at Cliff's house in Orinda before leaving the next day for Los Angeles, I received a phone call from another Orinda resident who was, but would hardly remain, a stranger to me. Her name was Therese.

It turned out that Therese had read my first NDE book, *Life at Death*, and wanted to talk to me about a professional matter concerned with that book. Since she had serendipitously discovered that I was staying very near her house in Orinda, she wondered whether I could come over to meet her while I was still in town. I explained that that would not be possible since I had to pack and leave the next morning. Therese countered by asking whether it might be possible for me to take some time on the phone now so she could explain just a bit about what she had in mind.

She had a very pleasant and gracious manner of speaking—there was certainly something very appealing, almost seductive, about her voice—so I readily consented. She then had a bombshell to drop concerning another invitation altogether.

Therese told me that she had been working with an oncologist and that they were both concerned with trying to find ways for terminal patients to die with less fear and with a sense of some kind of transcendent revelation similar to that which near-death experiencers often reported. In fact, what they wanted to try was to induce something like an NDE, and the means that they proposed to use for this purpose was the anesthetic, ketamine. Because Therese had read my first book on NDEs, she said she regarded me as an expert on the subject, so she had suggested to her oncologist colleague that she should ask me whether I would be willing to be a "professional subject" who would take ketamine under supervision in order to see the extent to which this drug might mimic an actual NDE.

Whoa!

In my mind I remember thinking, "Oh, God, wait just a minute."

I already was familiar with work that had been done with terminal cancer patients along these lines using LSD that Stan Grof and Joan Halifax had described in their book, *The Human Encounter with Death*. They had indeed shown that LSD employed in this way was sometimes capable of inducing an experience that had many of the same components and aftereffects of an actual NDE, including in most cases a reduction in the fear of death and an increased expectation of some form of life after death.

But ketamine was another story. I knew something about this drug from having read about John Lilly's experiments with it and from some other sources, and what I had heard had certainly made me wary of it. There was even a macabre and scary story about a well-known ketamine explorer who was found dead in a forest two days after becoming unconscious following an injection of ketamine.

I definitely had never had any interest to try it—if anything I was averse to doing so, particularly because I knew that it was administered by injection. Thoughts of heroin addiction flickered in my mind.

Besides, my days of using psychoactive drugs were by then long passed. I had experimented with LSD, peyote and psilocybin for a while during the 1970s, but I had taken them only about once a year, and had stopped for good in 1977. I had no desire to try anything new along those lines, and certainly not with anything like ketamine, which for me was a drug associated with real risk and danger.

"Ah, I don't think this would be for me, Therese."

Therese had an alternative proposal ready.

"Well, you don't have to make up your mind now, Ken. Just think about it, and let me send you a little literature on the subject, OK?"

She then happened to mention that the following spring, she would be coordinating a major invited conference on psychedelics at Esalen Institute in Big Sur and wondered whether I would have an interest to be there, particularly because John Lilly himself would be attending it. She mentioned that it would be held during the very first half of June, 1985.

Now here's the kicker.

Therese did not know when she tendered this invitation that I would actually be at Esalen at exactly that time. I had first been to Esalen in 1983 when its co-founder, Michael Murphy, had asked me to come out to do a program on NDEs. It was successful and Michael and I hit it off. He had recently been in touch with me again to invite me this time for a much more extensive engagement at the institute.

He wanted me to come for three weeks in the late spring of 1985 as a scholar-in-residence so that I could conduct a workshop on NDEs and attend and present my work in other workshops and seminars that would follow mine, including a month-long workshop that would be conducted by none other than Esalen's then permanent scholar-in-residence, Stan Grof. I had loved being at Esalen on my first visit, so naturally I jumped at the chance.

So I already knew what Therese didn't—that I would be there at the same time her conference would be held.

It is a cliché among the people in my world to say "there are no coincidences." Being contrary, I usually reply "except for accidents and chance events." But in this case, however, I couldn't help feeling a little unnerved when she invited me to attend. It already seemed like destiny had decided to take a hand in my affairs.

Naturally, I told her I would love to come.

Naturally, she was delighted.

We agreed to table the whole business about ketamine for now. In due course, however, she would send me some materials pertaining to the conference. And that, for the moment, was that.

Fast forward to June, 1985.

By now, I had already spent a very engrossing week at Esalen and had become very involved with a woman I'll simply call L. with whom I was then staying. One morning, several days before Therese's conference, L. told me that Therese's roommate, S., would be arriving in order to set things up at the conference. Since L. and S. were already good friends, L. invited me to come along to meet her.

That evening the three of us met and slipped into a warm pool together, sans clothes of course—Esalen style. We were alone except for one fellow who was at the end of the pool. At some point, S. whispered to L., but in my hearing, "Would you like to do a little K tomorrow?"

"What's K?" I asked.

"Ketamine," L. whispered in my ear.

"Uh-oh," I thought.

Of course, I was supposed to be "saving myself" for a possible ketamine experience, which I hadn't ruled out. It had been on the agenda for Therese and me to discuss after she arrived.

L. quickly expressed her enthusiasm for having a ketamine session the following evening. She knew that a grand house on her property was temporarily vacant and L. had the key and permission to use it.

I was very conflicted, and more than a little afraid.

I explained all the reasons for my hesitation, but briefly, urgently, and sotto voce so that the fellow who was still at the other end of the pool couldn't hear. Not only was I concerned about violating an implicit understanding about remaining a "ketamine virgin" for Therese, but I was really worried about having to take it by injection.

S. said to me, "Ken, I have taken it about 200 times. It's perfectly safe. I know how to give injections. Meet me for breakfast tomorrow and I'll answer all your questions."

By now, I was virtually living with L.—things happen fast at Esalen, and now I was already on the verge of taking ketamine with her and S.—so the following morning I had to hustle to meet S. for breakfast.

"I have a lot of questions," I began.

"I'm sure I can answer them all," S. replied.

She did give me the feeling I could trust her.

That was something I had quickly learned during my short stay at Esalen. You had to trust. If you were going to take a leap in the dark, you had to assume that someone would be there to catch you. S. radiated confidence; I felt I would be safe with her and that she would answer my questions truthfully based on her own extensive experience with ketamine.

In the end, after she had explained a great deal to me, I felt reassured. But there was still one problem.

Therese.

I mentioned this to S.

"Call her," she said.

When later that morning I was able to reach Therese, who would be leaving for the conference in just a couple of days, she was very upset. She really didn't want me to do it—it would bias my reaction to the kind of ketamine test under controlled conditions that she was still hoping I would assent to. She urged me to decline. There was also some evident bad feeling between L. and Therese, as if they were rivals of a sort (which was indeed the case, as I soon learned).

I neither consented to Therese's request nor rebuffed it. I just didn't commit myself one way or another. I think I evaded the whole matter and simply told her I would consider it and think it over. The conversation ended on a note of irresolution. I didn't think Therese was happy with me or the prospect I might be doing ketamine with L.

By that time, however, I had come to feel very comfortable not only with S., but very close to L. And because there was already a strong bond of friendship between S. and L. and a growing sense of camaraderie among the three of us, I rather resented Therese's attempt to place a block of sorts in the path of what seemed a natural progression. I decided to follow the call of my desire rather than to honor what wasn't exactly a pledge to Therese. I would do it.

What the hell! This was Esalen. At Esalen, you took chances, trusting you would land on your feet.

That evening, after dark, for it was still early June, the three of us made our way down to the large house L. had commandeered for our session. Immediately I was struck by its burnished beauty. I remember a very ornately designed banister with a series of balusters that led down to the lower portion of the house where the bedroom was located in which we would be situated once we had received our injections of ketamine. In the nearby bathroom, S. got out the syringes and the little vials of ketamine but before she began the injections, L., who was always the most eloquent of the three of us—she just had a gift of spontaneous flowery incantations—took a few minutes to do a kind of ceremony, asking blessings for a safe and fulfilling journey. Now we were ready to begin.

S. had explained that even at the sub-anesthetic levels we would be taking, once the injection had taken place, we must immediately go to the nearby bed, lie down and wait. She also said she had to be careful in order to make sure that there were no bubbles in the syringe because that could cause problems. I began to be very nervous. She would first inject L., then me (in my thigh) and finally herself. Were we ready?

Gulp.

Once S. had injected me, I made my way to the bed. L. was already supine to my left, I was in the middle of the bed, and S. would soon join us, and lie to my right.

I waited.

After only a few minutes, I began to see swirling colors—beautiful oranges and glowing peaceful reds. I was no longer aware of my body. It was as if I were gliding on a river of color, and then I was the colors; I had merged with them.

But next, I found I was holding L.'s hand with my left hand and S.'s with my right, and I was blending into them. I could feel their energies, their essence in me, because seemingly my own boundaries had dissolved. I said—we never forgot this—"The L. of Us and the S. of Us."

L. hissed softly but with emphasis, "Yes!"

We lapsed into silence.

I continued to surf the waves of ecstasy, but this was entirely different from what I had previously experienced on MDMA, which I had taken several days earlier with L. There were peaceful, floating, beautiful colors. Then at one point, everything went black—very black. I grew frightened; I thought I might be dying. Then, a radiant exfoliating burst of new colors and another level of the trip had begun. I was no longer aware of anything but beauty—no body, no Ken, nothing but being merged with the very sensations of the experience itself from which I was not separate, there being no "I."

Eventually—because I had no sense of time, I had no idea how much time had elapsed—I became aware that I was feeling the energies of L. and S. again. I was still holding their hands. But then—I remember this distinctly—my left hand began "making love" with L.'s hand. The way our fingers were moving together. She responded. This was love. I felt a little bad not doing the same with S., but it was L. was I drawn to.

It turned out about 45 minutes had gone by.

I was still very woozy and had to continue to lie there for a few minutes while the two of them got up.

There was a large, beautifully designed blue stone-inlaid circular hot tub nearby. Someone—probably S.—turned it on. Eventually, we all got into it and began talking softly about what we had experienced. We laughed over my phrase, "The L. of Us and the S. of Us." But it still seemed true—we had bonded, we had blended, we had become one. One in three persons, the Esalen trinity. (By the way, thirty-five years later, we are all still very deep and loving friends with one another.)

I spent the next day recovering—and reflecting on what I had experienced the night before. I had never taken anything like ketamine before—the experience was so qualitatively different from anything I had encountered with any of the psychedelics I had used during the '70s or with MDMA. I wasn't hooked, but I was exceedingly intrigued. Now, I was really looking forward to doing it again, this time with Therese.

And speaking of Therese, she was now due the next day. The people for the conference were already arriving, S. was now busy at work preparing the conference room and making various arrangements, and Therese was scheduled to arrive that evening. I needed to get the ketamine out of my head, so to speak, and ready myself for my meeting with Therese. I hoped she wouldn't be angry with me when she learned I was no longer a ketamine virgin.

She wasn't. And during the time of her conference, we quickly were on our way to becoming good friends, particularly because of another deep MDMA session we had together the night of the first day of the conference.

Therese, however, still wanted me to do ketamine with her and invited me to come up to her home in the San Francisco Bay Area once my stint at Esalen was over. Now I agreed with alacrity. I was on a ketamine roll.

The day after I had arrived, she proposed that we try an experiment. At that time, Therese was interested to explore various combinations of drugs. In this case, she suggested that we start with MDMA and use it as a kind of booster. When that drug had reached its peak intensity after about two hours, I would then be injected with ketamine. (S., who was in the area but had vacated the apartment temporarily so that Therese and I could remain there together, would be summoned to do the injection.)

Was I game?

"But what about that ketamine session with that oncologist of yours?"

"Oh, we can put that off for a while."

I had a little hesitation, but since I had already bonded so much with Therese at Esalen, not for long.

Therese's apartment had obviously been set up for such sessions. My impression was that this was the way she conducted some of her work with her clients. And since I had already come to be feel very comfortable there, I was ready to relax with her, be close to her physically and begin my second MDMA encounter with her.

S. came in to wish us well, and then went elsewhere, presumably into her bedroom.

Therese and I lay down on one of her very plush rugs and waited for the MDMA to take effect. By this time, I was familiar enough with the drug to know how it would affect me. Once more, I felt myself bonding with Therese, with her essence, and the feelings just built and built with waves of love lifting me into a world of pulsating ecstasy.

At some point, S. quietly came in and injected me, but not Therese, with ketamine, but this time the dose, by agreement, was much higher than that I had taken it at Big Sur. This, too, was part of the experiment.

And this time, not surprisingly, my experience was very different, radically so. Although it started in the same way, with those beautiful shimmering colors into which I soon merged, I then found myself—although I could only recall this afterward—experiencing what I subsequently came to label "the creation of the universe." Somehow, I seemed to be an indissoluble part of "the Big Bang," except it was a soft feeling of being, not seeing, something like an expanding balloon that contained the germ of all the galaxies that were then first forming. It was as if, encoded into the star-stuff of which I was composed, was information about the very origins and evolution of the universe, which I was now tapping into. (Afterward I couldn't resist the admittedly wild speculation that this information must somehow be contained in our very cellular structure, but I had no such thoughts then. I was not capable of thinking at all.)

I remember that the energy of this soft expansion was not neutral—this creation was infused with a feeling of love. (Again, afterward, I was inclined to feel that this was probably due to the effect of MDMA.)

At this point, there was no "I." There was only the experience of oneness with the nascent universe as it was in the process of formation. Any sense of time had completely disappeared. Not only that, any sense of being human, much less a particular human called Ken Ring, had also vanished. There was only this experience, but no one was observing it.

At some point—it must have been perhaps a half hour later from what Therese, who had been observing me, told me—I began to have a faint inkling of a kind of descent through an array of what seemed to be galaxies all around me, as if some invisible force, a kind of gravity, was causing a sense of downward motion—although in fact, there was still no sense of "I" or anything human. Just this feeling of a descent through star-systems.

After a time, I had the first intimation that there was something called "earth," which appeared to be my destination, and with that came the slow realization that I was something—a person! That I was human, that I was heading back toward earth. But my identity was still not clear to me.

I later learned that S. had been there during this whole session, and that she had had a tape-recorder handy in case I said anything of interest. It's good that she did because what happened next surprised everyone.

I didn't come back as myself, Ken Ring.

I returned with another identity altogether. I was a Dutch

tugboat captain who appeared to have lived in the 19th century, and I spoke English with a distinct accent (that later seemed to be like that of the famous Austrian comic film actor, S.Z. (Cuddles) Sakall, a staple in films of the forties, most famously Casablanca.

When I started talking in this accent, I heard Therese hiss to S. "Is the tape recorder going? We have to get this!"

I have a very clear memory of what I was experiencing at this time.

First, it was as if in my final descent toward earth, as I was slowly parachuting down, as it were, I had landed not on the ground, but had got stuck in the branches of a tree. On the ground was Ken Ring, and I, as the tugboat captain, was aware of him. But Ken Ring was no longer who I was.

Second, I remember saying and repeating, "This is a distinct personality, a distinct personality." I could not just see this man; I was him. I could feel him as if I indeed lived inside of him. I knew that he was a "cold man." (Not at all like Ken.) That he was lonely, and somewhat embittered. And that he was actually envious of Ken Ring. About him, he said, "Yah, Ken Ring, the guy that likes the ladies."

I knew what he looked like. I could see his face, his sideburns and whiskers. I could see him on his boat, and I could see him in a tavern where he made his remark about Ken Ring's fondness for ladies. I knew he was Dutch, even if it his accent was more like that of an Austrian. And I knew I was him, not me.

You know how when you are driving in a car listening to the radio and you begin to lose the signal? Well, something like that began to happen next. I felt that the tugboat captain, whom Therese later labeled "the immigrant," was beginning to fade out and as he did—to continue the metaphor I used earlier—it is as if I was now being sucked out of the tree and down into the body and person of Ken Ring.

Plop! I was back. I recognized—with relief—that I was Ken Ring again. But I remembered everything about "the immigrant." And Therese had recorded my words and accent.

In all, over the next year, I wound up doing ketamine nine times, including my first experience in Big Sur. In five of those sessions, "the immigrant" was present during the penultimate stage I passed through on my way to myself. He was always the same, and he always, as far as I can now recall, spoke in the same accent and had the same personality—cold, unfeeling, somewhat cruel, and lonely.

I leave it to you to interpret who—or what—he was. And why he was so often a part of my ketamine experiences as they terminated.

My subsequent experiences with ketamine, sometimes with Therese, but mostly with others, were similar, but on the whole, not quite so intense as my initial ones had been though still full of marvelous and enthralling sensations and periods of ego-dissolution. Whenever I would enter the K-state, I would recognize it immediately as distinctively sui generis. It represented a world of its own, radically different from any of my other experiences in altered states of consciousness and utterly beguiling.

I might have used words such as "captivating" or "enchanting" were it not for one further experience I had under Therese's aegis the next year.

Remember her wish to have me become a volunteer for a ketamine session with her oncologist colleague? Well, even though I was no longer a ketamine "virgin," but almost a ketamine veteran by now, she still wanted me to undertake this journey, if only for the sake of satisfying her colleague's professional interest in my report.

So one day in the winter of 1986, at this doctor's office in the hospital, I would be given the anesthetic with a special infusion that would allow the doctor to titrate me—that is, he could control the amount of ketamine to be administered so that it could slowly be increased to its maximum. During this process, he would tape-record any utterances that I might emit and afterward, once I had recovered, he would interview me. His main interest would be to determine the extent to which I felt my experience mimicked that of an actual NDE.

Therese, of course, had accompanied me there, and she would remain at my side during the entire session.

In going through my boxes of memorabilia recently, I was surprised to come across a cassette tape of this session and a two-page letter from the doctor summarizing my experience and what he felt he had learned from it. I didn't have the patience to re-listen to the tape, but I did read his letter, which brought back some aspects of the experience for me, though it was one for a number of reasons that I remember, with horror, very well.

Although some of the excerpts from the tape that the doctor's letter includes make it clear I was again experiencing vivid colors at the onset, when the dosage was increased, I was already indicating that I was "farther out now... whirling in the cosmos... like part of a galaxy... moving through vast, vast, vast spaces... like floating nebulae... going further out into space... scintillating. I see more light...,"

Then nothing for a long time, but what I remembered afterward was something that gave me a sense of profound metaphysical fright. What I became aware of when the dosage was apparently at or near its maximum was that human beings were not real. It as if they were mere projections, like the images on a screen. But people were deluded because they had come to identify with the images in the same way that when we watch a movie, we see people, not images. But only the images are real, not the people. We were no more than simulacra—the whole of existence was not as we supposed. Instead, it was empty—just full of moving images. And who or what was behind the projector? Nothing...

I am certain that I have never experienced anything more unnerving and psychologically destabilizing in my life. I felt that all points of ordinary reference and meaning had dissolved and that it left me, or what I had thought of as me, completely void.

The doctor writes, "At this level, the process of ego dissolution appeared to start. Pertinent comments included the statement 'I'm gone... gone... gone' and somewhat later repetitions of the word 'collapsing.' Later [there were] long howling vocalizations. During this period the speech was very dysarthric, but there was a plaintive and possibly dysphoric quality to it... The first sign of recovery was a chuckle or laugh which sounded almost like crying. Then the first clear vocalization, 'I'm alive... I'm alive.'"

What I remember at this point was seeing Therese's elbow. I reached out for it the way a man drowning in an ocean and overcome by fear reaches for the edge of a raft.

Although I obviously felt I had in a sense returned from death, what I had experienced was in no way like a transcendent radiant NDE. If anything, it was the opposite, and it left me with a feeling of something close to dread. What if what I had perceived was somehow a kind of ultimate truth about the nature of things that was blessedly veiled from us during states of ordinary consciousness?

Certainly, I had never before experienced anything like that on any of my previous trips with L. or Therese nor would I experience anything remotely like it in any of my subsequent ketamine sessions. In fact, I've never known what to make of it. It occurred to me afterward that maybe I had never had so much ketamine in my system, that perhaps I had had too much this time. Or perhaps I had been given a glimpse of something that was an essential, if unutterably frightening, part of our universe.

All I know is that that experience haunted me for days afterward and that I have never forgotten it.

Years later—more than three decades now—what do I make of these experiences? To be sure, I can't draw any generalizations about ketamine experiences on the basis of my own idiographic encounters with this drug. I don't want to claim that they have any ontological significance either. Mine were what they were, and while others may have had experiences that seemed to mimic at least some aspects of NDEs, that certainly was not true for me.

Nevertheless, I still regard ketamine as providing the means of access to a distinctive world of revelatory experiences that usually left me in a state of rapturous wonder even if upon recovering it was hard to retain much of the contents of these extraordinary voyages, which were in any event almost impossible afterward to capture in the net of language.

I remember at the time of Therese's Esalen conference that John Lilly, one of the participants, was hardly ever present. Dressed in a kind of brown monk's robe, he seemed mostly to be in his VW microbus (if memory serves) injecting himself, as I was later told, every 15 minutes or so with ketamine.

I remember thinking at the time thoughts along the lines of: "How sad. Such a brilliant man," etc.

But after my own experiences with ketamine, I was inclined to see things very differently. At least on the basis of my own experiences, ketamine gives you access to a world that is so fantastically alluring and full of wonders that to me it makes perfect sense to want to explore it, just as adventurous naturalists of previous centuries were keen to travel to unknown and exotic lands.

I'm glad I did.

When a Jew Goes to Germany

Just after returning to Connecticut in 1984 from a trip to the Far East, I received an invitation to speak at a conference in Germany. Germany! This was a country I had never thought to visit for reasons that will be obvious—it was on my verboten list. What Jew would not have strong feelings about Germany?

Still, I was tempted because the conference themes—birth, sex and death—were all of interest to me, and many of my new American and Tibetan friends in the consciousness movement would also be speakers or attending, and there were to be several notable European speakers participating as well. It seemed too good an event to miss, and yet... I would have to go to Germany.

I temporized and wrote the conference organizer that I would have to think about it, making up some polite excuses about possibly conflicting commitments. But after a while, I succumbed to the lure and, despite my reservations, I agreed to go.

The conference itself was scheduled for a week in August somewhere in Bavaria near or in the Black Forest. A few days before the conference, after I had made all my preparations, I suddenly became very sick with something that was either the flu or pneumonia. (I wondered at the time whether the timing of my illness was influenced by psychogenic factors having to do with my ambivalence.) Anyway, I would have to cancel, and that was that.

It being too late to write (this being before the days of email), I had to call the conference organizer, a man named Dieter. He could hear how sick I was when I called to give my regrets. However, he refused to accept them. Instead he told me simply and in exactly these words, "You must come."

When he spoke the phrase, he was not imploring me nor was he giving me an imperative ("you must come or else..."). It was as if he was saying to me, "You must come because it is spiritually necessary for you to be here." Honestly, this is exactly what I thought at the time, not afterward. He then quickly went on to say, "We will take care of you." This was a very direct, no frills conversation. Struck by his tone and manner on the phone, I told him I could not promise anything, but I would try.

When it came time to leave, I was still quite sick, but I decided to trust what Dieter had told me and take my chances. When I arrived, dog-tired and still ailing, in Frankfurt, some people—a married couple who would be going to the conference—picked me up at the airport and took me immediately to their home where they put me to bed and indeed "took care of me."

By the next day, somehow, despite my jet lag, I was feeling substantially better, and I drove down with the husband to the conference site itself, which was located in a small town—something like Todtmoos, although I'm not sure that's the right spelling—near the Black Forest.

Not long after I arrived, I met Dieter. Talk about an archetypically-looking Nazi! He was thin, had wispy blonde hair, sunken cheeks and a ghostly pallor. Really, he seemed like a spook, and even his accent gave me the creeps. Still, he was very warm and welcoming, and despite everything, I couldn't help liking him.

After that, I went into the main conference hall to check things out, and shortly afterward found myself talking to a German journalist, Michel, who told me he had wanted to interview me for a magazine he worked for. We agreed to do the interview itself some days later, but I noticed right away how at home I felt with him.

Eventually, there was some kind of pre-conference gathering that evening where the conference attendees were all seated at a series of rectangular tables. Since I was by then kind of hanging out with Michel, I sat with him and some other people, mostly Germans, whom he knew. In the immediate cluster of people I found myself with, I felt unusually at ease. In fact, the feeling of rapport was so striking as to be almost uncanny.

I soon learned the reason that I felt so strangely comfortable with my new colleagues. Sitting at that table that evening with those strangers who seemed somehow so warm and familiar to me, I quickly learned that several of them had recently been experimenting with exactly the same drugs to which I had recently been introduced at Esalen, MDMA, now popularly known as Ecstasy, and ketamine. It was almost as if a bond of sorts had been unconsciously established between us because of our common experiences—even before we had become aware of them. So much so that it almost felt like we were like brothers and sisters in a way or at least spiritually kindred souls. I couldn't know then how much truth there was to be in that perception.

The conference started the next day and was very engrossing. Over the next few days, I had a lot of wonderful and stimulating encounters both with my previous friends and with some of the speakers I had hoped to meet there, but the deepest connections I was having were with this cluster of people I had met the first night. After that night, I would sometimes see them in a group context, but at other times, I would go off with one or another of them for a more extended conversation.

The day after my own talk, for example, Michel drove me to a restaurant away from the conference grounds so we could have some privacy and where he could tape record an interview with me. We decided to eat our lunch first and do the interview afterward—but the luncheon conversation was so absorbing to us that the interview itself was almost an afterthought.

Now, here's where it gets interesting. First, there was an obvious physical resemblance between Michel and me, even though he was about 15 years younger. But, second, it was clear from the way Michel described his childhood that we had had very similar tastes and interests even as children. However, there came a point in Michel's life where he had made a critical decision that completely changed his life. A friend of his had been screwed by someone in a business deal and wanted to get even. This friend had induced Michel to help him, and the ultimate outcome was that Michel and his friend were apprehended in some kind of illegality and other mischief, and Michel went to prison because of it.

As he continued to talk (and I chimed in about my life), it occurred to both of us that we were like brothers, except whereas he had chosen a dangerous and wayward path in life, I had chosen a safe and conventional one. We looked at each other agape because here we were, so many years later with similar interests and similar tastes, if very different backgrounds, but feeling almost as if we had been brothers all along who had only now, though this chance set of circumstances been reunited. And, as you will see, Michel and I remained in touch for a long time afterward, too, and never lost this brotherly feeling for each other. The strange thing is that neither of us had had a brother in our lives, yet felt this sense of brotherhood between us almost as soon as we began to talk in earnest about our lives and the paths we had followed.

Another person in this group was Angela, a woman in her mid-thirties, who, like Michel, was a journalist but also was serving as a translator at this conference (which was conducted in English). She and Michel were friends, were in the same group of shamanistic voyagers, and had once, I think, been lovers, though Angela was then married to somebody else. I had a very strong connection with Angela, too, and we also had some very soulful conversations during the conference, though they tended to be more light-hearted and playful at times.

As the conference progressed, it seemed to take on more the quality of celebration. Of course, during the days, there were the usual lectures and workshops, but in the evenings there were sometimes special events and entertainments, and soon enough, I realized, there were always parties. Not long after the conference began, I found myself going to the parties of the Germans (and not those of the Americans I already knew, who were partying else-where). Of course, although the conference was held in English, the German parties were not, and not having any German myself, I was completely clueless linguistically. But none of that seemed to matter. The Germans took to me readily—even the ones who weren't in that original cluster—and I felt very at home with them.

Again, there was this uncanny but yet unmistakable sense of belonging, or kindredness, and I had the best times at these parties, just soaking up the ambiance and good cheer. Once, I remember, I was sitting across from Angela at a small table with some other people, and she impulsively leaned across it and gave me a long, lingering kiss.

Another night, at one of these parties, I took a stroll outside with another one of the persons in the original group, a woman named Karin. Although Michel and Angela spoke perfect English (Angela's was even without an accent, as she had lived for a while in the States when growing up), Karin spoke only broken English, so our communications were sometimes a little tricky. Neverthe-less, I found myself telling her that I was a Jew (something that I hadn't mentioned to the others at that time), that I had had a very hard time deciding to come to the conference, etc., but that the experiences I had been having ever since I arrived had been extremely healing for me, and that my previous attitudes toward Germany had already begun to unravel. Karin didn't say anything. She just looked at me with deep compassion in her eyes, and then, without the least hint of anything erotic, she embraced me for a very long time.

The energy of this conference and everything I had been expe-riencing just continued to build as the end of the week drew near and my connection to these Germans grew stronger. On what was to be the last full day of the conference, Michel told me that that night a few of them had planned to gather to do a special ritual ceremony to mark the close of our week together. There would be eight of us—Karin, Angela, and Michel and several other people, including one American student of shamanism, who had married a German woman in this same crowd. The plan was to meet in Angela's room, which was the largest and the most commodious, and to do an evening-long ritual.

When we assembled, the American student of shamanism did a kind of purification ceremony, which took quite a while. After that, we all ingested MDMA, and a few hours later when the MDMA had reached its peak, we all took ketamine—a double drug session like the one I had experienced with Therese the year before, and, believe me, a very potent one. MDMA lasts about five hours, but ketamine is relatively quick in its action (it takes less than an hour to run its course), and for it, we all lay down in a large circle, holding hands. I remember Angela was on one side of me and Karin was on the other for this last part of the evening ceremony, and as I had with L. and S. at Esalen, I could feel a sense of merging energies with Angela and Karin. It would be far too difficult to describe in detail the kind of inner experiences these drugs produced in me that night, so I won't even try. Let it suffice for me to say that they were very powerful and deeply bonding.

Eventually, however, the various people in our group (two of them were couples) drifted off to their own quarters, and in the end, I was there with my two closest companions, Angela and Michel. It was now about 3:30 in the morning, and just then the phone rang. Angela, startled, thought it might be her husband, checking up on her (they later did get a divorce). But, no, it turned out to be Dieter. He was calling to find out how we were doing.

It was then I learned that Dieter and his cohort had been having their own similar ritual in another room. After she hung up, Angela told Michel and me that Dieter wanted to come over to pay us a visit.

The odd thing is that after I had met Dieter at the beginning of the conference, I had scarcely seen him. Of course, he was busy with his conference duties, but he seemed never to be at the German parties I attended and he wasn't a part of the German clique that I had joined almost immediately.

I remember Dieter's entrance to our room vividly. Almost surely because of the effect of the drugs I had taken that night, I saw a golden haze around Dieter's body as he walked through the door. Whether this was actually his aura or an artifact of my perception I have no way of knowing, but for whatever reason I was aware of it. The next thing was I heard Dieter call out my name, Ken, like a lover. I mean, it was like this—K...e...n, softly but with great feeling. As he intoned my name, he came over directly to me. I had been sitting on the floor, but I instinctively rose to greet him. Wordlessly, he extended his arms to me and drew me to him. A very long silent embrace ensued, and in that embrace, Ken and Dieter disappeared. They no longer existed. Neither did Germans or Jews, men or women, or any particularities of personal identity at all. They only thing that was present was Love, a love that melted away all distinctions. In that embrace was summed up everything I had experienced at the conference, and in that gesture, I was finally healed of all my past harsh feelings about the Germans. Later I thought of Schiller's line, "One embrace for all the world."

The conference really culminated for me that night with that epiphany. Dieter had told me that I must come and that they would take care of me. How could I—how could he—have possibly known how necessary it was for me to be there and how prophetic his words would be?

There is an amusing coda to this story, though. The next day, somebody (I didn't know) was supposed to give me a ride back to some town where I was to catch a train to Frankfurt from where I would be departing for the U.S. But things got bollixed up and my ride never showed. What to do? No worries, said Michel, "I'll take you."

Now another thing about Michel that I didn't tell you earlier is that he had already been in one very serious car wreck (it had killed his girlfriend at the time) and had told me he was still a somewhat reckless driver. And you know how they drive in Germany, anyway! Still, I had no fear, and I wound up having one of the most incredible car rides, over the back roads of Germany, at speeds that sometimes exceeded 120 mph, that I have ever had in my life. It was necessary to drive that fast for me to make my train, which I did with about ten minutes to spare. I never had any fear—only a sense of exhilaration—and afterward thought how appropriate that I should have this last ride from the conference with my daredevil brother.

I stayed in touch with all of these people for years afterward and visited them again a couple of times, when we once more did various drug trips together (sometimes with LSD, sometimes with ketamine), but one of my favorite subsequent experiences with hem occurred in California three years after that initial trip to Germany.

I was at another conference, this time in Santa Rosa, and was standing around in one of the halls between sessions talking to some friends. Suddenly, from behind, someone was hugging me. And I knew right away who it was! Yes, Dieter! I could tell immediately from his embrace, even though I couldn't see him, that it was he. It was unmistakable. He hadn't forgotten either.

Of course, I should add the obvious. I know the people I met at this conference were not "typical" of most Germans and that the circumstances under which I met them were exceptional, too. I don't mean to "generalize" anything from this set of experiences. All I can tell you is that, however unusual these events were, I could not help but think they were somehow "orchestrated" to help me get over a longstanding emotional block when it came to Germany. And they did. I've felt differently ever since.

This, however, isn't the end of my encounters with the Germans at that conference. A few years ago, I was to receive a most unexpected letter from another German I had briefly met there. And my subsequent relationship with him seems to me now to be the perfect and fitting capstone to the love that I experienced at that gathering.

At that conference I was very taken with some of the art that was on display, particularly with a mandala that had been painted by an orange-clad young German named Vinzent, who was then a follower of an Indian guru by the name of Bhagwan Rajneesh. I loved Vinzent's work and bought the painting on the spot. Afterward Vinzent had it sent to me, and it still hangs just few feet away from me in my office. But that was the last contact I had with Vinzent—for almost thirty years!

Then, one day, in 2014, I received an e-mail from him—out of the blue, as they say. Vinzent turned out not only to be a painter, but an astrologer, and he was asking my permission to include my astrological chart (he somehow seemed to know my birthday) in a book he was then thinking of writing. That letter initiated one of the most extraordinary and loving friendships I have ever had with a man. There was a kind of deep kinship between us that became apparent almost immediately, and it resulted in some remarkable letters, at least on his part, about his work and his inner spiritual life. They led me to treasure this correspondence and to treasure him. Over the past five years we have exchanged many letters, the result of which is I have come to feel that, like Michel, Vinzent, too, is a brother of mine, and certainly one that I very much cherish.

Sometimes, one can't help but think that there is a guiding benevolent force in our lives that orchestrates events that are designed to heal us and arranges things such that the people we are destined to meet appear at just the right time. It's not just the Lord that works in mysterious ways. It's the way Love works, too.

Medium Hot

In July of 2011, after receiving a painting from an old friend of mine who used to live with me in what we then called "The Near-Death Hotel" in Connecticut during the early 1980s when I was deeply involved in my work on near-death experiences, we began to have a few friendly and nostalgic exchanges by email. My friend's father happened to have been an art historian and that prompted me to mention that my own father, Phil, had been an artist, and that I had written a privately printed memoir about him called *My Father, Once Removed*. Since the memoir also dealt quite a bit with my own life in relation to my father, my friend said she would love to read it, so, shortly afterward, I sent her a copy.

The main thrust of my book was that, although my father had lived with me for only the first few years of my life and then had died at a young age, I had long felt his presence in my life, and in a way I could not quite explain but could not deny either, his love and guidance for me. After reading my book, my friend wrote to me as follows:

> Once I read the book, it is very clear you and your father have a very strong bond. Also, we can only speak by personal experience. Where I go when I have a need to KNOW my father is truly with me is to a good medium. They are kind of hard to find (a good one). I know of two that are VERY good. [She then gives me their contact information.] I have

had a couple of readings from one of them and my father came through clear as a bell. I cannot of course guarantee anything she might be able to communicate to you. I can only tell you she is good at what she does. My experience has been that this is the best way to KNOW they are with us a LOT of the time.

I didn't doubt the impact of these readings on my friend, but I had always shied away from mediums and psychics and had never sought a reading. Besides, after writing that book about my father and subsequently discovering quite a bit about his life that confirmed many of my intuitions about him and his love for me, I no longer felt any need to seek any kind of medium-mediated contact with him. So, I in effect demurred when I wrote to my friend concerning her urging such a course for me:

What I wonder about is whether I would be a good candidate for it since I am so left-brained. You have such a great openness to these realms and you are so loving yourself— no wonder you can enter into these states of consciousness and GO THERE. What a blessing. Well, I won't rule it out if the opportunity should come my way—it's only that I don't feel the need for it. But maybe I shouldn't be closed to this sort of thing, eh?

Within days of this exchange, I heard from another dear friend and colleague of mine, another woman who had had a long involvement in the field of near-death experiences and who had published several books on the subject. Her father, too, had recently died and she had earlier written to me when he was close to death about her deep connection to her father in the days prior to his death. Although my friend had had a difficult relationship with her father when she was a child, in later years they had grown very close and her father was very open to the implications of near-death experiences as he approached his own death. He was not afraid, and according to what my friend had told me, he had died serenely and in peace.

I was sure my friend would grieve his death, but because she is a very critically-minded and sophisticated European woman and was of course thoroughly versed in near-death studies, I was surprised to learn that after her father's death she was desolated by it and wanted to find for herself some evidence that he was safe and secure in the afterlife. I was really taken aback by her response since I felt that surely, she of all people would not require this kind of reassurance. But there it was—she was no different in this respect, it seemed, than many people who suffer the death of a loved one and want some kind of a sign that he or she still exists and remains connected with the living even after death.

In any case, my friend was now writing to me about how she had gained the knowledge she so fervently had been seeking. She had consulted—a medium.

> I must tell you something beautiful that happened to me. You know how inconsolable I was with the death of my father. I asked a friend to indicate to me a good medium because I desperately needed to establish a contact with him and restore my spiritual convictions which I had completely lost.
>
> Last Friday I received the report of the medium and it is simply unbelievable. It's a beautiful text of 2 1/2 pages, made of 2 kinds of messages: (1) the statement that he is still alive and that the after-life exists: "You were right my daughter, the after-life does exist, you can believe in it. I was surprised but I feel so incredibly well." (2) Facts which the medium could not know or guess. Many of them. Completely accurate, some of them referring to things we said just some hours before he died.
>
> Ken, I am not sad anymore, I cannot be sad! I know everything is well, just the way it is supposed to be. I feel

100% in peace, and so incredibly happy. I feel completely connected to my father, I can feel him, see him smile, being next to me, all the time. I thought I had lost him and I have found him. But not exactly the father I knew, but the person he was in the last days of his life. I then had the very strong feeling that he was sublimated, as if he had already been touched by the grace. That's exactly what I felt during his last days. And this is the being I feel next to me. I must say that this is like a miracle to me and I am infinitely grateful for this.

Needless to say, although I was very happy for my friend, I was even more struck by the fact that within two days I had received two communications from old friends connected to my NDE world who had reported such intensely impactful and subjectively convincing experiences of their deceased fathers after having received a reading from a medium.

This gets even stranger for scarcely a week later, during a visit from still another old friend whom I had first met when he had brought me and several other NDE researchers together with Raymond Moody in 1977 after which he and I had founded an organization to study these experiences, I was to hear another such story. At lunch one day, my friend—not knowing anything about my recent communications with others about their experiences with mediums—began telling me about his. The short version of his tale concerned a good friend of his who had recently died. My friend had consulted a medium and what she had told him had simply blown him away. I have now forgotten some of the specific details my friend related to me that day over lunch, but I do remember his saying how much of it was evidential and how profoundly he had been affected by the reading he had received.

Boing!

It was at this point that I could not refrain from mentioning that this was the third such account I had come across within the last two weeks. What was the universe trying to tell me?

After hearing my story, my friend urged me to make contact with the medium he had consulted—someone in New York—and later provided her email address and phone number. I said I'd think about it, but I really didn't. I just filed the medium's contact information away and more or less forgot about it.

And now for the clincher. Would you believe that a week later, I had another visit from a colleague, a philosophy professor this time, whose main professional interest for some years had also been the study of near-death experiences. I had read one of his articles years ago and we had become fast friends ever since. In any event, while he was visiting from Chicago, my friend and I met for lunch in Berkeley and began schmoozing. At one point, he asked me whether I was familiar with spiritualist churches.

I allowed as how I was—I had attended of couple of services many years ago when I was first becoming interested in what were then called "altered states of consciousness." I knew that their services were conducted by mediums and that after the religious portion of the service was concluded, the medium—often a woman—would give readings for some of the members of the audience.

This is what had happened to my friend who was attending his first such service, and when he received a reading from the medium, he was so forcibly impressed by it that he decided to make an appointment for a private reading a week later.

Now some background: My friend has made it a practice to write dialogues after the manner of Plato, which deal with perennial issues in philosophy. For this purpose, he actually makes use of historical figures, such as Plato and Socrates. I have read a couple of these dialogues and found them powerful and provocative. However, my friend told me that prior to meeting with this medium, he had been utterly blocked when trying to complete his latest such work; the dialogue had just stopped flowing and it was frustrating my friend enormously.

When my friend first attended the church service, and it came to be his turn to receive a message, the medium who had never laid eyes on him said something like this, as best he can remember: "There's a gentleman here in spirit who's been helping you with your writing. He says that you've been dilly-dallying around and wants you to get back to your writing desk." At that point, my friend added, he had written only 9 or 10 pages in over 3 years. The medium then added something to the effect that the spirit was concerned with his legacy, "even if I didn't care about such things."

My friend continued, and now I quote:

I was completely blown away, and have still not integrated this into my psyche. I then scheduled a private half hour reading with her. She talked fast and non-stop. She said that gentleman was here, wearing a lovely white robe, which would have been a toga, and he was upset that people—meaning academic philosophers, I presume—do not understand his writings. Now, there is just no way she could know that Plato and Socrates were spiritual teachers whose teachings are completely misunderstood by western philosophers. She is a social worker, and I assume she has her MSW. But like most practical do-gooders, she has no knowledge of western philosophy, and would not know the difference between Plato and Mickey Mouse's dog. Then, in that reading, she went on to describe my father, and a good friend who had recently died from obesity.

My friend said he was utterly amazed at what she told him—indeed he said that it had been a "life-transforming event" for him—and afterward, when he resumed work on the dialogue, it came out of him like a flood (he has since finished it and it runs to 793 pages!). It was almost as if he was "channeling" Plato himself, he said, beaming. I could see how much he was affected by this.

At that point, I told him my story.

On my way home, I thought: How many times do I have to hear the same message before I decide to act on it?

As soon as I got home, I got out the contact information I

had been given for the medium in New York and called her up to arrange for a reading.

The woman I reached whom I will identify here only by her first name, Laura, sounded rather young, but friendly and lively on the phone. [She is in fact a very highly regarded medium who has since published two popular books about her work.] She said she'd be glad to consider doing a reading for me, but as she was about to leave on a vacation with her family, she suggested that I first look at her website to get some information concerning how she worked and what I might expect from a reading and then, if I were interested, I could get back in touch with her. I read over her website, was impressed with her credentials and professionalism, and emailed her back to make the arrangements. We agreed that she would do a reading for me just after her return from vacation, on August 22 at 9 a.m. Pacific Daylight Time.

Laura said she didn't need or want any information from or about me. She only needed to know my name, that was all. Her website made it clear that when it came time to do my reading, she would first "read my aura," and after that she would make contact, if possible, with some of my relatives "on the other side" to see what messages they might have for me.

Two weeks later, at the appointed time, Laura called me and gave me some initial instructions concerning how she would proceed, which pretty much conformed to the information I had already read. She advised me just to relax and let the process unfold as it would.

What follows is a partial but reasonably full transcript of the reading. My comments and questions during the reading are in parentheses. Comments in brackets made after the reading relate to my clarifications and interpretations of some of Laura's remarks.

Looking at Aura. Oh, my God, your aura is quite magnificent, to say the least. It goes up in a giant U, and I don't see that typically. I feel that on some humanitarian level, you must have reached a lot of people or they're telling me you're going to reach a lot more people. In other words, your energy is very expansive. It's like a rainbow, but not the usual rainbow—it's colors upon colors. At the base, there's yellow ... may indicate two or three minor medical issues going on for you right now. Above that, there's green, and green has to do with openness to new ideas. Your aura's very interesting. It's not a normal aura. Normally, I see one color above, one to the right, one to the left. Yours is like this gigantic expansive aura, like a cone on top of you ... You're going to bring change to others. Your energy is going off to the world in some way. Above that, there's blue and white, and at your core, your astral body is a beautiful, beautiful blue color. Blue for me is a sign of nobility of spirit. Blue for me is for someone who is here on a much more advanced level. You're here to help humanity. Blue ... often means a person to whom others spill their secrets, confide in ... You have this balancing effect on people. People just open up to you and spill their secrets. You have a very balancing, healing effect on those people. It's interesting because above you, I see white, and white for me has to do with soul testing, with the reason we are here. And it's interesting because it's tied to this blue, which means helping others. Your soul test wasn't just about you. It's almost as if you are in a teacher role, to help other people. To me there's definite teacher energy to you, but it expands beyond a normal classroom. You're here on this earth in a physical form on a very advanced spiritual level. I don't feel that you were a super-religious person as a child or anything like that, I don't think it's tied to religion at all. But there's a humility about you, a humbleness. It's very beautiful, what I'm seeing. But you are definitely a teacher to others, but it expands beyond your lifetime. It's going to extend beyond your lifetime, beyond you. It's not just that you've mastered your own soul test, but you're going to help other people master their soul test. Above that, there's pink, and pink has to do with love. But it's not just directly attached to you, it's like it's love for humanity, or something. And I feel that above this white/blue soul test is this pack [?] of love. I need to tell you that whatever work you've done here is going to resonate after you cross and bring about love and healing. Wow, sorry to stay in your aura so long, but I don't often see something like this.

Now, on your right, what you're going into, I see orange. And orange has to do with creativity, appreciation for art. You're about to go into this period of creativity, too. I feel like writing—are you writing now? (I have written, yes.) Are you currently writing something? Working on writing? Are you counseling or collaborating with someone? I almost feel like you are helping to guide someone or contributing to something someone else is doing? [I had recently been in touch with a doctoral student about collaborating on a research project on NDEs and had been advising her in other ways about various professional matters.] (I think that could happen, yes.) I see that this is coming this year. By November that will be more clarified. I don't know if someone who is connected to you is writing something or including you or asking for your assistance ... The other thing I want to say is that I see ... science around you. Are you very interested in science? Your guides are telling me that you're very educated. I don't know if this makes sense, that you'd be, like, decorated, like an honorary degree? I feel like awards (well, recently, I have been honored for my work). OK, I feel that there's more to come, though. I think it's going to be a big deal, like a major award or a major honorary degree. There's something big coming, all right. That's what I'm feeling because they're decorating you.

[At this point, Laura begins picking up on the presence of various relatives of mine. From what she told me after the reading, it was as if there were a group of them gathering around and they all seemed to want to communicate at the same time. Multiple voices as in a Robert Altman film. But principally, they were my mother, my father and my first wife, Elizabeth, the only one of my wives who has died. In life, she and my mother were quite close.]

Your mom is stepping in from the other side. There are a lot of people there all at once. Mom and dad are both there. She wants to tell you that September is important. Is September a birthday or anniversary or crossing date? (Not that I'm aware of.) I feel around the 23rd, OK? ... There's someone behind her, very strong. Like a Mary. [This is presumably my aunt Mary, my mother's older sister, who was very close to my mother during life and like a second mother to me. She was a very strong personality in life and was in effect always my mother's protector.] (Yes, Mary definitely connects.) On your mom's side, right? I think there's someone with an E, Elizabeth, actually. You were very close with this Elizabeth? [Elizabeth was my first wife who had died a couple of years ago. Like me, she was a psychologist.] (I was close to Elizabeth at one time, yes.) Did you work together? (Ah, we were married.) There's something like being interested in the same things or working together. It's more like intellectual interests. (We did have some intellectual interests in common.) Did you have three children together? (I have had three children, but I only had one with Elizabeth.) Are there two children of one sex and one of another? (That's right.) You were married to her first? (That's right.) Did you divorce? (Yes.) She's telling me that you separated here on earth, not because she crossed, right? (That's correct.) She also says she sorry about being stubborn about things. (Ha, ha, tell her I forgive her!) I feel like when she was here, she 100% thought she was right about things, but when she crossed and did her life review, she kinda felt a little bit like "Oh, things could have been different, I was stubborn." She's kind of joking about it. She also brings up a "D" name. (A "D" name?) Yes, is there is David? [David is my son.] (There is a David, yes.) Is that a child for you? (Yes.) She brings it up as a child. Also, there's something that sounds like Kathryn. (That's amazing, Kathryn's another child of mine.) In some ways she watches over. I mean, it's not just Kathryn, but also David. She also mentions someone with a M name. Is there a grandchild with a M name? [David's young son is named Max.] (Yes, there is a grandchild with an M name.) Is it a little bit different of a name? (Yes, it is a little bit different.) Do two of your kids have kids? (Yes, that's correct.) Two of the children are put together, and one is separated out. Do two children live closer and one elsewhere? (Two of my children are closer to each other, and one of them is more or less separate.) Is it Kathryn who is more separate? (Yes, that's right.) [Speaking of Elizabeth who is doing a lot of the talking after my mother let her in ...] I don't feel like you two stayed very close after the divorce. (That's correct.) I don't feel that there's a great connection. [This is true; we were estranged for a long time.] I have to let you know that she's sorry for what she contributed to that. She also realizes that she was stubborn about that, by not holding things precious, but also that she's also at peace with everything. In the end any love that existed, that's what's amplified [?]. She sees the kids, she watches over them, that sort of thing. (That's really nice to know, thank you.)

Dad's staying in the background. Dad crossed before your mom, yes? (That's correct.) I also feel like, very intelligent was your dad. (Yes.) I also feel like he handed something down to you. Do you have his name, his middle name? (Well, I had his name, but not his first name; our first names are different.) I also feel like he's been crossed for quite some time. [My father died in 1953.] (Yes, that's true.) Did he have an illness, like in the stomach area? (Not that I'm aware of.) I'm also getting something from the chest area. [My father died of a heart attack.] On Dad's side of the family, was there a military connection there? With the war? (My dad was in the military, yes.) I have both sets of grandparents here, but there are strong ties to another country. Did your grandparents emigrate here? (Yes, that's true.) I feel like it's around Poland or somewhere (You're very close—Lithuania.) [Lithuania was sometimes a part of Poland.] It's your grandmother who's coming through with that. Did you have a grandmother who was born there? (Yes.) Very strong woman, yes? (No!) Emm. I also get that there's a R name coming through. (Connected to the grandmother?) Yes. (Yes, her name did begin with R.) Was it like Ruth? (Yes, perfect!) I have to tell you she tells me that you are peacemaker. She tells me that's a role you've stepped into. I'm supposed to tell you, and I think she brings this up because she was from another country, one thing that

you learned is that we human beings are not from any one particular country. I mean, we got too caught up with this, our identity.
We can look at ourselves in our identity as fellow human beings
to one another, and not be so [identified with our own country],
but we are all connected. Somehow—remember the writing I was
talking about? (Yeah)—somehow the writing might be connected
with this. It's a very advanced way of thinking, a very healing
way of thinking, a way that we human beings need to connect to
one another on. You're more aware of that and that's one of the
messages you're going to be trying to share ... Did you do writing
on this? (Yes.) To me, you started this process, and whatever it is,
others are going to pick it up from here, but you're still involved.

I also see you being asked to speak somewhere ... There's
going to be more to come, or you're going to be interviewed or
something. You've laid the groundwork, but now you're going to
be asked about it.

Your mom is talking about a picture in an oval frame. Do you
have a picture of your mother in an oval frame? [I later remembered that I did have such a photograph in one of my albums, but
I didn't recall it at the time.] (No, but I do have a photo of another
relative who is in an oval frame.) Is this in your office? (Yes, it is.)
She's very happy about this, and is it a black-and-white picture?
(Yes, it's her father.) She's very happy about that. Is there a William
there? He's attached somehow. (Yes. Attached to her father?) Yes.
(Yes, William was his son.) William's also on the other side. [He
was very close to me when I was growing up and was the first big
influence on my intellectual life.] (That's right.) There are together.
This is their way of telling you that they're all hanging out together
... But they're making me feel, like, were they all closed-minded
to or ignorant of this whole idea of heaven, the other side type of
thing? [They were all irreligious and as far as I know none of them
believed in life after death.] (Definitely!) It's almost like you've
been here, they said. (In a manner of speaking.) I almost feel like
you could describe it better than me. Does that make sense to you?
(Emm, yep; afterward I'll tell you why.)

I hear this "thank you" all the time coming from the other side. It's giving me chills. It's somehow that you're teaching others about the other side. Somehow, I feel you know more than I do about the other side. Do you understand? (Yes.) There are children over there who are thanking you for—like bringing peace to their parents. (I understand that, too.) Do you do grief counseling or work with the bereaved? (Not exactly, but I can relate to what you are saying.) I know, because there's a lot of them, but you're not related to them, but it's thank you on behalf of the children, thank you for the work you are doing. You're very, very unique. Because you—I feel like a lot of people once they cross and do their life review realize that all this was real, this is how I could have helped people, this is how I could have done things differently in my life—it's almost as if you have that knowledge, but you're here (Right). You help bring other people to that knowledge. It's very beautiful what I'm seeing. (Thank you.) Very beautiful ...

[After a bathroom break ...] One of your grandchildren will take after you. (Oh, how nice.) It seems to be about writing, too. You've involved with writing, correct? (That's right.) Is one of your grandchildren writing, too? (They're too young.) It's gonna be one that is involved in writing, somehow. Or following in your footsteps. (Are you sure it's a grandchild?) I think it's going to be a grandchild, but does your son do that, too? (Yes, he does.) They're telling me that your son already does this. Your son has a child, too, yeah? (That's correct.) OK, it's going to be handed down again. (Ah, OK.) It's almost as if I'm just supposed to let you know this, that this will come, too. It's almost like a beautiful chain that goes on. Your son has a son, too? (That's right.) It's a beautiful connection that I'm seeing. Does your son think alike or is very much alike? (We're alike in some ways, yes.) Are you interested in the same topics, and does he do education? (Yes, he does do education.) Is this the David? I hear David again.

Mom [who seems to have been imparting the above information] has crossed for a while now, yes? [She died in June, 2001.] Did she get to know David well? [Fairly well, but not too well.]

It's like she knew him around the age of 20, right around there. I also want to say—was mom put in a care facility when she was ill. (Yes.) Did she have an issue with Alzheimer's (Well, she was somewhat demented at the end.) When I see her [then] she was not of clear mind. I feel like what mom is trying to show me is that when she was still here, she was physically on earth, her mind was half there. When she crossed, did you try to get there in time or something like that? (Yes, I tried to but was unable to.) I need to let you know that she sees that you tried to get there in time, but I feel that it wasn't meant to be. You weren't there when she crossed, is that right? (I wasn't, and I was not able to get there.) OK, I just need to let you know that that's OK. That's how it was supposed to be. I also feel like your mom wanted to cross with a little more privacy than other people. That was something that she wanted. [That would be in character for my mother.]

Do you have prostate problems? (Ha, ha, well, I do have prostate problems, but only benign prostatic hypertrophy, but just last night I started to read a book about a guy with severe prostate problems ...) Did they talk about laser surgery of something? (Well, it has been discussed ...) She [mom] seems to be indicating that there's more to come, that there's going to be some kind of treatment, that you shouldn't shy away from it, but should listen ... I don't see anything serious for you ... And I'm supposed to tell you— do you exercise a lot by walking? [Tape needed to be changed at this point, but I was urged to keep walking, as that was the best exercise for me. Walking is in fact my main form of exercise, as it was for my mother.]

[When Laura resumes, but before the tape starts recording, she begins talking about my personal guides. There are two of them, both male. They are powerful, very advanced beings. One has a scientific background. At his point, side two of the tape begins ...] The scientist feels to me like somehow in the science field, but also interested in the afterlife. And I want to go back about 100 years. Like he's on the team with your guides. Like there's a connection to France there? [I have long felt a connection to France, more than any other country.] There are some very unique things about my reading for you. [And there are apparently other helpers as well—she wasn't clear here.]

Is there a John or a Jack? I want to be this [in the category of] colleagues. Not family. [Not clear if this person is here or there, but she thinks the person is in the same field—presumably, as I now suppose, John Audette who has been a longtime colleague in my NDE world and who recently visited me.] Is there, like a Bruce you work with? (I have worked with a Bruce, yes.) [Bruce Greyson, another NDE colleague, also connected to John.] Somehow you and Bruce do the same thing or you help each other. Were you both at some conference recently? (No, but we've been together at conferences.) [And I was invited to be at an IANDS conference with Bruce—also John—early next month, in September.] I don't know if there's another one coming soon ... But somehow, you're all on the same playing field. It's almost as if the other side knows that. If this were a baseball team, these people are all on it and are all working for the same kind of goal.

Is there a Diane here you're connected to? Are you very close to her? (Yes, in an odd sort of way.) [Presumably Diane Norton, a longtime NDEr friend who has been very loving to me over the years, but whom I have treated rather indifferently at times. I had, however, just written her a letter.] I feel like somehow that relationship definitely helps you grow. (Hmm, interesting.) She's more important than she seems.

[At this point, Laura asks me if I have any specific questions for her.] (I'd like to know if you can give me any information about my father.) Well, first of all, I feel like he crosses before his time. Somehow you and he had abbreviated time together. (That's very true.) And I hear an apology for that. He apologizes to you, that's what I'm getting. To me, it's like in a way he was letting you down. This could be like he crossed without having enough time with you as father. It's like, "I'm sorry." He crossed very quickly, too. (Yes.) Was that from a heart attack? (Exactly.) OK, and there was no goodbye, correct? (That's right.) And you were much younger, right? (True.) [I was 17 when he died.] I just feel like there's an apology for that. I feel like he's saying he should have taken care of his health better. I don't feel that he's that old when he crosses at all. [He was 41, just as his career as an artist was taking off.] There's a tragedy around him. (Yes.)

He was a very smart man, yes? (Yes.) (Can you see him?) Let me look. I don't think he was that tall. Was he under six feet? (Yes, he was.) He had dark hair, yeah? (Yeah.) Did he have dark eyes, too? (I think so.) At one point, did he wear a mustache? (Yes, he did have a mustache.) There's something funny about it or he thinks he looks silly with a mustache. He's joking about the mustache. There's something about a train. Did he collect trains? (That sounds more like my stepfather.) Did your stepdad collect trains? (Yes.) OK, this is his way of letting him in, too. Somehow your stepfather was around in your life a lot more to raise you than your biological dad was. (Yes.) He's grateful to him. For helping you, for nurturing you, for being there, OK? Could your stepfather be very stubborn about things, though? (Extremely.) And did he yell? [My stepfather was very bellicose and choleric; he did yell a lot.] (Yes, exactly!) Like, yaah! He's happy that he was there, but he wishes he could have—well, that side of his personality could be very difficult. (So you're saying that my dad knows this about my stepdad.) Oh yeah. (Does my dad have any particular message for me?) Obviously, he's very, very proud of you because obviously you've achieved more in the family than anyone else. Did you get an advanced college degree? (Yes, I did.) And nobody else in the family had done that, you understand? [That's true; I was the first.] It's a really big deal to them. (Huh, no kidding?) A really big deal to them on the other side. And your biological dad's mom is really, really proud of you.

Your biological dad was a hard worker, yes? (I think he was, yes.) I feel like he was trying to build something while he was still here. I don't mean like trying to build a house, but trying to build something on his own ... and it was cut short. (Yeah, it was.) Like it was left incomplete. (You're very right.) He wasn't so happy about that. He was happy about other things. It was like, "oh, man!" When he crossed, it was like, "Hey, wait a minute. You're kidding me. First of all, this is real. Second of all, I'm not going to be able to finish that?" You understand? He was annoyed about that.

Do you know if your mother had a miscarriage? (She might have, but I can't be sure. I wouldn't know.) OK, it's what your biological dad is telling me. Is there a brother for you? (I don't have any brothers.) He's bringing that up—it might be his way of telling you that. (I kinda always felt that I had an older brother.) You probably did but you didn't know. But you look like your dad, though. (I think I do look a little bit like my dad. I've always identified with him.) And also, you've dreamt of him, yes? (I've had many thoughts about my father. I might have had dreams about him, but I can't recall them offhand.) It's also interesting in that he says he helps you with your work from the other side. Somehow organizes things on the other side that helps your work here, you understand? (So he's helping me?) And he has helped you. He's helped you for twenty years. Because he couldn't do it here physically, he's had to do it from the other side. [I always felt this and several years ago wrote a memoir about my dad whose main theme was my sense that he had been a continuing, loving and guiding presence in my life.] He also thanks you for not being angry at him. I don't know if you understand that. (I've never been angry at him.)

(Does he say anything about his own name?) Oh, did you take your stepfather's last name? (Yes.) He's says that's fine. His last name was longer. (Yes, it was longer.) Was his last name Jewish or something? (It wasn't particularly Jewish. Not like Goldstein or Silverstein ...) But he was Jewish. Was there like a Kaufman or something? (His last name was Kurman.) Oh, that could be it, then! But it's fine that you didn't take his last name. He's happy with what you did. [I've always been glad to have been Kenneth Ring and not Kenneth Kurman.]

He says you're not closed-minded at all. You don't look at life like I'm this religion or that religion. You kind of swim through things, through religion, and through people. You're not based in only one, you understand? You celebrate humanity. Very impressive.

Do you wear glasses? (Yes.) Do you need to get your prescription changed? Did you just do that? (I do it very often.) Well, he's just bringing it up. He's watching out for you. (Well, I feel a real connection with him.) Well, he loves [?] you a lot, and as I said, he's been helping you for the last twenty years. I think you're very connected to him.

How are you tied to the other side? The way I'm getting it is the way a medium would. (I'll tell you afterward.) It's very interesting to me. Because he's helping you organize things the way one of my guides would help me, you know what I mean?

(I have one question you might not be able to answer, but I'd be curious. I'd like to know that in the unlikely event of my death, will I see my father or will I have some connection to the various people you described to me?) Well, absolutely, but he's laughing at you! "You asking me that when you already know the answer to that!" I mean, he's joking with me, and he sighs, and says [apparently tongue-in-cosmic cheek], "first, there's going to be a tunnel, and then, if you like, I'll greet you first, and then you're going to see all of us there ..." It's almost like he's laughing at you, you understand? You gotta believe that they're all going to greet you. I don't think it's going to be any time soon. I think there are a lot more connections and things that you're doing here. You're still very involved in things.

I also see you on TV. Were you—this is going to sound bizarre— OK, were you on Larry King or something? (That's amazing, yes, I was on Larry King.) Really?? Was this like 20 years ago? [Damn close—it was in 1992, 19 years ago.] I'm getting something like, your dad helped to arrange getting you on Larry King. I was arguing with him, "What, Larry King?" I thought maybe I was getting it wrong. I'm also supposed to tell you that if you chose to, you could still be doing media, but you've backed away a little bit. (Yeah, exactly.) You chose to back away from it? (Yes.) You're definitely going to be invited to speak somewhere, too. (I wouldn't be surprised.) You're in California, but I could see you going to the other coast, like to Virginia? (I was asked to speak in North Carolina, but I declined.) OK, but I think they are going to ask you again. It's not going to go away. It's nothing you have to do; it would just be kinda cool. Just so you know that. You also don't like to fly? (That's very true. I don't like to fly anymore.)

At this point, Laura asked if I had any more questions, but as we had already been talking for 80 minutes and her reading was only supposed to be an hour long, I said I thought we should stop here, I didn't want to impose on her any further. So I turned the tape recorder off after which we chatted for a few more moments and I thanked her for what had been a very meaningful reading for me and one, as I told her, in which she had related many accurate things about me and my family members that she could not have known. Afterward, I gave her reading a lot of thought, especially as I was transcribing it and again, now, as I have been writing up this report.

One more concluding note. Not long ago, in another memoir in which I had discussed some recent discoveries about my father's life, I ended my remarks by writing the following:

> I have always felt his love as the primordial fact of my life, even when he was forced to part from me, and even after his death. Even now, as I write these words. And when I die, I hope I will have my own confirmation of this when, at last, I may see him once more with his arms outstretched, waiting to welcome me home.

This reading has only added to my sense, now bordering almost on a firm conviction, that when my time comes, my yearning for this reunion will indeed be fulfilled and I will again find myself embraced by my father and will feel his love once more, only more intensely and with the greatest joy.

Animals

Introduction

In my house there are two bathrooms, one for me and the other for my guests, who are, fortunately, only women these days. In the guest bathroom, facing the toilet is a small bookcase and in the top row of that bookcase is my collection of books about animals, one of my favorite subjects, for I find the world of animals endlessly fascinating and full of wonder. My guests seem to as well because at least three of them lately have raided this bookcase and borrowed some of my books. Ken's lending library seems to the result.

I've written about animals, too. I even wrote an illustrated book about the cat, Petunia, that my girlfriend Lauren and I share (though she retains custody of Petunia). And, naturally, I've written some blogs about animals, too. Here are four of them.

Confessions of a Retarded
Animal Lover

Nature and I are two. —Woody Allen

I've always loved that quip of Woody's, probably because I identify with it. For much of my life, and even to some extent today, I have felt not only removed from nature but alien to it. Some years ago, I wrote a memoir about my father from whom I was separated at an early age and who died when he was scarcely forty years old. I called it *My Father, Once Removed*. If I were to write about my life in nature, I could give it a similar title.

Didn't Thomas Carlyle, who was not a fan of things mechanical, somewhere assert that "machines are inherently aggressive?" Well, I could say something akin to that sentiment about nature— that it is inherently frightening, at least to me. But I know I'm not the only one who thinks this way about nature. I remember when I was young reading the books of a man named Eric Hoffer—he was a self-educated longshoreman whose books were very popular when I was a kid—where he said much the same thing about nature in trying to counter the typical romantic blather about it. Nature is fine on a sunny day in the park, but if you get caught in a sudden thunderstorm in the woods, it is not your friend; it could kill you.

I don't know how I got to feel this way, but unlike many kids, I did not grow up with animals. In neither my mother's home nor that of my aunt's where I also spent a lot of time when I was growing up were there any pets. Not having a father, no one took me camping, fishing or hunting either. I even flunked out of cub scouts because I couldn't figure out how to tie a knot properly. I knew that I was descended from a long line of Lithuanian rabbis; what I was good at was reading books and studying. That was the world where I felt at home. Jews are urban people anyway. We didn't farm; we made money (although I was never much good at that either, come to think of it).

I also had another problem growing up that helped to make me a misfit in nature. I was born with a congenital nystagmus that left me with very poor vision and a wayward sense of balance. No one even discovered my visual problems until I was six years old. Before that, I guess I was walking around like a child version of Mr. Magoo.

You can't become much of a naturalist if you can't see. I can't tell you how many times I would be walking with a friend who would suddenly stop to point out a beautiful bird in a tree. I could see the tree. Or I remember a time when I was walking by the Pacific Ocean in Monterey with a good friend when she stopped to look at how the sea lions were cavorting. I could see the water. I could never see well enough to make out anything. In order to learn to appreciate nature, of course I had to read books about it, such as Annie Dillard's Pilgrim at Tinker Creek. I could be in nature, but I could never experience it the way most people could. Where nature was concerned, I was a hopeless retard!

But that was to change when I was in my mid-thirties. It was then that I had my first LSD experience, which took place mainly when I was ambling around in the woods not far from the University of Connecticut where I was teaching.

That experience was a revelation to me at many levels, and it totally changed my feelings about nature. I remember looking at a certain tree and realizing as if for the first time that it was alive—and holy. For a long time after that experience, I could no longer look at trees in the same way I had been used to. And after that, I spent a lot of time tramping through the nearby woods. I would go there as often as possible, both for pleasure and as a place of refuge. I would drag my kids there, too, who were not keen to go and would complain. But I was at home in nature now, and when I could travel to places, such as Colorado, where there were mountains, I learned to love to hike up them. Of course, I was never much of a hiker, given my physical limitations, but hiking became one of the supreme recreational pleasures of my life. It's only been in the last few years that I was no longer able to hike. I miss it terribly.

My views about animals have changed, too, and I will get to that since that is what I really want to focus on in this essay but first I need to say a little about my feelings about the two types of pets we are most familiar with—cats and dogs.

It's often said, simplistically, that there are two kinds of people in the world: dog people and cat people. Well, I am definitely a cat person. And I always have been. Even though I didn't grow up with them, once I got married and had kids of my own, cats became a part of my life. I feel about them the way the ancient Egyptians did. They are divine creatures, and truly one of the jewels of evolution's experiments. There's an old song from South Pacific, "There is Nothing Like a Dame." For me, there is nothing like a cat. Nietzsche said "Without music life would be a mistake." I would say the same for cats. A catless world would be an abomination. I trust I have made myself clear.

As for dogs, I would be happy to live in a world without them. They may be "man's best friend," but they are not mine. Oh, I know there are touching stories about men and their dogs, one by Thomas Mann called in fact "A Man and His Dog," or the famous story by J. R. Ackerley, about his dog Tulip (though it was actually named Queenie), and many others. Fine, to each his own. But, frankly, some dogs look like unmade beds to me, and I really can't abide their slobbering tongues, their panting, their fearsome teeth, their annoying barks, and their slavish loyalty. When my second wife suddenly arrived one day with a large matted four-legged thing, who proceeded to jump on me, seeking out my gonads, I immediately named him Albatross, and his name, shortened to Alby, stuck. I'm sure he was responsible for our fighting like cats and dogs ourselves (you will know who was who) and in part for our later divorce. I'm sorry if I have offended you, if you are a dog lover, but I hope to redeem myself in my next blog when I will have some wonderful things to say about dogs who don't live with me.

In fact, I will soon have some wonderful things to say about animals, period, because in recent years I have become fascinated with books about animal intelligence (or "animal cognition," as it is now usually called) as well as the emotional life of animals. Indeed, I now have a slew of books in my library—well over a dozen—dealing with various facets of the lives of animals and am currently reading a new one on animal languages. For somebody who didn't grow up with animals, I am now growing old with them, and what I have learned about them has been a source of endless wonderment and enchantment. Of course, I admit I am really not spending my time with actual animals; I am limited merely to doing my usual thing—reading about them. But that's been enough to thrill me with what I'm learning about them and why I'm keen to share some of that knowledge with you in the remainder of this essay.

The thing that's new in animal studies, and what has particularly excited me, has been the focus on the inner lives of animals. Perhaps surprisingly, in recent years animal researchers have learned a great deal about how animals think, what they feel, what kind of emotional lives they have, and most intriguingly, about the structure of the languages they use to communicate with one another and to us. Consider, for example, the titles or sub-titles of the following books, which are representative of these new directions in the exploration of the lives of animals.

Mama's Last Hug: Animal Emotions and What They Tell Us about Ourselves by Frans de Waal. (De Waal is world famous for his forty years of research on chimpanzees.) In this illuminating book, de Waal shows us how similar the emotional lives of chimps are to our own. After beginning with the very moving story of the death of the chimp, Mama, de Waal shows us that humans are not the only species with the capacity for love, hate, fear, shame, guilt, joy, disgust and empathy. There is no sharp dividing line between us and them; we all animals after all and we share a continuum with all life.

Beyond Words: What Animals Think and Feel by Carl Safina. (Safina, a MacArthur Fellow and a marvelous writer—I even wrote him a fan letter and he responded most graciously—in this book writes about the inner lives of elephants, wolves and killer whales.) I can't resist quoting just a short passage from the book jacket, which echoes de Waal's sentiments:

> *Beyond Words* brings forth powerful and illuminating insight into the unique personalities of animals through extraordinary stories of animal joy, grief, jealousy, anger, and love. The similarity between human and nonhuman consciousness, self-awareness, and empathy calls us to reevaluate how we interact with animals.

The Soul of An Octopus: A surprising Exploration into the Wonder of Consciousness by Sy Montgomery. (Montgomery is another accomplished writer and naturalist. She lives with a flock of chickens and a border collie—and did you know that one border collie learned the names of a thousand toys and understands grammar? Yes!) Of course, when it comes to octopuses (yes, that's the plural—not octopi!), we encounter a creature vastly different from ourselves. For one thing, their brain is distributed through their arms, but Montgomery, too, wants to explore their emotional lives and how they come to experience and navigate the world. I defy anyone not to be amazed and utterly captivated with the story that Montgomery tells of these extraordinary beings whose evolutionary history is so different from ours. And yet....

Modern research into the lives of animals has taken us a long way from Descartes (or Des-car-tees, as my best friend, Stan, in junior high was wont to call him until I gave him some French lessons) who thought that animals, because they could not speak and therefore could not think, were soulless creatures, mere machines (in fact, he called animals bêtes-machines), incapable of experiencing pain.

Did that man ever look into the eyes of a dog?

Of course, Descartes was famous for his dictum, *cogito ergo sum*: I think, therefore I am. But why doesn't someone ever pose this question: If Descartes had said instead, "I do not think," would he then conclude that he didn't exist?

I think Descartes, as great a philosopher as he may have been, is over-rated. He may have been a smart cookie, but at least where animals were concerned, he was an arrogant anthropocentric nincompoop.

But he got his comeuppance. The fabled Queen Christina of Sweden, who was fascinated by Descartes' ideas, invited him to come to Sweden so she could learn from him. Against his better judgment, Descartes allowed himself to be lured there in the fall of 1649. As a brutally cold winter set in, he was obliged meet with the queen in her unheated library very early in the morning, and because she was the queen, Descartes had to appear bare-headed. Naturally, he developed influenza, which turned into pneumonia, which turned into death. So ended the life of a great philosopher who knew everything about how to think but would die without knowing that animals could think, too, and would never be stupid enough voluntarily to venture into territory which could be expected to be a mortal threat.

Well, so much for our Cartesian diversion. Let's return to more intelligent creatures. Take bats, for instance.

Free-tailed bats use echolocation to navigate and to catch prey. They emit sounds that are too high-pitched for human ears to detect. And they sing, too. In recent years, digital technology has revealed that bats are now believed to be the mammals with *the most complex form of vocal communication* after humans.

These bats not only sing, but each male bat creates his own

distinctive song to court females. And these songs are extremely complex and varied, and are constructed like human sentences. The language of bats, therefore, has its own syntax.

I learned all this from reading a fascinating book I alluded to earlier on the language of animals by a Dutch researcher and philosopher named Eva Meijer. She also revealed to me the secret lives of the lowly prairie dog.

Prairie dogs live in underground tunnels with different areas for sleeping, giving birth, and getting rid of bodily wastes. Because they have to be vigilant for predators when they surface, they have developed various complex alarm calls that sound a bit like the twittering of birds. Did you ever wonder why these animals are called prairie dogs? It's because when they are out in force vocalizing their alarm calls, it sounds like the barking of dogs.

But these calls also contain information about the predator, and it is so highly specific as to be almost unbelievable. According to Meijer, in the case of a human predator, for example, they can communicate that it is a human, what color clothes he is wearing, and if he is carrying something like an umbrella or a gun. Different parts of the call change meaning depending on the order of its elements, so that the language of prairie dogs has a simple grammar. Meijer says that research into the language of prairie dogs shows that they use verbs, nouns and adverbs in meaningful ways.

Take that, Descartes!

I wish I had the space to talk about the wonders of larger animals that are more familiar to us, such as chimps and elephants (I have read a number of books about each of them, which have been fascinating to me), but for now, let me mention another creature that is familiar to us all on a daily basis: the crow.

Crows are among the most intelligent of birds. A number of studies have shown that they can solve complicated puzzles and devise and use tools. They are extraordinarily clever and tales of their prodigious memories are legion. If you threaten or actually injure a crow, that crow will never forget you and will attack you on sight. I have read a number of accounts of this sort of thing, but one of the most fascinating comes from one of the best books on birds you could ever read, Jennifer Ackerman's *The Genius of Birds*.

I just can't resist quoting this story, which I will lightly edit and slightly abridge here:

> A brilliant string of studies over the past five years ... at the University of Washington has revealed the extraordinary abilities of American crows not just to recognize individual humans by their faces but to pass along to other crows information about those whom they deem dangerous. In one experiment, teams of people wandered through several Seattle neighborhoods wearing different sorts of masks. One type of mask in each group represented the "dangerous" mask. The people wearing the dangerous mask captured several wild crows. Other people, wearing "neutral" masks or no mask at all just meandered along harmlessly.
>
> Nine years later, the masked scientists returned to the scene of the crime. The crows in these neighborhoods—including those who weren't even hatched at the time of the capture—reacted to the people with the dangerous masks as if they were a threat, dive-bombing, scolding, and mobbing them.

Moral: Never mistreat a crow or you will pay for it. And also don't volunteer to carry out any such experiments wearing a threatening mask. You may decide that some scientific experiments are just not worth having to fend off savage crow attacks!

Well, there are so many remarkable stories about animals I would love to regale you with, but this blog can't go on forever, any more than I can, so let me conclude with one more topic, which many of you will know has long played a special role in my life: death. In this case, the death of animals.

Can animals actually die? Of course, they can, you would say.

That's obvious! But not to some philosophers. Martin Heidegger, who along with Ludwig Wittgenstein, is generally regarded as the most important philosopher of the first half of the twentieth century, famously held that animals, because they presumably have no concept of death, cannot die; they simply disappear.

Honestly, these philosophers! Some of them deserve to be attacked by a swarm of vengeful, screaming crows.

I have already referred to the fact that animals are capable of empathy, so it won't surprise you to learn many animals mourn those who have died. Chimps, for example, and the mourning rituals of elephants are well known. (I could easily write pages about elephants in this connection; the stories I have collected about them are deeply moving.) What isn't well known is that giraffes and foxes also mourn their dead. There is even a remarkable story about a gorilla who used sign language to describe the death of his parents by poachers.

And there are our crows again whose mourning of their dead comrades is especially affecting. I have read several very touching stories, especially in Ackerman's book, about the way crows gather around the body of a dead crow, and often return to drop twigs or a piece of grass over its body.

In fact, when I was talking about such rituals to my girlfriend Lauren a few days ago, she volunteered that she already knew all this from her own experience and proceeded to tell me about something she had witnessed herself a few years ago. After listening to her account, I asked her if she would be good enough to write it out for me so that I could use it in this essay. Lauren indeed was "good enough," so here it is in her own words:

> There is a set of wires that intersect in front of my house. One goes to my home, and another is attached to a pole across the street that crosses in front of my view, which would otherwise be exposed to a panorama of the Golden Gate Bridge and the bay. One day I heard a terrific uproar at the front of my residence and wondered at the commotion.

As the cacophony continued, I investigated only to find crows sitting on the wires abutting one another bawling, rocking back and forth, and in utter distress. There must have been forty of them in lamentation. Why were they crying so piteously?

In a moment of bravery, I walked out my front door, down my steps, and peered into the street at the object of anguish. There to my surprise was a huge crow without a mark on his body, but dead. I looked up at the mourners and said to them, "I am so sorry that your friend has gone." With those words, the crows inexplicably and suddenly became quiet. I picked up the body, which was surprisingly heavy, and said, "I will take care of his body. You may lament him, but I will take guardianship over him." The crows reciprocated with a soothing cooing sound. I was stupefied that my words and actions had such an impact on these beautiful highly intelligent avians.

I walked with their friend to my backyard noticing that five of them followed me up the driveway and settled in a tree under which I placed his body. They bobbed and swayed and cooed quietly while I went about my preparations. Inside I found a length of fabric with which to wrap his body and returning I picked up a shovel with which to dig his grave. I dug as deep a hole as I could, perhaps a foot and a half deep all the while the mourners remained unchanged, quietly grieving. When I had completed my regrettable task, I covered the grave with an old doormat knowing that one of the night creatures might dig him up. I then placed an antique fireplace grate over the mat to make sure the gravesite would remain untouched.

This is the biggest surprise of all: five of the crows returned each day for five days and remained all day to mourn their friend. Then I noticed that there were only three who came to lament his passing, and they too remained all day for three days. While I can never be sure, I suspect that one still comes each day to pay her respects, and I welcome her.

I need to bring this blog to an end soon, but not quite yet.

Obviously, I could offer you here only a few tidbits, as it were, about the lives of animals based on my reading of books about them. But I hope I have said enough to intrigue some of you to read some of these books yourself. (If you would like a complete list of such books in my own library, please write me.) Of course, books are no substitute for actual physical encounters with animals, but most of us can't easily arrange to have an elephant in our backyard or to burrow underground looking for prairie dogs. Anyway, in my case and at my advanced age, I am pretty much forced to follow my usual practice—to spend time learning about animals, once removed, in my belated efforts to become an animal lover after all these years *malgré moi*. It is never too late for an old dog to learn new tricks.

And speaking of dogs, I haven't forgotten my promise to say some good things about them in my next blog, which will be about the psychic life of dogs and especially cats, wherein more wondrous stories will be told about the amazing sensitivities of those we call our pets, including what happens to them after they die.

It's Reigning Cats and Dogs: The Psychic Lives of Our Pets

One day several years ago, as my girlfriend Lauren and I were out on her patio, a cute little stray kitten wandered in and stopped to look at us. Lauren who loves cats smiled encouragingly and bent down to greet our visitor who then tentatively approached. I immediately dubbed her "Petunia," though we didn't then know her sex. That was the beginning of a love affair—between Lauren and Petunia who quickly became Lauren's most affectionate and devoted companion, displacing me in that hierarchy to a secondary position.

Lauren soon discovered that not only was Petunia exceedingly affectionate, but she was clearly psychic, too. She always seemed to know, for example, when Lauren was planning to drive across the bay to visit me. And when Lauren would sometimes bring Petunia with her, the cat would invariably hide on the day Lauren was to leave for home. It got to be so that we would have to mime to each other so that Petunia would not know Lauren's plans.

There were, in fact, so many instances of Petunia's unusual, seemingly psychic, sensitivities that a few years later, I actually wrote a little illustrated book about her I called *Petunia, The Psychic Cat*.

Indeed, there is abundant evidence that cats are telepathic. Rupert Sheldrake, an exceptionally creative and curious English scientist, has collected many cases of this kind, and not only about cats, in one of the most remarkable books on animals I have ever read. It has a most intriguing title, too: *Dogs That Know When Their Owners Are Coming Home*. But there is a lot about cats in this book, too, and in the first part of this essay I am going to draw on it extensively. It begins with this story about a professor at a university of which I happen to be an alumnus:

> When the telephone rings in the household of a noted professor at the University of California in Berkeley, his wife knows when her husband is on the other end of the line. How? Whiskins, the family's silver tabby cat rushes to the telephone and paws at the receiver. "Many times he succeeds in taking it off the hook and makes appreciative meows that are clearly audible to my husband at the other end," she says. "If someone else telephones, Whiskins takes no notice."

This is not an isolated case. Sheldrake writes that he has collected fifty-nine cases (!) of cats who respond to the telephone when a particular person is calling, even before the receiver is picked up. In every instance, the caller is someone to whom the cat is deeply attached.

Here's another typical example:

> Seven years after she acquired Carlo, my daughter went to teacher training college and rang us infrequently. However, when the phone did ring and it was Marian ... Carlo would bound up the stairs [where the phone was] before I had picked up the receiver. There was no way that this cat could have known my daughter was to ring us ... He never did this at any other time and was not allowed upstairs anyway.

Many cat owners—about one-third, according to a survey that Sheldrake conducted—believe their cats are telepathic. The examples above and those to come will make it clear why so many cat lovers are convinced that this is so.

As the title of Sheldrake's book implies, he is particularly interested in anticipatory behavior in animals, especially dogs, who give evidence that they are aware when their owners will be returning home. These reports do not depend on anecdotal accounts alone; Sheldrake has actually carried out controlled experiments to establish the point. Here is a summary of a typical such experiment.

A dog owner is sent into town to wander about. At a certain time of her own choosing, she forms an intention to return home. Cameras have been placed in her home so that the movements of her dog can be tracked. Let's say the dog has been lying on a sofa. However, at the very moment the owner has turned around and has started her trek toward home, the dog suddenly jumps off the sofa and pads over to the door to wait for his owner to return.

There are many cases of such astonishing anticipatory behavior in dogs in Sheldrake's book and many other marvelous stories about the amazing things that dogs are capable of, so I highly recommend this book to any of you who are dog lovers. But, as I remarked in my previous blog about animals, since I fancy cats and am actually a bit averse to dogs, the rest of this essay will concern itself with the wonders of cats.

However, before moving on, I should note that cats, too, can exhibit in the same kind of anticipatory behavior as dogs. Here's just one such example:

> When the son of Dr. Carlos Sarasola was living with him in Buenas Aires, he often came home late at night, after his father had gone to bed with their cat, Lennon. Dr. Sarasola noticed that Lennon would suddenly jump off the bed and go and wait by the front door ten or fifteen minutes before his son arrived home by taxi. Dr. Sarasola made careful observations of the time the cat responded to see if the cat could be responding to the sound of the taxi door shutting. He found that the cat responded well before the taxi arrived. "One night I paid attention to several taxis that stopped at the front of my building. Three taxis stopped and Lennon

remained quiet with me in bed. Some time later, he jumped down and went to the door. Five minutes later I heard the taxi arrive in which my son was traveling."

Cats seem to be very sensitive not only to the emotional state of their owners—there are countless examples of that and this is well known—but are especially telepathically attuned to accidents, illness and death. Here are a couple of illustrative cases that Sheldrake provides.

In May 1994 I sat outside on the veranda, and my three-year-old cat, Klaerchen, lay beside me purring comfortably. My eleven-year-old daughter had gone out with her girlfriend on her bicycle. Everything seemed harmonious, but suddenly Klaerchen jumped up, uttered a cry we had never heard before and in a flash ran into the living room where she sat down in front of the telephone. The phone soon rang and I got the news that my daughter had had a bad accident with the bike and had been taken to the hospital.

We had a beautiful Carthusian tomcat that we all loved, but he loved my husband most of all. In the summer holidays we went camping in Denmark and left the cat at an animal home in Switzerland [where we lived]. In Denmark my husband, who was forty-eight years old and had never been ill, died of a heart attack. When we went to pick up our cat the lady told us she knew exactly when a tragedy had happened to us and then gave us the exact day and hour, which she could not have known! Our tomcat had withdrawn into a corner and whined in a way he had never done before, staring at a certain point in front of him as if he observed something special, his whole body shaking.

Cats seem to sense the onset of death, even when there may have been no discernible sign of it beforehand. Again, there are many examples of this kind of premonition in cats, and we will soon consider in detail a couple of such cases, but for now, here is one last brief such account from Sheldrake's book.

> Dorothy Doherty says that the day before her husband collapsed and died, their cat continually rubbed around his legs. "I remember him saying, 'What's wrong with her today?' As she had never been so persistent before, I have often wondered if she knew what was to happen."

About the certainty of that kind of presentiment, there was no doubt in the case of Oscar the Cat, whose remarkable story was sent to me by colleague. It was originally written by Dr. David Dosa, a geriatrician at Rhode Island Hospital and an assistant professor of medicine at the Warren Alpert Medical School of Brown University, and published in a journal in 2007. Here's the story, which was entitled "A Day in the Life of Oscar the Cat." You will find it charmingly written, almost like a fable, but it nevertheless is based in fact.

Oscar the Cat awakens from his nap, opening a single eye to survey his kingdom. From atop the desk in the doctor's charting area, the cat peers down the two wings of the nursing home's advanced dementia unit. All quiet on the western and eastern fronts. Slowly, he rises and extravagantly stretches his 2-year-old frame, first backward and then forward. He sits up and considers his next move.

In the distance, a resident approaches. It is Mrs. P., who has been living on the dementia unit's third floor for 3 years now. She has long forgotten her family, even though they visit her almost daily. Moderately disheveled after eating her lunch, half of which she now wears on her shirt, Mrs. P. is taking one of her many aimless strolls to nowhere. She glides toward Oscar, pushing her walker and muttering to herself with complete disregard for her surroundings. Perturbed, Oscar watches her carefully and, as she walks by, lets out a gentle hiss, a rattlesnake-like warning that says "leave me alone." She passes him without a glance and continues down the hallway. Oscar is relieved. It is not yet Mrs. P.'s time, and he wants nothing to do with her.

Oscar jumps down off the desk, relieved to be once more alone and in control of his domain. He takes a few moments to drink from his water bowl and grab a quick bite. Satisfied, he enjoys another stretch and sets out on his rounds. Oscar decides to head down the west wing first, along the way sidestepping Mr. S., who is slumped over on a couch in the hallway. With lips slightly pursed, he snores peacefully—perhaps blissfully unaware of where he is now living. Oscar continues down the hallway until he reaches its end and Room 310. The door is closed, so Oscar sits and waits. He has important business here.

Twenty-five minutes later, the door finally opens, and out walks a nurse's aide carrying dirty linens. "Hello, Oscar," she says. "Are you going inside?" Oscar lets her pass, then makes his way into the room, where there are two people. Lying in a corner bed and facing the wall, Mrs. T. is asleep in a fetal position. Her body is thin and wasted from the breast cancer that has been eating away at her organs. She is mildly jaundiced and has not spoken in several days. Sitting next to her is her daughter, who glances up from her novel to warmly greet the visitor. "Hello, Oscar. How are you today?"

Oscar takes no notice of the woman and leaps up onto the bed. He surveys Mrs. T. She is clearly in the terminal phase of illness, and her breathing is labored. Oscar's examination is interrupted by a nurse, who walks in to ask the daughter whether Mrs. T. is uncomfortable and needs more morphine. The daughter shakes her head, and the nurse retreats. Oscar returns to his work. He sniffs the air, gives Mrs. T. one final look, then jumps off the bed and quickly leaves the room. Not today.

Making his way back up the hallway, Oscar arrives at Room 313. The door is open, and he proceeds inside. Mrs. K. is resting peacefully in her bed, her breathing steady but shallow. She is surrounded by photographs of her grandchildren and one from her wedding day. Despite these keepsakes, she is alone. Oscar jumps onto her bed and again sniffs the air. He pauses to consider the situation, and then turns around twice before curling up beside Mrs. K.

One hour passes. Oscar waits. A nurse walks into the room to check on her patient. She pauses to note Oscar's presence. Concerned, she hurriedly leaves the room and returns to her desk. She grabs Mrs. K.'s chart off the medical-records rack and begins to make phone calls. Within a half hour the family starts to arrive. Chairs are brought into the room, where the relatives begin their vigil. The priest is called to deliver last rites. And still, Oscar has not budged, instead purring and gently nuzzling Mrs. K.

A young grandson asks his mother, "What is the cat doing here?" The mother, fighting back tears, tells him, "He is here to help Grandma get to heaven." Thirty minutes later, Mrs. K. takes her last earthly breath. With this, Oscar sits up, looks around, then departs the room so quietly that the grieving family barely notices.

On his way back to the charting area, Oscar passes a plaque mounted on the wall. On it is engraved a commendation from a local hospice agency: "For his compassionate hospice care, this plaque is awarded to Oscar the Cat." Oscar takes a quick drink of water and returns to his desk to curl up for a long rest. His day's work is done. There will be no more deaths today, not in Room 310 or in any other room for that matter. After all, no one dies on the third floor unless Oscar pays a visit and stays awhile.

Note: Since he was adopted by staff members as a kitten, Oscar the Cat has had an uncanny ability to predict when residents are about to die. Thus far, he has presided over the deaths of more than 25 residents on the third floor of Steere House Nursing and Rehabilitation Center in Providence, Rhode Island. His mere presence at the bedside is viewed by physicians and nursing home staff as an almost absolute indicator of impending death, allowing staff members to adequately notify families. Oscar has also provided companionship to those who would otherwise have died alone. For his work, he is highly regarded by the physicians and staff at Steere House and by the families of the residents whom he serves.

~

Moved by this story when I first read it, I sent it to my daughter Kathryn who, like her father before her and possibly because of him, has always loved cats and lived with them for most of her life. Kathryn was not surprised to read his story in part because she had one to match it.

This is what she wrote to me after reading about Oscar the Cat. In it, she will describe what she witnessed after she brought her mother, Elizabeth, who was ill with cancer, to live with her and her husband, Bill.

When we first brought Elizabeth back to the house, she was extraordinarily sick—barely functioning, barely talking. We set her up in the little bedroom and she stayed in bed. Little Princess was a cat that lived down the street. She didn't have a good home life and for a while before Elizabeth came, she would come up to our house and we would pet her on the back patio, but she would never come in and we would never feed her. Then she would go home and come back when she wanted—sometimes that next day, sometimes a few days later. The day that we brought Elizabeth home, Princess came up came on the back patio, walked in the back door and went right straight to Elizabeth's room. The cat had never been in the house. She jumped up on the bed and she walked around Elizabeth and then settled right down next to her.

Elizabeth had had surgery and her stomach area was very tender. But this cat knew not to walk on her stomach. Princess would walk across her shoulders, would curl up by her head, by her side, and by her feet, even lying on her legs but never on her stomach. Princess stayed with Elizabeth so long that the neighbor who owned the cat started calling around the neighborhood trying to find the cat. The cat finally decided that she should go home. But the next day she was back and she continued to come back every day and stay with Elizabeth all day.

Elizabeth loved cats. Even in her befuddled state she was absolutely thrilled that the cat was with her and she would smile when the cat walked in the room and was just happy to have her there. This went on for a couple of weeks. But Elizabeth was so bad that I had to put her in a nursing home and while Elizabeth was gone the cat would come in and go to her room and look for her.

Sometime during this period when Elizabeth was in the nursing home, the woman who owned the cat was going to move and she was looking for somebody to take all of her animals—she had three cats and one dog. Bill and this neighbor did not get along at all, but when we heard that she was going to give the cats away, we contacted her through a different neighbor and they told her that we were interested in taking the one cat. She finally called Bill and said that we had to take two cats because they were sisters but we said that we only wanted the one cat. She told us "Well, you can't have either one then." A couple of weeks later she called us and said we could have the one cat and she would leave the paperwork in the mailbox and we could have the cat when she moved. So she left the paperwork in the mailbox and was supposed to bring the cat by but instead she called us and said "Well, sorry—the cat jumped into the moving van with us so we just took her." We had already told Elizabeth that we were getting the cat for when she came home and she was, of course, devastated.

Two weeks later our neighbor (who had facilitated the deal) called us at the apartment and said "Aren't you taking care of your cat?" "We said, what cat?" He said the cat you got from the neighbor. We said we didn't get the cat—she took her with her. He said "Well, the cat is right here in my yard and she looks terrible— she's all messy and matted." We said we would be will be right there!

We went the home and there's the cat. We took her to the vet, got her cleaned up, shaved and she became our little Princess. Elizabeth was thrilled—couldn't wait to get home to see the cat. The cat immediately recognized her, stayed with her constantly and they were a happy couple for the entire time that Elizabeth was there. Elizabeth was definitely this cat's charge.

Elizabeth had gotten well enough during part of the time that she was home to use her computer. She had a printer, and after she died, I noticed there was a printout on the printer that was entitled "When cats grieve." The article from the Internet was all about how to take care of a cat after their master died. So goes the story of Princess and Elizabeth. But it didn't stop there.

Nita [Bill's mother who also lived in the house], who did not like cats and put up with the fact that we had adopted little Princess really did like little Princess a little bit. When Nita got sick and started to go downhill, Princess would jump up on her lap and sit with her during the day and comfort her just like she had done with Elizabeth. And when Nita was much closer to death, little Princess would climb up on her bed and stay with her just like she'd done with Elizabeth.

So believe me, we know that cats really do understand when people are sick and they do try to take care of them in a lot of cases. Elizabeth was happier and I believed lived longer because Princess cared for her.

After Elizabeth died [she had to be moved to a hospice before her death], Princess constantly went into her room looking for her. It was probably the better part of a month before she stopped. She did the same thing when Nita died, but not for as long.

Princess knew she was supposed to find and take care of Elizabeth and she did. It's not like we brought her into the house. She marched right in the open back door and ran through the house like a kitty with a purpose to find Elizabeth. Elizabeth suffered a lot while she fought her terminal battle and little Princess softened her struggles. She could bring a smile to Elizabeth's face when no one else could. She was one of Elizabeth's last thoughts as she left us that article so we could take care of Princess's own grief. As we found out, cats grieve too.

~

Our pets grieve for us when we die, and God knows that when one of our beloved pets die, we are broken-hearted and mourn for them. I have seen so many women weep with anguish on such occasions, and we men, too, are not immune from deep grief on suffering the loss of pet. Indeed, the death of a pet with whom we have shared such an intimate life for many years can be more devastating than the death of a person, and often is.

We form such deep bonds with our pets, and they with us, that to experience a final, wrenching separation is often hard to endure. Never to see our pets again? That is a sorrowful thought indeed.

But.

For many people, whether they have heard of near-death experiences or not, the thought that we may after death be reunited with our own loved ones is a powerful source of hope and often a deep-seated belief. And the many accounts of NDEs we now have where such encounters have been reported only bolster those beliefs. I know that, for my part, I cherish the hope that when I die, assuming I can ever get around to it, I will see members of my family again, particularly my father whom I lost, seemingly for good, when I was a child.

But then we love our pets, too. Is it too much to hope that we will never see them again as well? Or is it possible ....

Be sure to check out my next blog to find out the answer to the question whether when a pet dies, does he or she really disappear for good?

Do Our Pets Have an Afterlife?

We all know what happens when we die—we don't.

At least that's what most of us believe, whether by religious faith or because we've been convinced by the collective testimony of near-death experiencers or perhaps for other reasons. But whatever the basis of our beliefs, we hold that life isn't a dead end. Upon death, we just continue to exist in another form.

But what about our pets? The philosopher, Martin Heidegger, as you may recall, argued that animals don't die; they simply disappear, he said.

But do they? Are they so unlike us—creatures without a soul, according to Descartes—that upon their physical death, they simply cease to exist?

Don't be too sure. Let's look at the evidence first before we reluctantly consign our pets to perpetual oblivion.

Janice Holden is the current President of The International Association for Near-Death Studies, an organization I co-founded almost forty years ago, and the longtime editor of *The Journal of Near-Death Studies*. She is certainly a recognized authority on NDEs. In a recent interview, she asserted that although she was unaware of any systematic research dealing with the perception of pets during NDEs, nevertheless, there are numerous reports that people were reunited with beloved deceased pets during their NDEs. I have also been assured by P.M.H. Atwater, another well-known NDE researcher, that it is not just dogs and cats that are perceived by NDErs, but pet birds as well.

Here, however, in line with my previous blogs, we will focus just on cats and dogs. And for this purpose, we can draw on the work of Jeff Long, another prominent NDE researcher. Jeff also hosts the most important and widely regarded NDE website, The Near-Death Experience Research Foundation (or NDERF), and has collected quite a few cases of this kind. Let's now just consider several of those in his files.

I will not take the space here to quote the entirety of these NDE reports or give the circumstances of their occurrence. Instead, I will just quote the relevant portions concerning their perception of deceased pets.

Michael

As I raised my head up from the ground to look around, I saw my deceased dog from my childhood bounding towards me. I remember exclaiming her name at the top of my lungs as I saw her bounding towards me. It was overwhelmingly wonderful. I felt completely at peace and totally happy. I was so excited to see her again, and I did not question the experience at the time. It was as if she had never died and she had always been waiting for me to wake up from my nap in the grass. The thought "why is my dead dog here?" never occurred to me. The thought "where am I and why am I laying in this field of grass?" never occurred to me. Everything was simply as it was supposed to be.

The experience was very brief, but VERY real. An entire reality was just as real as our world is now. There was not a single aspect of that experience which did not feel real.

Tracy

A dog's tail weaved through the tall grass. A beautiful fuzzy puppy wagged her tail at me. At first, I did not recognize her. I had never seen our dog as a puppy. I was so happy to see her. We had to put her down two weeks prior to my daughter's birth. She had injured her hip. We had given all the surgery we could to keep her, but it did not make her quality of life better—it had become much worse. We had her put down on my due date. Our hearts were so heavy with the loss of the dog that generously shared her life with us for 12 years.

Kustav

I saw a piece of floating land in the distance. It had one pine tree and covered in snow. I was still so cold, but decided to go to that tree. Below the tree, I heard a meow. I looked down, and saw Elmar! Elmar was a white Persian cat. I could not believe it. He was watching me. His beautiful green eyes and long, luscious white fur. Suddenly, I realized I had hands. I was surprised by this. I picked up Elmar. While I held him, he purred. No longer did I feel cold. His fur completely warmed me up and I felt the energy of his love. It was just like old times. I began to cry in feeling of happiness. I could even smell him exactly the way he used to smell. I put him down, and could tell from his purring and rubbing up against me that I would be o.k., whether that meant returning to life or staying on this floating Island. Then, I realized Elmar's eyes had the same look as I remembered when something got his attention.

Wayne

There was a Boston terrier dog standing beside her. We had always had Boston Terriers as pets when I was a kid but I didn't recognize this particular dog.

As a side-note, I went through a big box of old family photos and I found the dog with my grandmother. Her name was Trixie and she was our household pet when I was born in 1956. I don't remember her though as she was put to sleep around 1958. It was definitely, absolutely Trixie with my grandma.

Jonathan

I then became distracted by figures to my right which were all my former pets (dogs and cats that had died) climbing over each other to get to me, they gave me the impression of me just getting home from a long trip as they seemed very excited to see me.

Yvette

I'm in a park. Green grass was everywhere. It was very pretty and very clean. I see a black cat running up to me. It's my Amigo, my black cat who had passed away 6 months earlier. He runs towards me and leaps into my arms. He feels exactly the same. He was always a solid cat from his years on the streets. I hold him tight. I am so happy to see him. Joy fills me!! I cry a little bit. I hold him, hugging him, kissing him. He's rubbing his cheek on my face. I am so happy to see him. He is so happy to see me. This happiness is as if I've never felt before. I could feel his love and adoration. I have never felt happiness like this before in my life. It was peaceful, comforting, and so fulfilling.

Scott Janssen is a hospice social worker who has also reported cases of this kind in a recent article on this subject, "Near Death Experiences: Will Our Dogs be Waiting For us?"

Here is just one such case.

Alma

> I remember leaving my body. I could see myself on the
> ground below and the ambulance guys working on me. It
> was all very strange. Then I felt myself moving away. I
> saw a beautiful light and heard this amazing music that just
> brought me such peace. Eventually I found myself in a big
> yard where I'd grown up. I saw Sadie, my best childhood
> friend, a cute little Schnauzer. She was running toward me,
> wagging her tail. I'd missed her so much when she died.
> Yet, there she was, coming to greet me. She was licking me
> like crazy and I was laughing with joy.

I don't need to adduce more such stories, do I, in order to
establish the answer to my question. Yes, Virginia, our pets truly
do seem to have an afterlife.

But do our pets really live after they die? Perhaps they are just
figments of our desires and we simply hallucinate them once we
ourselves pass over to the life beyond this one.

Well, consider: Reports of NDEs often involve the perception of loved ones who appear to greet us when we pass over. You
might argue that we hallucinate them, too, but hold on. Not so fast
with your skepticism.

What about those cases, and there are more than a few, when
an individual is greeted by someone she doesn't know or recognize, only to be told afterward that that was your grandfather (who
died before you were born and whom you never knew). Or say a
person returns from an NDE and reports that he was greeted by his
sister—only he never had a sister. Except that his mother now tells
him what he never knew. He had a sister but she died at the age of
two before he was born. Or suppose you see someone during your
NDE whom you know still to be alive, only to find that he died
three days before when you were ill, and so forth.

No, we are typically greeted by those who have formed a deep
bond with us or we with them. And isn't it true that we often have
formed a very deep bond with our pets and they with us? Why

shouldn't those bonds also prevail after death, just as they do with the people we have loved and been attached to?

The bonds we form with our pets in life are not severed by their death. Our separation from them is only temporary. If we can trust these accounts of pets observed during NDEs, it means that we will indeed be reunited with them after we die. And for any animal lover, what could bring greater joy than to see our beloved cat or dog once more to greet us when we pass over?

A Whale of a Story

If you've been following my recent series on the lives of animals—admittedly, an escape and distraction from the dreadful sorrows of our time under the COVID cloud and the cruelties and violence in America these days perpetrated by us human animals—you will know that so far I have concentrated on the smaller and familiar creatures in our everyday world. So we have explored a bit about the lives of bats, prairie dogs, crows, cats, and the occasional stray dog who has managed stealthily to stroll into my stories. Now maybe it's time to increase the scope of our focus to something in the megafauna range where we find animals of truly super-size dimensions. How about if we swim with whales for a while?

Lately I've been re-reading portions of the book, *Beyond Words*, that I alluded to in an earlier blog. Just to remind you, it was written by the naturalist and ecologist, Carl Safina, who works as a self-confessed hard-headed scientist but can't help writing like a poet.

One section of his book describes his experiences while spending time with a man named Ken Balcomb who is a well-known marine biologist and one of the world's leading experts on killer whales, which he has been researching for the last forty years. Balcomb lives up near Vancouver Island where in one of the straits off the particular island on which he lives, many killer whales make their home. Balcomb spends a lot of his time hanging out with these whales, whom he now knows well enough to identify individually, and Safina spent a lot of time hanging out with him, learning about these marvelous creatures.

Just as I drew extensively on a book by Rupert Sheldrake when I was writing about cats, so I will base this essay almost entirely on what I learned from Safina's book. But to prevent confusion, let's get one thing straight from the outset.

Killer whales (often called orcas, though Safina prefers to call them killer whales) are actually dolphins. They're just whale-sized denizens of the ocean. In fact, they are the largest species of dolphins in the world. They can range in size from 23 to 32 feet and can weigh up to 6 tons! Like elephants, they can live up to 50 or 60 years, though some, if rarely, have lived beyond 80. Killer whales, like bats, use echolocation to communicate and hunt, but they can also communicate by making sounds that can travel for many miles.

As their name implies, they are ferocious predators. Up where Balcomb lives, there are two main types of killer whales. One is called "residents" and they feed primarily on salmon. The other, dubbed "transients," feast off of mammals. These two types tend to steer clear of each other.

One last thing before we begin to explore the lives of these mammoth but magnificent mammals. Their name is misleading. Although they can indeed be savage when it comes to their prey, they can actually be very gentle and playful, as we shall see, and there is no record of any human being having been attacked much less killed by any killer whale in the wild. In fact, quite the opposite, as we shall also discover.

For a brief introduction to some of the basic facts about the nature of killer whales, let's begin with what Safina has to say about them on the first page of his account:

[Killer whales are] intelligent, maternal, long-lived, cooperative, intensely social, devoted to family. They are, like us, warm-blooded milk-makers, mammals whose personalities are really not much different from ours. They're just a lot bigger. And notably less violent.

Now let me begin to elaborate on some of these features and eventually illustrate them through some of the stories about killer whales that Safina relates.

First, consider the social structure of the resident killer whales who particularly fascinated Safina. Like elephants, their basic social unit is a family headed by a matriarch around whom swim her children and her daughter's children. But where the family unit differs from that of elephants is in regard to the male killer whales. They never leave their mothers; they remain with her for their entire lives. Thus, the mother-child bond among killer whales is extremely strong as long as the mother lives. But if she should die, so often do her children, especially her male offspring; they can't live without her nurturance and guidance. The death rates for male children, thirty-years-old or higher, are anywhere from three to eight times that of comparably aged males with intact families.

Now, let's talk about how killer whales behave.

One of the most striking things about them, and from an early age, is how sexual they are. They often masturbate against objects and males regularly engage in sex play with one another. They just seem to love sex, as one whale researcher commented: "Dolphins love to have sex and they have it a lot."

Not surprisingly, dolphins are very playful. They seem to love to cavort. Balcomb jokes that "they love to party." And their play tends to be frolicsome, and not aggressive at all. In contrast to chimps, for example, Safina says that they are more peaceful and goes on to comment:

For all their heft and dental weaponry, when they find themselves in close proximity they either socialize or leave. Researchers have long been impressed by the absence of aggression among free-living killer whales.

As the foregoing comments imply, dolphins have a highly developed need for social contact. Some researchers think it is even stronger and more intense than in humans. And research shows that if killer whales are deprived of social interaction, they suffer and can go into physical decline.

One of the points that Safina makes repeatedly about killer whales is that each of them has a distinct personality. They are individuals, just as we are, with their own personal ways and behaviors. And many researchers who have been able to "get up close and personal" with killer whales have been struck with their undeniable presence. Here are just a few such observations:

> Dolphins and humans have not shared a common ancestor for millions of years. Yet for all the seeming estrangement of lives lived in liquid, when they see us they often come to play, and we greet them and can recognize in those eyes that someone very special is home. "There is someone in there. It's not a human, but it is someone," says [whale researcher] Diana Reiss.

> [One researcher said] You realize this is not a reptile … This is somebody. When he looked at you, someone else said, his gaze "had need in it, and your empathy lit up right away." People saw "an awareness, a presence, a longing" [for contact].

> It was hard to accept that level of awareness and intention in something that did not look in any way human. A sense washed over me that this orca was just as aware of living as I was … This was overwhelming.

Finally, according to Ken Balcomb:

> A whale's stare is much more powerful than a dog looking at you. A dog might want attention. The whales, it's a different thing. It's more like they're searching inside you.

And any number of persons, whether they be researchers or simply others who have interacted with killer whales, have commented on the sense of awe and wonder that they inspire.

One reason that killer whales evoke these reactions must surely be their obvious *intelligence*. Safina devotes a whole chapter to this subject, and although it's clear that the intelligence of killer whales is different from ours, it is equally evident that it is highly developed. Furthermore, their neocortex has a greater amount of surface area relative to total brain size than humans brains do, and although humans have more cortical neurons than killer whales, the difference is only marginal. In any case, there is no doubt about how intelligent they are; they are fully conscious beings—like us.

And there is more to their intelligence, too. As with some of the other animals we have considered in this series, there is strong anecdotal evidence that they are telepathic. And since my previous blogs have explored this subject—which professionals call "animal psi,"—let's now take some time to recount some of the stories that not only suggest that this faculty is highly developed in killer whales, but often gives rise to a sense of the uncanny.

Because Safina is an avowed skeptic in these matters, he can't resist entitling a long chapter in his book, "Woo Woo." Nevertheless, by the time he reaches the end of it, he is forced to admit that there are mysteries here he cannot quite explain away. And although he hangs onto his skeptical worldview, his last words are, "What in the world is going on?" Well, let's see what you make of it.

In fact, Safina seems to go out of his way and against his own prejudices to make a number of references to animal trainers who have worked with dolphins who cannot shake their sense that dolphins are telepathic. So we find statements like the following: "Then something happened that made me careful about my thoughts about whales ever since ... They can read your mind. We trainers see this kind of stuff all the time." And again, "When the trainer at Marineland of the Pacific said that killer whales can read your mind, she wasn't joking." Another researcher, who had given no indication that she was about to finish her work, wrote "the dolphins seemed to know that we were leaving and gave us a grand send-off. I have often wondered how they knew." And still another trainer, who confessed she was stupefied at how dolphins had seemingly intuited what she had wanted them to do (perform a novel trick) said "we don't know how they do it." Safina himself could only wonder: "dolphin telepathy?"

Safina does recount some stories to illustrate these mysteries that seem to point to the telepathic sensitivities of these whales but because of space limitations, I would prefer to focus on one other remarkable type of their behavior: rescues of people or other animals in distress.

Perhaps one of the most paradoxical things about killer whales, despite the fact that they have been hunted down and savagely killed by humans for many years, is not only do they not respond in kind, but only with kindness itself. As Safina remarks, "The fact is, killer whales seem capable of random acts of kindness." However, I don't think that's quite accurate. Their acts of kindness are not random; they are targeted and deliberate.

For example, Balcomb told Safina of a number of instances, including one where he himself was involved, of getting lost in terrible fog without a GPS, when suddenly a group of killer whales appeared. Balcomb followed them for fifteen miles and found, when the fog lifted, he was home. In some cases, whales have led lost sailors safely to their port without even knowing the seaman's destination—or did they?

For another, let me quote one that Safina himself was told by his own editor. He was kayaking off the Georgia coast when…

"The wind and tide suddenly changed and conditions became challenging. He didn't know the area well and was beginning to grow worried. Soon dolphins appeared, flanking him, seemingly piloting him. He went with them, and they brought him to an inlet where he could get to safely."

Now let me cite one such story at length in order to provide a sense of how uncanny some of these rescues seem to be.

Once, Alexandra Morton [a whale researcher] and an assistant were out in the open water of Queen Charlotte Strait in her inflatable boat when she was enveloped by a fog so thick she felt like she was "in a glass of milk." No compass. No view of the sun ... A wrong hunch about the direction home would have brought them out into the open ocean. Worse, a giant cruise ship was moving closer in fog so reflective Morton could not tell where its sound was coming from. She imagined it suddenly splitting the fog before it crushed them.

Then, as if from nowhere, a black fin popped up. [And then several more.] As they clumped close to her tiny boat, Alexandra followed in the fog like a blind person with a hand on their shoulder. "I never worried," she recalled. "I trusted them with our lives." Twenty minutes later, she saw a materializing outline of their island's massive cedars and rocky shoreline ... The whales had taken Morton to her home.

Morton felt changed. "For more than twenty years, I have fought to keep the mythology of orcas out of my work. When others would regale a group with stories of an orca's sense of humor or music appreciation, I'd hold my tongue ... Yet there are times when I am confronted with profound evidence of something beyond our ability to scientifically quantify. Call them amazing coincidences if you like; for me they keep adding up ... I can't say whales are telepathic—I can barely say the word—but I have no explanation for that day's events. I have only gratitude and a deep sense of mystery that continues to grow."

Why these killer whales are motivated to help us we can never know with certainty, but what is certain is that they do and such stories are legion. For another kind of frequent helping behavior, consider this remark of Safina's: "From antiquity to recent times, stories recounting dolphins pushing distressed swimmers to the surface are too numerous to track." And then he proceeds to give some examples.

In some cases, they can even alert human beings to a life-threatening situation before it turns fatal. Consider this case:

> One foggy day, the biologist Maddalena Bearzi was taking notes on a familiar party of nine bottlenose dolphins who'd cleverly encircled a school of sardines near the Malibu pier. "Just after they begin feeding, one of the dolphins in the group suddenly left the circle, swimming offshore at a high speed. In less than an instant, the other dolphins left their prey to follow."
>
> Berzi thought this was very odd, so she followed, too. The upshot? She found "an inert human body with long, blond hair floating in the center of the dolphin ring. Berzi again: "Her face was pale and her lips were blue as I pulled her fully dressed and motionless body from the water."
>
> Somehow she survived and said that she had been intent on committing suicide. The dolphins wouldn't let her. They saved her life.
>
> Why? All Safina could say is "Such things are profound."

But after recounting these and other cases, Safina is left to try to puzzle them out.

> How do we explain the facts of so unexpected a truce [between killer whales and humans], so unilateral a peace? It seems to me that it is, yes, a big leap to go from the fact of no aggression to the idea that killer whales have chosen to be a benevolent presence and occasional protectors of lost humans. But what do whales think? How is it that

all of world's free-living killer whales have settled upon this one-way relationship of peacefulness with us? Before I encountered these stories, I was dismissive. Now I feel shaken out of certainty. I've suspended disbelief. It's an unexpected feeling for me. The stories have forced open doors I had shut, doors to that greatest of all mental feats: the simple sense of wonder, and of feeling open to the possibility of being changed.

Perhaps just from reading these stories, you, too, would be moved to wonder why these huge animals who can indeed be killers when it comes to other sea life have nevertheless formed such a regard for the welfare of human beings, which almost seems—dare I say it?—like a kind of love.

Toward the end of his book, Safina lets a psychologist by the name of Paul Spong have the final word about these killer whales, which pretty well sums up Safina's own view about them.

Eventually my respect verged on awe. I concluded that Oricinus orca is an incredibly powerful and capable creature, exquisitely self-controlled and aware of the world around it, a being possessed of a zest for life and a healthy sense of humor and, moreover, a remarkable fondness for and interest in humans.

This would seem to the point to end this essay, but there is more to the story of these killer whales that must be added.

They are in trouble, and Ken Balcomb has been in mourning because he can see the writing on the water. It appears that these wondrous creatures to whom he has devoted his life, like so many species, may be doomed to extinction.

Why?

There are several factors at play here. To begin with, in the 1960s and 1970s, many young whales were captured, which has led to a long-term problem. Without these whales to mature and breed, the population has been decreasing. Now their numbers, already down to 80, are continuing to decline. Balcomb says they are losing one or two a year.

But that isn't the worst thing. These resident killer whales feed off salmon, but there is no salmon protection act, and the stocks have been declining because of over-fishing. When the salmon go to humans, they are not there in sufficient quantity to support these whales. On learning all this, Safina is moved to write ruefully, "First we took their children, then we destroyed their food supply." Balcomb tells him that in one of the three existing pods there is not one matriarch left to breed, and Safina remarks: "He looks at me while it sinks in: this whole family is doomed." Furthermore, over 40 percent of baby whales have died before they reach the age of even one year. If these trends continue, these pods will cease to exist in a few decades.

And that's not the end of it either. We are also poisoning the oceans with our toxic chemicals, and they, too, are sickening and killing these whales. [According to Rebecca Giggs, in her book, *Fathoms: The World in the Whale*, the earth's most toxified animals are the killer whales who live in Washington's Puget Sound.] And since whales are at the top of the food chain, they are particularly vulnerable, and the baby whales that are born are the recipients of this bitter fruit. No wonder so many of them die young.

As if that isn't enough to break your heart, let me quote this passage to illustrate the latest assault on the lives of these whales.

Balcomb shows Safina some photographs of a three-year-old female named Victoria, and says of her:

"A sweet little whale. A favorite of whale watchers here, very playful. Jumping all the time. Very outgoing and vivacious. A real charismatic whale. Just a sweetie.

Found dead. Look at these photos." Her young corpse looks battered to death. Hemorrhages all over her head, blood in her eyes and ear canals. These next images show her ear bones actually blown off their attachments. I'm

trying to assimilate these images while Ken is saying …
"We had whales on the hydrophones. It was night. Then we
heard the navy sonar. And then, an explosion."

Ken explains: "When the shock wave hits, rapid com-
pression of air in internal spaces such as the ears creates
enough of a vacuum to make the adjacent blood vessels—
which are pressurized—burst. Once burst, that's it; they
just continue bleeding … At less than a hundred yards,
military sonar alone can also create fatal hemorrhaging."

Our U.S. Navy is killing these whales. It is continuing and
getting worse. Balcomb believes that, worldwide, *thousands of
whales are being killed in this way.*

There are more gruesome stories like Victoria's in Safina's
book, but there is no point to give further examples. You can
already see what we humans are doing to destroy these creatures
who only want to befriend and play with us.

This, it seems, is what we humans do to our animals, and with
impunity since they have no political rights. We either exploit them
or eat them or, what we appear to do best, kill them. It goes without
saying that there are many good and caring human beings, but as a
species, has there ever been a more deadly predator on earth? We
seem to have a penchant for destroying everything including now
our own planet.

As for our megafauna, there are few left now. Our elephants
and rhinos may well be extinguished by the end of the century, and
we can only hope that our whales will survive somewhat longer.
In the meantime, as we suffer from an increasingly hot planet, they
will have to cope with living in waters that are not only no longer
healthy for them but full of dangers they have no way to avert. Let
us treasure them while we can.

Jews and Music

Introduction

Beginning in the 19th century and extending for most of the 20th, Jews played an outsized role in the development and promotion of classical music. Indeed, the history of classical music cannot be written without an account on how Jews, especially wealthy ones in Vienna and Berlin, helped to create the world of classical music of today. But did you know that also most of our greatest classical musicians from this time were also Jews?

A couple of years ago, I decided to write a book on this subject, which I called, somewhat puckishly, *When Jews Ruled the World— in Music*. This section features some excerpts from that book. Some of the stories I relate are droll and funny, so I hope you'll be entertained by them even if you don't give a fig for classical music.

Composers I Have Known and Loved

When I was a kid, I had no interest in classical music and I don't even remember hearing any in my home as I was growing up. But there was one particular event that occurred when I was about eight years old that was to foreshadow my later passion for classical music. I had discovered a book my mother had in her library that featured biographical sketches of the world's great composers. I don't remember its exact title, but I can still see the book in my mind's eye and feel its heft. For some reason, even though I was not yet familiar with classical music, I loved reading about these composers, and since I had a head for dates, I soon memorized the years of their births and deaths. In those days, the great composers started with Bach and ended with Stravinsky (who was then listed as 1882--), and seemingly constituted about a dozen in all. Early in my life, then, the stories of these men (and they were of course all men) impressed themselves upon me vividly. It's odd—I don't remember many books I read as a child, but the memory of lying across my bed absorbed in my mother's book of great composers is still clear to me. From the outset, it seems, I was fascinated with the lives of composers.

After I began college, although I never lost my interest in music, I pursued other subjects, eventually becoming, as I've mentioned, a psychologist and then a professor. I taught for many years at the University of Connecticut, had a successful career eventually focusing on the study of near-death experiences, and finally, in

114

my early sixties, having taken early retirement, returned to the Bay Area in California where I had grown up.

I took some time to wind up my professional career, finishing a couple of books I had been working on, and then wondered what to do next. I gave no conscious thought to music, but one day, during a period when I had been ill for quite a while, I found myself reading about Camille Saint-Saëns. In short order, I found myself completely engrossed in his life story about which I had not previously known much, and in my enthusiasm thought I might share a few of my thoughts about him in a little essay I would write just for the fun of it, mainly for my friends. Well, without recounting this whole improbable adventure, suffice it to say that I wound up writing an entire book about him and got it published by the sheerest fluke without even seeking a publisher. I even collaborated on a screenplay about him, which, although the film never got made, did get a fair-to-middling review from the William Morris Agency. Anyway, I had a ball working on this project during which time I confess that I eventually succumbed to the biographer's disease: I had fallen in love with Camille.

Really, I had done all this as a lark to begin with, but I found that writing about Saint-Saëns had triggered something in me—something new and something old. I had become interested in composers again and felt a yen not just to read about them, as I did when I was a kid, but to write about them—despite having no professional credentials in music whatever, only the chutzpah of an academic who apparently had no qualms about venturing into territory where he had no right to tread.

So before too long I had started work on a much more ambitious book, this time about three composers, Leos Janacek, Peter Tchaikovsky and Edward Elgar, and their women muses. My aim was to restore a proper recognition to the collaborative fructifying role those women had played in helping to bring forth much of the music these composers wrote, a great deal of which might never have taken the particular and enduringly compelling form it did without the creative stimulus that their muses provided. I felt that such women deserved to be more than footnotes to a distinguished composer's career; in my view, they had a right, as it were, to appear on history's stage beside the artists they lived to inspire and to share posterity's applause with them.

That was fifteen years ago. Despite getting a number of laudatory reviews, I could never find a publisher for this book—the only time in my career as an author of almost twenty books, I had failed to do so. One reviewer said gently that had I written this book in, say, in 1937, when "people cared about classical music," I could easily have found a publisher, but these days …

Recently, again finding myself at loose ends, I decided to begin work on another book having to do with classical music, which was published earlier this year. And, naturally, it includes one chapter about some composers, all Jewish, I had never written about, two of whom you are about to meet. Composers, like many artists, are often a bit daffy and some of them have really remarkably dramatic lives that most people never learn about. Of course, everyone knows about Beethoven, but how about Louis Moreau Gottschalk?

Not many people know that Gottschalk was the most celebrated mid-19th century American composer, but he was, hands down. Born in 1829 in New Orleans, he was the son of a Jewish physician and Creole mother, and he was quickly found to be a prodigy at the piano. Eventually, he was to write almost exclusively for the piano, and in time he became a sensation at the Parisian salons but then I am getting ahead of our story. So let's return to New Orleans before we get to Paris where Gottschalk was first to shine and wow the ladies, which in time may have led not just to his downfall but to his death.

Gottschalk's precociousness as a pianist was recognized early and by the time he was eleven, he had made his debut before a crowd of New Orleans' music lovers. However, his father recognized that if Gottschalk's talent was to be developed, he would have to go to Paris for training. But at the age of thirteen, he was rejected a priori by the head of the Conservatory, Pierre Zimmerman, presumably on the basis of his American nationality ("America is a nation of steam engines," Zimmerman sneered), but possibly because of his "mixed race." Zimmerman didn't even give the kid the chance to play. He was simply dismissed. But others, including several notable composers, were soon and duly impressed. There was Chopin, for example, who reportedly said, "Give me your hand, my child; I predict that you will become the king of pianists." His prophecy was close to the mark. Liszt was also very taken with Gottschalk's obvious gifts as a pianist, and Berlioz, too, "predicted a great future" for him and even offered to teach him composition. Take that, Zimmerman! With such accolades from such prominent composers, Gottschalk was soon able to find very able piano teachers to nurture his development and within a couple of years, he was already something of a young celebrity with the Parisian salon crowd.

The critic Harold Schonberg summarizes his early stature as a pianist as well as giving us a sense of his personal charisma:

> Gottschalk's talent at the keyboard was of a supreme order. He soon became not merely a good pianist but a great and celebrated one ... and for a while he had a tremendous vogue in Europe. He was slim, handsome, aristocratic, extraordinarily talented, and he blazed a trail through early Romantic pianism. Many competent critics called him the equal to Liszt. The flashy young American, the first internationally famous pianist to come out of the United States, was the man of the hour.

Indeed, Gottschalk was such an attractive personality and so prodigiously gifted that during the 1840s, he was not only in great demand as a soloist in Paris, but throughout France, Spain and the Americas. And his success continued into the next decade. For example, according to music critic Arthur Holde, "his performances were regarded as so sensational that he was able to give 80 concerts in the 1855-56 season alone." Gottschalk was the

American Liszt—a rock star both in the salon and on the concert stage.

And we know the temptations that lie in wait for rock stars. In those days, it wasn't drugs. But as in our own time, it was the lure of women, and all commentators invariably mention his many affairs and some of the scandals he managed to get involved in during the course of his regrettably short but always adventuresome life.

One notorious one was with the American Actress Ada Clare, originally a Southern belle from an aristocratic family who eventually moved to New York where in time she would be known as "The Queen of Bohemia." And sure enough, she had a very public affair with Gottschalk and had a child by him "out of wedlock," as the phrase then was. The affair was said to have "shaken the foundations of New York society." Apparently, the foundations held, and Gottschalk went on with his career as she eventually did with hers. Oddly enough, both died young, Gottschalk at forty, Clare, at thirty-nine.

And then there was his close call in San Francisco some years later. Schonberg gives this amusing account of it:

> The citizens were stirred up when there were reports that Gottschalk had made free with one of the respectable young ladies of the city. He hadn't, or at least he claimed he hadn't, but rather than face a posse of vigilantes, he fled to a ship and sailed to South America [ending up in] Rio De Janeiro.

Gottschalk was indeed a peripatetic pianist, seemingly always on the go. By 1865, he estimated that he had traveled 95,000 miles by rail and given about 1000 concerts. Apparently, however, his frequent travels were sometimes occasioned by exigencies unrelated to the demands for his musical performances.

Here, however, I need to interrupt the narrative arc of Gottschalk's short but drama-filled life by saying something about his music, which was as singular and distinctive as was the man himself.

Gottschalk's music was very popular during his lifetime and his earliest compositions created a sensation in Europe. Schonberg comments that when his music began appearing on the continent, audiences could not get enough of it. And renowned pianists of the day vied with each other in their zeal to play his exotic compositions with their strangely beguiling Caribbean flavor. Early pieces like Bamboula, La Savane and Le Bananier were based on Gottschalk's memories of the music he heard during his youth in Louisiana. A number of them are said—for I have never heard them—to have "a wonderfully innocent sweetness and charm." Some, perhaps many, were "mere" salon pieces, meant to entertain his audiences, and did, but others, giving listeners a sense of the optimism and exuberance of American life, were significant and worthy creations in their own right. Schonberg, for one, expressed a real appreciation for what was of unique value in Gottschalk's work:

> Probably no composer in the world at that time, not even Berlioz or Liszt, had Gottschalk's rhythmic originality. His rhythms were profoundly original because he was working in an Afro-Cuban rhythmic world that had not been explored by any serious composer up to that time.

But before I conclude this account of our composer, we must now return to Gottschalk's life and recount the story of his strange and enigmatic death, which seems somehow so fitting to the character of the man and the life he led.

In 1869, we find him in Rio to which he had fled after his Don Giovanni-like escape from the clutches of an aroused San Francisco citizenry following his latest tryst with a woman of former virtue. There he had established a series of very grand concerts. One night he was performing at one, and had just sat down to play one of his own works. And the title? *Morte!* [I am not making this up.] As he started to play the piece, he collapsed. A few days later he was dead.

I have read various speculations as to the cause. One writer suggested it was simply because of "excessive strain and nervous exhaustion." Others say it was yellow fever. Schonberg opines that it was probably peritonitis. But several commentators have said that the real cause of Gottschalk's early death was—that he was murdered! By a jealous husband.

We will never know, for if it was a murder, it was never solved. But the romantic in me would like to believe it is true. It would be so karmically appropriate. I like to think of Gottschalk in the lead role of a certain Mozart opera. And you know which one. [Well, since you may not habla opera, I'll just tell you: Don Giovanni of course.]

Gottschalk was a truly seminal composer of verve, charm and panache, an American original. The first American to make a splash in Europe with his winning personality, his marvelous pianism, and his memorable and catchy music, he is certainly someone whose music still deserves to played for and enjoyed by modern audiences, and is.

Gottschalk's life was certainly full of drama, but for weirdness, was there anyone stranger than that bugbear of modern music, Arnold Schoenberg?

I admit it. I am a triskaidekaphiliac. Perhaps you are not familiar with that formidable term. Suppose I were to tell you that I was born on Friday, the 13th, and because of that, I have always considered 13 to be my lucky number. So now you have presumably divined my psychiatric condition. I have an inordinate fondness for the number 13.

Schoenberg was my opposite: He suffered from a really bad case of triskaidekaphobia. So bad that it killed him. We will get to that.

But first, I suppose I must state a few obvious and well-known facts about Schoenberg. Unlike Gottschalk, Schoenberg was not only famous in his lifetime but has remained famous after his death. He is widely acknowledged as one of the most influential and important of composers in the first half of the 20th century. He is most famous for the invention of what to me is one of the most hateful devices of modern music, the twelve tone system that gives equal weight to each note of the chromatic scale. That's his claim to shame. It brought about a revolution in modern music. To me, it brought about the end of music and the beginning of something that drove mass audiences elsewhere to find their listening pleasures. All this is familiar fare.

Whether Schoenberg was "great" depends on your point of view, but certainly when the definitive history of 20th century music is written, Schoenberg's name will be a prominent entry. He's a composer who really made a difference.

But he was also a very strange man. So rather than simply treading over familiar ground in order to tell you something about Schoenberg, I'd like simply like to relate to you one story about him that will help you to understand just how strange he was.

Schoenberg was a Jewish refugee from Vienna who was forced to leave when the Nazis came to power and, like many European Jewish musicians escaping the scourge of Nazism, he settled in Los Angeles. Quite a few of these men wound up writing for the movies, but not Schoenberg; he played tennis instead. And continued to compose, to teach, to paint (Schoenberg was also a gifted painter) and to polemicize. But he also lived with a demon.

It was his fear of the number 13.

Schoenberg was born on September 13, 1874, and in what would be his last year, 1951, he would be turning 76. But of course in Schoenberg's phobic mind, he couldn't help thinking of his age as 7+6=13, a fateful dreaded number. And, as it turned out a fatal one, since he wound up dying on July 13 of that year.

But that's just the beginning and end of the story. What makes it even more curious and spooky is what came in between.

Throughout his life he fastidiously avoided rooms, floors and buildings with the number 13. He even refused to rent a house because its street address had been 13 Pine Street. This was not a superficial concern, but rather a powerful, all-consuming obsession that was central to his entire belief system. His musical manuscripts show the customary measure numbers, but starting with the composition of the 13th song of the cycle *Das Buch der Hängenden Gärten* (Book of the Hanging Gardens), Schoenberg began to substitute the number 13 with 12a in the measure count. Then there was the case of his opera, *Moses and Aaron*. Oops, that makes thirteen letters! For Schoenberg, that also made for a big problem. But he found a way to solve it. Simple but effective: He just left out one of the "a's" in Aaron, so the title of his opera became Moses and Aron. Now you know why.

As Schoenberg got older, the degree of his triskaidekaphobia increased and spread into all aspects of his life, from the mundane to the existential. He absolutely dreaded his sixty-fifth birthday in 1939, because that year was a multiple of 13. In a letter dated 4 March 1939, Schoenberg wrote: "Indeed, I am not so well at the moment. I am in my 65th year and you know that 5 times 13 is 65 and 13 is my bad number.

In 1950, on the occasion of this seventy-sixth birthday, Schoenberg received an ill-omened note from his fellow composer and musician Oskar Adler. Adler stipulated that since Schoenberg's age of 76 added up to 13 (7+6), it would be a critically dangerous year. According to friends and family, this ominous suggestion severely depressed and apparently stunned Schoenberg. His obsession was taking a dangerous form.

Things finally came to a head on *Friday*, the 13th July, 1951. On that day Schoenberg stayed in bed all day. He was sick, anxious and depressed, but he wasn't going to take any chances. His wife Gertrud reported, "About a quarter to twelve I looked at the clock and said to myself: another quarter of an hour and then the worst is over."

But it wasn't. Gertrud reported to her sister-in-law Ottilie the next day that her husband had actually died at 11:45, 15 minutes before midnight, just as he had feared. The curse of triskaideka-phobia had struck!

I think that Schoenberg must have been a character in a story by Edgar Allan Poe all along and just didn't know it, don't you?

When the Music Stops

These days classical music no longer has the cachet it did when I was growing up. In that era when the tenor Mario Lanza was in top form, when Toscanini was conducting—on primetime TV—his famous NBC Orchestra, when classical pianists like José Iturbi and Oscar Levant were appearing in Hollywood films, when Leonard Bernstein (Lenny!) was at the height of his celebrity with his entertaining television series, "Young People's Concerts"—that was when classical music in America had reached its popular zenith. It was also the age when I just beginning to become passionately interested in classical music, which has never ebbed.

Of course, that's still another thing that makes me something of an old fogy, one of those graybeards who now, apart from young Asians, make up the preponderance of audiences for symphony concerts. But, as I say, it was very different when I was young and enthralled by the spell that that kind of music had over me.

Perhaps because I am now old, I have lately been thinking a lot about that period in music and recently found myself writing about it, too. And perhaps just because I am old, one of the things that has struck me is how many of the most celebrated composers and some of our greatest classical musicians died young. Think about all the great composers who died in their thirties: Mozart at 35, Weber at 39, Schubert at 31, Mendelssohn at 38, Chopin at 39, Bizet at 36, Gershwin at 38, and the greatest English composer until Handel (who was German of course) came along, Henry Purcell, who died at 36 of a chill he caught when his wife had locked him out their house. What an incalculable loss to music for them all to die so young!

These composers, of course, are long dead, but since I am not yet, I can still remember some of the instrumentalists—among the most outstanding of their time—who also died their thirties, all of them evoking a deep wave of anguish throughout the musical community in those years when the shocking news of their deaths became known. As it happens, all of these men were Jews, which is not surprising since during much of the twentieth century, it was largely Jews who dominated the field of classical music, but that is another story. And maybe it's not surprising that I found myself writing about these men and other Jewish musicians because I am nominally Jewish myself, still another story that I am happy to elide, at least for now. Which should make you happy, too.

But perhaps the stories you would find of interest concern some of these exceptional young musicians whose lives and careers were tragically aborted by their early deaths. They have never been forgotten, though their names may not be familiar to you. But at least this way, you will be able to learn why their deaths were so mourned at the time and why they are still revered today. Here are brief profiles of three of them.

Michael Rabin

Has there ever been a more precocious prodigy of the violin than Michael Rabin? The son of a Juilliard-trained pianist mother and a father who was a violinist in the New York Philharmonic, baby Michael could beat time perfectly with his feeding spoon by the time he was a year old. As soon as he could crawl, he would position himself under the piano, listening intently for hours while his parents played sonatas and, with their friends, trios and quartets. At three years of age, he gave evidence of perfect pitch. He was able to pick out on the piano the note corresponding to the sound of any grunt, steam whistle or automobile horn. He astonished his mother by memorizing when to turn the pages for a César Franck sonata after hearing it only once.

His mother began giving the boy piano lessons when he was five. Soon afterward, while visiting a doctor who was an amateur violinist, Michael noticed a tiny violin, began tuning it and playing it on his own, and burst into tears when an effort was made to separate him from it. The doctor allowed him to take it home. His father then began giving the boy lessons, and by the fourth lesson he had concluded that Michael's native talent was far superior to his own and managed to solicit guidance from the greatest violinist of his age, Jascha Heifetz.

After a lesson with the master, Heifetz was so impressed with the boy's obvious ability that he advised his father to have Michael study with Ivan Galamian, a renowned violin teacher, who later said that Michael had "no weaknesses, never." Galamian, who would eventually teach such famous violinists as Itzhak Perlman and Pincus Zuckerman, also asserted that Michael was his most talented student "ever." After studying with Galamian, Michael continued at the Juilliard School. At the age of ten, he was ready to tackle the formidably difficult *First Concerto of Wieniawski*.

His Carnegie Hall debut took place in January 1950, at the age of thirteen, as soloist in *Vieuxtemps' Concerto No. 5*, which had been a Heifetz specialty. Two years later he performed *Paganini's D major Concerto*, with Dimitri Mitropoulos conducting the New York Philharmonic. Mitropoulos called him on that occasion, "the genius violinist of tomorrow, already equipped with all that is necessary to be a great artist." George Szell, the illustrious longtime conductor of the Cleveland Orchestra, also raved about Rabin's playing, saying that he was the greatest violin talent that had come to his attention in the past thirty years. (Rabin's 1958 recording of *Paganini concerto* is considered by many to be this work's most definitive performance on disc.)

Perhaps Rabin's most famous and revered recording is of another Paganini work, his caprices. A musician friend was kind enough to burn a CD of these works for me some years ago, and I can attest to their magnificence. Rabin plays with a ravishingly pure tone. Another record connoisseur has recounted his first exposure to this performance with the following account:

> When I put on the old LP and Rabin lit into the first caprice, I felt an influx of adrenaline. The playing had overwhelming verve. His tone ... was fiercely dramatic. I will never forget the final trill of the 24th caprice, a superb flourish to cap one of the best virtuoso performances of all time. Thereafter, I paid visits to the record archives The Tower Records cut-out bins—anywhere I thought I might make contact with his spirit ... You can now obtain a separate disc of the Caprices ... an enduring testament to a marvelous talent.

Rabin went on to have a stellar career, playing in all the major cities in the United States, Europe, South America and Southern Africa—at least for a while. But something was wrong. For reasons still not understood, by 1959, when he was still in his early twenties, he suddenly ceased recording. He did continue to perform publicly and apparently still with his accustomed superb artistry, but soon there were stories circulating about Rabin's emotional instability and a troubled personal life. It seems that he had a difficult time adjusting to the change from a child prodigy to performing as an adult virtuoso. And more disturbing stories began to make the rounds in the late '60s when there were rumors of Rabin's chronic drug use. He also displayed some puzzling neuroses during this time including a fear of falling off the stage.

But there seems to have been a reason for Rabin's phobia of falling. It appears that he had developed some kind of neurological disorder, which could well have been epilepsy. It was ironic that it was at the very site where he had had such a tremendously successful debut, Carnegie Hall, that in the early 1970s, during a recital, he suddenly lost his balance and fell forward. Not long afterward he died from a fall in his New York apartment when, during what seems to have been an epileptic convulsion, he slipped on a rug and struck his head on a table.

Rabin was only thirty-five years old (Mozart's age when he died). The coroner found barbiturates in his blood afterward. Such a tragic end to what had been a brilliant career, and another instance of how early genius can sometimes exact a terrible toll on a musician's life.

William Kapell

Among Jewish pianists, too, there is one whose early death was especially devastating and was a grievous blow to the world of music. The death of William Kapell at 31 sent shock waves of heartbreak throughout the classical music community and occasioned deep and anguished mourning at the time of his death in 1953. He had been widely predicted to become and perhaps already was the greatest pianist of his generation—and then, in an instant, he was gone.

His brief life can be easily summarized.

Kapell was born in New York in 1922 into a family of Polish-Russian Jews; his parents ran a bookshop on Lexington Avenue. The boy won his first competition at the age of ten; his prize, a turkey dinner with the pianist José Iturbi. And he would go on to win every competition in sight. In 1941, Kapell won the Philadelphia Orchestra's youth competition as well as the prestigious Naumburg Award. The following year, the Naumburg Foundation sponsored the 19-year-old pianist's New York début in Carnegie Hall, a recital which won him the Town Hall Award for the year's outstanding concert by a musician under 30. He was immediately signed to an exclusive recording contract with RCA Victor.

He was already being touted "as the best American pianist of his generation." He went on to play with many of the foremost conductors of his time, including Eugene Ormandy, Leopold Stokowski, Fritz Reiner, Serge Koussevitzky and Guido Cantelli (who, ironically, would suffer the same fate as Kapell few years after the latter's death, when at 36, he, too died in a plane crash). Kapell also played chamber music with the best—Jascha Heifetz, William Primrose, Pablo Casals, Rudolf Serkin and Artur Schnabel (with whom he had previously studied).

Incidentally, when Kapell had earlier approached Vladimir Horowitz for lessons, the legendary pianist demurred, saying that there was nothing he could teach him.

After this death, one music critic gave his brief assessment of Kapell's artistry:

> During a professional career of barely 12 years Kapell emerged as the most prodigiously gifted and exciting American pianist of his generation. In his artistry it was impossible to separate awesome technique from fierce integrity and deep insight. Every note mattered in a Kapell performance. His pianism uncannily balanced contrasting qualities. It was impetuous yet sensitive, white hot yet poetic, cogent yet instinctive, assured yet intense. And on the concert stage his brooding good looks added to the allure.

"His playing had that indefinable thing known as command," the critic Harold C. Schonberg wrote in his book "The Great Pianists", adding that before his death Kapell was "well on his way to being one of the century's important pianists."

Another commentator provided this account of Kapell's dedication to his performances:

> Early on, there was a tendency to typecast Kapell as a performer of technically difficult repertoire. While his technique was exceptional, he was a deep and versatile musician, and was memorably impatient with what he considered shallow or sloppy music making. His own repertoire was very diverse, encompassing works from Bach

to Copland, who so admired Kapell's performances of his Piano Sonata that he was writing a new work for him at the time of the pianist's death. Kapell practiced up to eight hours a day, keeping track of his sessions with a notebook and clock.

I have also read several appreciative commentaries on Kapell's discography, which was actually fairly extensive and diverse, given his short life, but I think I have provided enough accolades already to establish what a gifted and dedicated a pianist he was. He appears to have given as much close attention to his recording life as he did to his live performances.

In August of 1953 Kapell traveled to Australia for an extended tour. Over 14 weeks he played 37 concerts, both solo recitals and concertos. Kapell played the final concert of his Australian tour in Geelong, Victoria, on October 22 in a recital which, in a macabre prefiguration of what was to come, included a performance of Chopin's "Funeral March" Sonata. He left Australia seven days later. On his return trip to New York, where his wife of five years and their young son and daughter were awaiting him, the DC-6 Kapell was flying in, attempting to land in a heavy fog, clipped a forested mountain 35 miles south of San Francisco, plunged into a ridge and fell apart in flames. Everyone on board perished.

The aftermath of Kapell's death was summarized in this Wikipedia entry about him:

> The fascination with Kapell's playing has continued in the decades since his death. Pianists including Eugene Istomin, Gary Graffman, Leon Fleisher and Van Cliburn, and many others have acknowledged Kapell's influence. Fleisher stated that Kapell was "the greatest pianistic talent that this country has ever produced."
>
> Kapell's estate sued BCPA, Qantas, (which had taken over BCPA in 1954), and BOAC (which was alleged to have sold Kapell the ticket). In 1964, more than ten years

after the crash, Kapell's widow and two children were awarded US$924,396 in damages. The award was overturned on appeal in 1965.

As Rabin was to violinists, so Kapell was to pianists—a meteoric talent of unsurpassed excellence that had far too brief a span in which to soar but whose place is secure in the pantheon of pianistic immortals.

Emmanuel Feuermann

When fleeing from the Cossacks during a pogrom, Jews could always carry a fiddle, but it was more difficult to tote along a cello, which might be one reason that there are far more outstanding Jewish violinists than cellists. Nevertheless, even though the cello doesn't have the glamor of the violin, just as contraltos must often play second fiddle (sorry!) to sopranos, there are still quite a few very gifted and famous Jewish cellists, and here you will get to know a little about perhaps the greatest cellist who ever lived.

"This is murder!" Toscanini shouted.

Had Emmanuel Feuermann, the greatest cellist of his generation, greater even than Pablo Casals, many musicians said, actually been killed?

Well, only in a manner of speaking, though for Toscanini, the cause of his death, at the age of only thirty-nine, was tantamount to murder. Feuermann had gone into the hospital for what was to have been a routine operation, simply to remove a hemorrhoid, but the procedure had not only been botched, but wasn't even carried out by a surgeon. Feuermann never should have died, but now he was most certainly certifiably dead, and Toscanini and others who knew and revered Feuermann were distraught. Like Michael Rabin some years later, a brilliant career had been prematurely ended by a freak, absurd accident.

His tragic early death was a grievous loss to the world of music, as is attested by the many tributes Feuermann received afterward.

The legendary cello teacher Julius Klengel with whom Feuermann studied as a young teenager wrote of him after learning of his death, "Of all those who have been entrusted to my guardianship, there has never been such a talent ... our divinely favored artist and lovable young man." Jascha Heifetz with whom Feuermann famously collaborated for several years declared that talent like Feuermann's comes once every one hundred years. Indeed, after Feuermann's untimely death it took seven years for Heifetz to collaborate with another cellist, Gregor Piatigorsky.

Artur Rubinstein was equally emphatic: "He became for me the greatest cellist of all times, because I did hear Pablo Casals at his best. He (Casals) had everything in the world, but he never reached the musicianship of Feuermann. And this is a declaration." During his first tour of the United States in 1935-36, Feuermann reaped enthusiastic reviews from music critics. After a 1938 Proms performance in London, critic Reid Steward of The Strad wrote "I do not think there can any longer be doubt that Feuermann is the greatest living cellist, Casals alone excepted ..." Even Casals himself extolled Feuermann: "What a great artist Feuermann was! His early death was a great loss to music."

The stature of the pall-bearers at Feuermann's funeral, who included some of the greatest musicians of the time, attest to the esteem in which this beloved cellist was held. Besides Toscanini, they were conductors George Szell and Eugene Ormandy; pianists Rudolf Serkin and Artur Schnabel; and violinists Mischa Elman and Bronislaw Huberman. A quartet including Erica Morini and Frank Miller played the slow movement of the Beethoven string quartet, Op. 74. I wonder if there was ever another funeral of a musician where so many musical eminences were gathered to honor one of their own peers.

So much for Feuermann in death. Who was he during his short life and where did he come from?

Feuermann was born in 1902 in Galicia, Poland, into an extremely musical family. A brother, Zigmund, was a child prodigy on the violin and his sister, Sophie, was also a prodigy at the piano. Feuermann's father played both the cello and the violin, and when young Emmanuel started playing the violin, he insisted on holding it vertically like a cello, and for the cello he was made. His epiphany came when he was ten years old when he heard Casals play. He demanded his mother buy the music Casals had performed so that he could learn it and began to practice it with intense concentration. By the very next year, at age eleven, he was ready to make his debut, and he started at the top, with the Vienna Philharmonic under Felix Weingartner, when he played a Haydn cello concerto to great acclaim. He thus started at the top and he stayed there for the rest of his life.

I will not bother to trace Feuermann's career in any detail, but just mention a few highlights and salient facts of about his life and importance as a musician.

Feuermann's early career took place in Europe where he played and taught, eventually becoming a professor at the Berlin Conservatory in 1929 where he taught until 1933. You can guess what happened then. Once the Nazis took power, he was summarily dismissed because of his Jewish heritage. Feuermann was then forced to move to London and eventually came to the United States where in 1935 he made his very successful American debut, wowing the critics. However, he made the mistake of returning to Vienna at the time of the Anschluss in 1938. The violinist Bronislaw Huberman had to help Feuermann and his family (he was then married with one child) escape to Palestine from whence they were able to return to the United States where Feuermann was to remain until his death. He then taught at the Curtis Institute in Philadelphia and in summers settled in Los Angeles, where he gave master classes. There he could be close to and collaborate with Jascha Heifetz and Artur Rubinstein, making up assuredly the greatest piano trio ensemble of all time. Even though eventually the distinguished Gregor Piatigorsky would take Feuermann's place, Heifetz later professed that for him, it was Feuermann who was incomparable.

Feuremann's importance to music does not merely reside in his fabulous career. He was also instrumental in establishing fundamental changes in cellist technique. For example, he worked hard to eliminate the nasal tone that had been thought to be a part of the natural sound of the instrument. And he seemed even to extend its register. It was even said that he could play the Mendelssohn violin concerto on the cello! And he stressed the role of the entire body in playing the instrument. Finally, along with his idol, Pablo Casals, Feuermann is credited with having established the cello as a solo instrument. Today, you can hear cellists like Yo-Yo Ma because of Feuermann's lasting influence on the importance of the cello.

Although Feuermann died in 1942, he still lives of course on YouTube where you can, for example, hear how he plays the upper register of the cello with incredibly nimble fingers in a super-fast recording of the Dvorak cello concerto that had to be played that way because of the constraints of the 78 records which was all that was available in Feuermann's day. You can also hear him play with Heifetz and Rubinstein.

And there are some priceless photographs of him, too, one of which shows him in a relaxed pose with Rubinstein and Heifetz who is seen laughing—the only time, apparently, that Heifetz was ever photographed laughing. But my favorite one of Feuermann must have been taken not long before his death in his late thirties. There you see him with his cello, looking very composed in his natty suit, a cigarette dangling insouciantly from his lips. That's how I like to remember him, the cellist who will never be forgotten as long as classical music endures.

So these are a few of the finest artists in classical music who ever lived whose young lives were cruelly snuffed out while in the prime of their careers. At least we have some of their recordings to remind us of their extraordinary gifts, but, really, that is small consolation. Sorry to end on such a downer, but if I have managed to evoke at least a scintilla of interest in the world of classical music in you—in case this was not already a domain you were very familiar with—I would be happy to regale you with some really amusing stories about some zany Jews who were very important in the history of classical music, not for performing it, but for their patronage. And one of them was perhaps the most highly regarded philosopher of the first half of the twentieth century, and certainly the strangest.

Have I intrigued you? Would you like to have some more stories from a vanished world before both it and I disappear? Let me know....

Why Composers Didn't
Need a Day Job

Becoming a composer of classical music isn't easy. Oh, it is easy enough to compose when you've got the musical talent and training and get the knack of it, but unless you're also a concert performer, usually on the piano, such as Franz Liszt, it's hard to make a go of it financially. To paraphrase a quip of Woody Allen's, composers can't live on inspiration alone; they also need a patron. And until foundation grants came into being in the 20th century, it was always the wealthy who carried the composer's freight. Without their support, most composers would have had to remain in their cold attics or give up to become waiters.

Of course, in the old days of the baroque period of music and into the classical era, where composers looked for handouts was in the purses of aristocrats. Oh, how many obsequious letters had to be written by composers to those whose purse strings they hoped to loosen. It was a degrading enterprise, but necessary if an ambitious composer was to make his way. And, of course, aristocrats would often employ composers, as in the famous case of Joseph Haydn who served for decades as a court musician for the Esterházy family of Austria where at first he was treated merely as a servant and took his meals with them—until he became the most famous composer of his day. But Haydn needed to eat, too, and not just compose. And patronage under the rule of the aristocrats could not only be humiliating but also unrewarding, and in more than one sense. You've probably heard of and listened to some of Bach's

Brandenburg concertos, six of Bach's most celebrated orchestral compositions. They were commissioned by the Margrave of Brandenburg (hence their name) who stiffed Bach who never received the German equivalent of a dime for them. Well, there are many more such stories, but that's not the story I want to tell you here.

Eventually, when the aristocrats were ushered off the stage of history, composers had to find other sources of funding. Enter the plutocrats, or more usually, the wives of plutocrats, very wealthy women who had a yen for classical music and the men who created it. So it was that beginning roughly in the middle of the nineteenth century, we encounter in the history of music the age of the patron. These days, these patrons are mostly forgotten or, at best, are mere footnotes to the lives of great composers, but in their day, they were indispensable. Without them, the world of classical music would have been much impoverished. Not just those whose work they sponsored, but we today continue to owe them a great debt. So they don't deserve to live only in oblivion. Let's bring out at least a few of them for a posthumous bow.

Of course, the rich are also often eccentric, and so it is with patrons. Perhaps the zaniest example of all was Tchaikovsky's patron, a woman by the name of Nadezhda von Meck. She became, after her husband's death, the wealthiest woman in Moscow. She was also mad about music and determined to further the work of the composers she favored. For a time, it was the young Debussy, whom she called De Bussy, but when she was introduced to the music of Tchaikovsky, that was it—kismet. She was to provide munificent support for him for fourteen years during the very peak of his career when he would compose his greatest and most enduringly popular works. Without her support, emotional and financial, it's doubtful that most of these works would ever have been written. During that time they exchanged hundreds of letters. Tchaikovsky would sometimes stay in her villas in Italy while she was absent. They had an extraordinary and intimate relationship— yet they never met!

Nadezhda was a recluse; Tchaikovsky himself was not only a

closeted homosexual but pathologically shy. They had an understanding from the beginning: they must never meet face to face,
and they never did.

The whole story of Tchaikovsky and his patron is absolutely
fascinating—and ultimately tragic—but it is by now well known.
(Indeed, I have also written about it at length in my books about
composers and their muses.) Rather than retell it here, however,
let me instead introduce you to a couple of other less well-known
patrons who nevertheless played important roles in the lives of a
number of now famous composers. They, too, were a little—and
maybe more than a little—dotty, but there is no doubt that they
were as eccentric in their own way as Nadezhda was in hers.

The Princess de Polignac

Winnaretta Singer, true to her name, was indeed a singular
person. Nevertheless, she might well have been lost among the two
dozen (!) children sired by her famous and obviously prodigiously
fecund father, Isaac Singer. Singer of course was famous not only
for the number of offspring he produced, but for something else he
fathered, the sewing machine. Actually, Singer didn't invent the
sewing machine, though everyone thinks he did, but whatever the
history of this world-changing mechanism, it made him an enormously wealthy man who could certainly afford to procreate as
many children as his wives could be induced to bear. Winnaretta
checked in as number twenty. She would prove to be one of the
children who in her lifetime would be become almost as famous as
he, though in her case "scandalous" might be a more appropriate
adjective.

The distinguished Singer family, as well as having its own
eccentricities and share of scandals, moved around a great deal,
mainly in Europe, both before and after Isaac's death in 1875. But
eventually Winnaretta made her home in Paris where at the age of
twenty-two she married a prince, though not (yet) the Prince de
Polignac. Unfortunately for that prince, Winnaretta had by then

become a lesbian. On her wedding night, it was later reported, she climbed upon an armoire and threatened to kill her unsuspecting groom if he came near. Apparently, Winnaretta relented somewhat, since the marriage lasted five years before it was annulled. But Winnaretta did not only have a hankering for ladies, but also for princes as well for she soon found another one who proved to be much more suitable since he was gay. Prince Edmond de Polignac was also an amateur composer and since Winnaretta was keen on music, their marriage was a match that suited them both. From all accounts, they were a very devoted couple, though they never did, finding their sexual pleasures elsewhere. But their mutual love of music and respect for each other's "proclivities" ultimately created a strong bond between them.

Though we will be mainly interested in Winnaretta's patronage of composers, her extramarital amatory life is fascinating, so I will allow myself to linger a bit more here to devote at least a couple of brief paragraphs to it.

In her affairs with women, which were numerous throughout her lifetime, Winnaretta had no qualms about being both flagrant and flamboyant. As I've said, and as is well understood, wealth can buy you more than trinkets; it can also purchase privilege and the freedom to do as one chooses without suffering undue risk. She had affairs with women during her own marriages and often during theirs. One incensed husband once stood outside Winnaretta's Venetian palazzo where she had been carrying on with his wife, and shouted, "If you are half the man I think you are, you will come out here and fight me." Winnaretta's response, if she deigned to give one, is not recorded.

She had affairs with painters and with members of royalty, such as the writer and socialite, Baroness Olga de Meyer, whose father was reputed to be Edward VII. The most celebrated woman composer of her day, Ethel Smyth, fell deeply in love with Winnaretta during their affair. And so on with writers, artists, musicians, etc. until her death. What a life!

But now let us move from Winnaretta's lively boudoir to her

glittering salon whose glamour would certainly rival any of those of other wealthy salonnières of her time. Just take a look at her guest list:

Winnanetta's salon was frequented by the famous dancer, Isadora Duncan, whose child was fathered by Winnaretta's brother, Peter Singer. Other celebrated artists included Jean Cocteau, Claude Monet, Sergei Diaghilev, Le Corbusier, and Collete. Among the musicians for whom Winnaretta became patrons and who attended her gatherings were Nadia Boulanger and pianists Clara Haskil, Dinu Lipatti, Artur Rubinstein and Vladimir Horowitz. Of course, her lover, Ethel Smyth, was sometimes in attendance, too. And guess who else?

Marcel Proust of course! Many of the author's evocations of salon culture were based on his experiences during his attendance at concerts in the Polignac drawing room.

And these grand occasions not only featured the illustrious guests I have mentioned but entire ensembles of performing musicians, singers and dancers: members of the Ballets Russe, the Opera of Paris and the Orchestre Symphonie of Paris also added to the musical fare and flavor of these evenings.

Finally, I must mention that Winnaretta was more than a patron of the arts; she was a talented musician herself who often performed at her salons as a pianist and organist. She was also an accomplished artist whose works had been exhibited at the Académie des Beaux-Arts. One of her paintings was even advertised as being a Manet!

It was in 1894 that the Prince and Princess de Polignac established their salon in Paris in the music room of their mansion on Avenue Henri-Martin. The Polignac salon came to be known as a haven for avant-garde music. First performances of some of the works of Chabrier, d'Indy, Debussy, Fauré and Ravel took place there. The Ravel episode deserves a little elaboration for it had far-reaching consequences for Ravel.

For the young and ambitious composer, whom his teacher Gabriel Fauré introduced to the Winnaretta salon, it became the social and professional springboard for a highly successful career. On their first meeting, Ravel presented Winnaretta with the dedication of his newest work, the *Pavane pour une infante défunte*. Instead of asking and waiting for her permission, Ravel had simply gone ahead and presented her with the score and dedication. In any event, Winnaretta accepted the dedication and became one of the most passionate supporters of Ravel's music. The pavane became of her favorite pieces and was played at her husband's funeral seven years later.

After her husband's death, Winnaretta used her fortune to benefit the arts, sciences, and letters. She decided to honor Edmond's memory by commissioning several works of the young composers of her time. Among them, Igor Stravinsky's *Renard* and Erik Satie's *Socrate*, which I've never heard or even had heard of until I read in one of the American composer Ned Rorem's diaries something to the effect, as I recall, that he regarded it the greatest piece of music he knew. However that may be, if it weren't for Winnaretta's patronage, who knows whether Satie would have been able to complete this composition. And did you know—I didn't—that she even interceded to keep Satie out of jail for some kind of indiscretion when he was composing *Socrate*? She could pull strings, too!

The music mad (or perhaps just plain mad) Wittgensteins of Vienna

She also supported the work of Darius Milhaud and other French composers including Francis Poulenc, Jean Françaix, and Germaine Tailleferre. And not just French composers. She also provided support for Kurt Weill when he was composing his *Second Symphony* and Manuel de Falla's *El ratablo de maese Pedro* was first performed at Winnaretta's salon with no less than the legendary Wanda Landowska playing the harpsichord.

How much does the world of music owe to the largesse of the wondrous Winnaretta, the Princess of Polignac!

The music mad (or maybe just plain mad) Wittgensteins of Vienna

Let us next consider the Wittgensteins.

Of course, these days the only Wittgenstein that most people know is Ludwig, the gnomic philosopher who is generally now regarded, with Heidegger his only serious competition, as the greatest and most influential philosopher of the first part of the twentieth century. However that may be, he was certainly the strangest. The eminent British philosopher and mathematician, Bertrand Russell, who knew Wittgenstein well and encouraged him to pursue philosophy, declared that he was "the most perfect example of genius he had ever known." He later told Wittgenstein's sister, Hermine, "We expect the next big step in philosophy to be taken by your brother." Russell later changed his mind, but that is another story, and not the one I have to tell here.

And what that story is concerns not just Ludwig, but the Wittgenstein family because most of them were extremely gifted musically and were passionate about classical music. For them, music was almost a manic obsession, and it seems to have driven at least some of them mad and to suicide. So it was not just Ludwig who was strange; the whole family seems to have been bonkers.

Consider this description from Terry Eagleton's account of the family life of the Wittgensteins:

The father, Karl, was a brutal autocrat as well as a high-class crook. He was an engineer by vocation, and his son Ludwig would later do some original work in aeronautics at Manchester University. A fabulously wealthy steel magnate, Karl rigged prices, bleeding his workers dry and doing much the same to his timorous wife Leopoldine. She once lay awake all night, agonized by an ugly wound in her foot but terrified of moving an inch in case she disturbed her irascible husband. She was an emotionally frigid mother and a neurotically dutiful wife, from whom all traces of individual personality had been violently erased.

The family was a seething cauldron of psychosomatic disorders. Leopoldine was afflicted by terrible leg pains and eventually went blind. Her children had their problems too. Helene was plagued by stomach cramps; Gretl was beset by heart palpitations and sought advice from Sigmund Freud about her sexual frigidity; Hermine had dodgy fingers; Paul suffered from bouts of madness; and little Ludwig was scarcely the most well balanced of souls. Almost all the males of the family were seized from time to time by bouts of uncontrollable fury that bordered on insanity.

But one thing is for sure: they were also mad about music.

The Wittgensteins, who, by the way, were extremely wealthy, seem to have been a musical family for generations. Ludwig's grandmother was the celebrated Jewish violinist Joseph Joachim's distant cousin; in fact, Joachim became an adopted son. Ludwig's father, Karl, was highly musical as was his wife, Leopoldine. The elder Wittgensteins eventually came to know Joachim's accompanist, Johannes Brahms, who became a family friend and gave piano lessons to some of Ludwig's aunts. By the century's close, during Brahms's last years, he had become a fixture at the Wittsgenstein Palais, where his clarinet sonatas and quintet had their first private performances.

A brief sidebar about Brahms who was a very contrarian character. In an age and on a continent where anti-Semitism was common, he was a philo-Semite. Not only was he long associated with Joachim, but he was also friends such Jewish composers as Karl Goldmark, although eventually their friendship cooled because Goldmark came to find Brahms's personality too abrasive. There is a famous story about Brahms when he was about to leave a dinner party. Before his departure, he was heard to say, "If there is anybody here I have failed to insult, I apologize!" But he certainly was a favorite at the Wittgensteins' home.

But the family's cultural life really centered on the grand

Musiksaal on the first floor of their main house. Besides Brahms's frequent presence, Joachim's famous quartet played in the Musiksaal several times each year. Clara Schumann, Richard Strauss, and Bruno Walter attended the Wittgenstein soirées, as did the most famous musical critic of the day, Eduard Hanslick. Contemporary revolutionary composers, such as Schoenberg, also came to the soirées several times, but Mahler, whose music Ludwig later dismissed as "worthless," came only once and was not invited back after he left before the end of the evening's entertainment.

Music was more than entertainment for the Wittgensteins, however. They were also important collectors as well as patrons. Their collection included autographed scores by Brahms, Schubert, Wagner, and Bruckner. A Bach cantata, two Mozart piano concertos, a Haydn symphony, and one of Beethoven's last piano sonatas were smuggled to Ludwig in Cambridge during the Second World War. One of Ludwig's sisters' sons successfully hid Schubert's "Die Forelle," Brahms's "Handel Variations," some Beethoven letters, Wagner's sketches for "Die Walküre," and other treasured musical mementos for safe keeping during this fraught time as well.

Unfortunately, as I have implied, the Wittgensteins' love of classical music had a dark side. Besides Ludwig, who was the youngest, there were four brothers, Rudi, Hans, Kurt and Paul. Hans was a prodigy whose extraordinary musical perception became evident at the age of four; Gustav Mahler's teacher, Julius Epstein, called him a genius. Both he and Rudi seemed destined for careers as keyboard virtuosi, but each was driven to commit suicide as young men. (There was speculation that Hans may have been homosexual. Rudi and Ludwig were known to be.) The third brother, Kurt, also died by suicide at the age of forty. After the tragic death of each of these children, Karl forbad their names from ever being mentioned again. Ludwig often thought of killing himself, even, he said, as early as the age of ten, as did his only other surviving brother, Paul. Paul, never considered the family's best pianist, nevertheless achieved great success for a time, even after losing an arm in WWI. But, he, too, was a deeply troubled man, sometimes suicidal, with many eccentricities and tics who suffered from his own version of "the Wittgenstein curse." But let us leave Paul's story for later and return now to Ludwig's whose own musical tastes and talents were peculiar and idiosyncratic enough.

Some of his musical gifts and sensitivities were both weird and remarkable.

He was an extremely acute listener. Once, on hearing a Schubert record playing at the wrong pitch, Ludwig interrupted his conversation to adjust the turntable's speed. He would also unhesitatingly correct others' inaccurate humming or singing.

Then there was his prodigious skill as a whistler! Yes, whistling was one of his specialties. Oddly enough for a Wittgenstein, Ludwig seems not to have mastered any musical instrument as a child, though as an adult he learned to play the clarinet well enough play Brahms's sonatas. But as a whistler, he was unexcelled and legendary. He would enjoy impressing his musical friends with his virtuosic whistling performances. Several Cambridge dons recalled hearing him whistle the solo part of an entire concerto while a pianist played the orchestral part. His repertoire included Brahms's "Variations on a Theme Haydn" as well as other symphonic works.

His taste in music was surprising and characteristically eccentric. He had no patience for or interest in contemporary music. For Ludwig, music seems to have ended with the end of the 19th century. Instead, he insisted there were only six truly great composers, all Germans or Austrians: Haydn, Mozart, Beethoven, Schubert, Brahms—and Labor. Who was Labor, you ask? A blind organist and family friend who was also the beneficiary of the Wittgenstein patronage. Ludwig himself seems to have been very fond of Labor, and when visiting Vienna, would sometimes prefer to spend time with him rather than with his batty family.

Needless to say, Mahler's music had no interest for him; indeed, as I have mentioned, he appears to have despised it. Likewise, and not surprisingly, Wagner's operas were not for Ludwig. He even had no use for the music of Richard Strauss, a family friend, who used to play piano duets with the young Paul. In music, Ludwig was strictly one for the classics in which fixed forms and tonality were adhered to as matter of course. In philosophy, he was an iconoclastic genius and broke new ground, but in music, he was not only content to tread on familiar ground; he insisted on it with an almost manically rigid and obsessive fanaticism.

How different he was from his brother, Paul, whose taste in music was completely different, but no less eccentric in its own way.

Between these two, who ceased to have any contact with each other after 1939, there was often great tension and displays of temper. One day, for instance, when Paul was practicing at one of the seven grand pianos in their winter home, he leaped up and shouted at his brother Ludwig in the room next door, "I cannot play when you are in the house, as I feel your skepticism seeping towards me from under the door!" They seem frequently to have been at loggerheads since their temperaments were so different.

Paul's real tragedy came later. As I've mentioned, he returned from World War I with only one arm, his left. Even so, he was determined to continue to play, and even while recovering, worked furiously and ingeniously to develop techniques that would enable him to perform. Once he had recovered, he often practiced for up to seven hours at a sitting. He was nothing if not driven and ambitious.

And in time, he was rewarded with considerable success, at least at first. At the height of his career, in the late nineteen-twenties and early thirties, Paul's concerts drew wildly enthusiastic reviews from respected critics. For a pianist limited to the use of only one hand, he was a phenomenon. Indeed, during his lifetime, for many years he was more famous than his brother.

It didn't last. His abilities seem to have become eroded, and in consequence, his reputation as a pianist suffered a sharp reversal.

Today, if he is remembered at all, it is not so much as a one-armed pianist, but as someone who commissioned a series of piano concertos for the left hand alone from some dozen composers, among them such famous ones as Richard Strauss, Sergei Prokofiev, Benjamin Britten, Paul Hindemith, Erich Wolfgang Korngold, and Maurice Ravel. Alas, today, only the Ravel is sometimes played, and even so it is far less popular than his jazzy *G major concerto*. But what is memorable about many of these commissions was Paul's disputes with some of these composers and the sorry fate of their offerings.

Robert Gottlieb gives an amusing account of these commissions, including the not altogether admirable pecuniary motives of some of the composers for undertaking them:

> Strauss extracted a particularly large fee, and Britten, at least, affected to be in it just for the money. ("I have been commissioned by a man called Wittgenstein," Britten wrote to his sister. "He pays gold so I'll do it.") Paul often insisted on changes to the music, especially when he thought that the orchestra had been overscored and would drown out his playing. (Britten groused, "The man really is an old sour puss.") There was also a colorful dispute with Ravel, who complained for the rest of his life about his dealings with Paul. There was worse in store for poor Hindemith, who wrote his concerto in 1923: Paul couldn't understand the composition, so he filed it away. It was discovered eight decades later, in a Pennsylvania farmhouse that had belonged to Paul's widow ... Paul couldn't fathom Prokofiev's concerto, either, and he shelved that, too.

Like his brother, Paul also had his share of eccentricities quite apart from his disputatious tendencies and fits of temper. Most of Paul's eccentricities were perhaps the normal ones for a loner who had been brought up amid vast wealth. He was a fiercely private man who liked to book entire railway carriages for himself, even when travelling with his family. His wife, Hilde, who was half blind and had been his pupil, bore him two children in Vienna before their marriage; the elder child had been conceived shortly after their first piano lesson, when Hilde was eighteen years old and Paul was forty-seven.

They were forced to flee Austria after the Anschluss in 1938 and eventually settled in New York. But Paul appears not to have lived with his family, at least not all the time. He set them up in a house on Long Island while he retained an apartment on Riverside Drive. Once, when his clothes were stolen from a hotel (used to the privileges of wealth, he had left them outside his room, assuming that someone would wash them), he sat around in bed sheets until someone pointed out that it might be possible to buy a new outfit at clothing store. Another time he apparently left the hotel wearing a hat that was still attached to its box.

Sometimes it seems as if Paul, lacking one of his arms, had only half a brain, too. He died at 73, outliving his now by far more famous estranged brother by ten years.

And with Paul ends this improbable and bizarre story of the musically mad Wittgenstein family. Despite their personal foibles and family tragedies, however, I do not mean merely to poke fun of them for we must remember how much they did to promote and support the musicians and composers of their time as well as to preserve the heritage of the great composers of the past. As such, they are only one, if certainly one of the most memorable, of the very important families of Vienna who made a lasting contribution to the history of music, not only in Vienna but of the world. They were just more looney than most Viennese wealthy patrons, but as in the world at large, so in the world of music, "it takes all kinds."

COVID

Introduction

By the time COVID hit during the first part of 2020, I had given up writing books and taken up the blogging life. Like many people at that time, I kept what I called "a COVID diary," although it really wasn't a diary at all. It was just a series of blogs I wrote during that fearful period. In this section, I include five of these essays in which I explored the challenges, and terror, of that time, though sometimes with a dash of perhaps ill-judged humor.

Plagues, Pandemics, Poxes and the Electric Toothbrush

Elizabeth Kolbert is a longtime staff writer for *The New Yorker*, an expert on environment issues, particularly those pertaining to the climate crisis, and the author of one of the most terrifying books of our time, *The Sixth Extinction*. In that book, she describes in horrifying detail what human beings have done in the newly named epoch of our time, the anthropocene, to destroy nature. We have done a very good job.

But none of that, fortunately, is our concern here. What is, is an article of Kolbert's I recently read that had to do with the history of pandemics. That stimulated me to do a little research of my own into this matter, and that is what I would like to share with you here. At the outset, however, I need to acknowledge my indebtedness to Kolbert for some of the information I will be presenting in this blog.

Those of you who are older, or perhaps as old as the hills as I am, may be familiar with some of this history, but for younger readers, this may be new territory. Let's begin to explore it.

Almost all of us who have grown up during the past hundred years or so have not had any personal experience with pandemics until now. We have of course grown used to the seasonal flu, which causes many people to die every year. But the flu doesn't stop the world; it goes on just minus thousands of people. A pandemic, however, not only stops the world but changes it in unpredictable and often decisive ways. History, as one author has recently suggested, is not just made by men, but by microbes. Of course, in our lifetime and relatively recently there have been outbreaks of serious respiratory diseases, also caused by coronaviruses, such as SARS and MERS, and the Ebola virus, the H1NI flu, and so on, but these were, fortunately, mostly regional illnesses and were relatively quickly quelled. Malaria, though a very serious disease (it kills about a half million people every year) is familiar to most of us only from reading about it. It is rare in the United States. So, by and large, we have been very lucky to live during these times. Most of us have emerged unscathed by serious widespread disease and life has gone on in its wayward way, as have we.

Needless to say, however (a phrase that always goes on to contradict itself), this has not invariably been the case. There is hardly anyone left on earth who survived the Spanish flu that began as World War I was ending in 1918 and didn't burn itself out until 1920. During that time it killed an estimated *50 million* people throughout the world, maybe more. By comparison, "only" about 20 million people perished in the war. That flu was a lot more deadly in scarcely more than a year than in the four years of "The Great War."

But pandemics like the Spanish flu go back a long way and it is sobering to become familiar with their history. These days almost everyone knows something about "The Black Death," the plague that after it started in Europe in 1347 was eventually to wipe out about one-third of the population of that continent. But plagues and other pandemics of world-changing consequence began to afflict vast populations of humanity long before that.

According to Kolbert and other sources, the first pandemic of which we have knowledge broke out in 541 near what is now Port Saïd in Egypt. It then spread to the west toward Alexandria as well as toward the east where it reached Palestine. And then it just kept going, and going. In early 542, it had reached Constantinople, which was then the capital of the Eastern Roman Empire under the rule of Justinian (who also caught the fever, but managed to survive it). The plague hit Rome the next year, Britain in 544,

Constantinople several more times over the next forty years and didn't burn itself out until the year 750, more than two centuries after it started. Can you imagine?

And what was it like for people who found themselves caught in the vicious vise of this devastating plague? Here is Kolbert's account of it:

> The earliest symptom of the pestilence was fever. Often, [according to one contemporary historian] this was so mild that it did not "afford any suspicion of danger." But, within a few days, victims developed the classic symptoms of bubonic plague—lumps, or buboes, in their groin and under their arms. The suffering at that point was terrible; some people went into a coma, others into violent delirium. Many vomited blood. Those who attended to the sick "were in a state of constant exhaustion. For this reason everybody pitied them no less than the sufferers." No one could predict who was going to perish and who would pull through.

When the plague came the first time to devastate Constantinople, Justinian had his hands full. Again, Kolbert:

> The Emperor paid for the bodies of the abandoned and the destitute to be buried. Even so, it was impossible to keep up; the death toll was too high. [One historian thought it reached more than ten thousand a day, though no one is sure if this is accurate.] John of Ephesus, another contemporary of Justinian's, wrote that "nobody would go out of doors without a tag upon which his name was written," in case he was suddenly stricken. Eventually, bodies were just tossed into fortifications at the edge of the city.

That's what plagues were like for those who lived in those times. And of course they were far worse when the Black Plague broke out. It not only blasted many millions of lives and changed course of history in Europe but it never stopped. It just kept going year and after year, century after century. In those times, people had to learn to live and die not with the flu, but with the plague.

The plague repeatedly returned to haunt Europe and the Mediterranean throughout the 14th to 17th centuries. According to one historian, the plague was present somewhere in Europe in every year between 1346 and 1671.

If you were unfortunate enough to live in London in 1665 when the plague broke out there, you had a one in five chance of dying. That plague itself killed perhaps as many as 100,000 people.

And the plague is still with us. There were two outbreaks of it in San Francisco around the time of that city's famous earthquake, and even in this century, there were two eruptions of it in Madagascar.

Plagues are not only horrible and horrifying to those who catch the virus; they can be just as deadly for those who are innocent of doing any harm. This is because during such times, it is easy and tempting to find scapegoats for the spread of the disease. Jews, of course, have always been a handy scapegoat in the history of Christendom. Here's just one example provided by Kolbert concerning what happened to the Jews of Strasbourg during the during the Black Death in 1349:

> Local officials decided that they were responsible for the pestilence—they had, it was said, poisoned the wells— and offered them a choice: convert or die. Half opted for the former. On February 14, 1349, the rest "were rounded up, taken to the Jewish cemetery, and burned alive." Pope Clement VI issued papal bulls pointing out that Jews, too, were dying from the plague, and that it wouldn't make sense for them to poison themselves, but this doesn't seem to have made much difference. In 1349, Jewish communities in Frankfurt, Mainz, and Cologne were wiped out. To escape the violence, Jews migrated en masse to Poland and Russia, permanently altering the demography of Europe.

Now although we now longer kill scapegoats, some people have begun to blame the Chinese for what President Trump, our leading xenophobe—and germophobe—likes to call "the foreign virus."

Returning to history, we move now from pandemics and plagues to poxes, specifically smallpox. Many people today associate smallpox with the kind of pustules (actually called macules) that afflicted the faces of 18th century European aristocrats or even some of our own "royal personages," such as George Washington. Far from it. Smallpox is one of the deadliest and most dreaded scourges ever to torment the lives of human beings, and it is still with us.

During the 20th century alone, it is estimated to have killed anywhere between 300 and 500 million people. Kolbert says it may have resulted in the deaths of a billion people during the course of its history, which goes back thousands of years to the time of the Egyptian pharaohs. It kills about one-third of those it infects.

Smallpox, too, has played a leading role in shaping the course of history, particularly in what used to be called "the new world."

Each race and many peoples have contributed their share of horrors to our world, but certainly the Europeans have done more than their share of heinous depredations in literally decimating (a word that is often misused since it means to reduce to one-tenth) the native populations of the Americas and Australia by bringing, and in cases deliberately inflicting, deadly diseases against which the indigenous people had no immunity.

For example, the Spanish inadvertently owed much of their success in conquering the Aztecs and Incas in Mexico in the 16th century to smallpox. Unlike the Spanish, the native Indians had no immunity to the disease, having never encountered it. It was far more fatal to them than the Spanish themselves as many native peoples succumbed to the disease. A century later, the North American Indians suffered a similar fate from a smallpox epidemic. True, the Europeans had the guns and brought the horses, but did you know that it is estimated that perhaps 90% of American Indians died of germs that the European invaders brought with them, most of all, it seems, from smallpox?

According to one historian:

"The discovery of America was followed by possibly the greatest demographic disaster in the history of the world."

Without question it changed the course history in permanent ways, as we have all now long realized, and native people, while they survived, realized most of all to their enduring sorrow.

And this same shocking story played out elsewhere as well, for in the 18th century, smallpox also took many of the lives and destroyed the culture of the aborigines when it reached Australia, the last corner of the world to have escaped its ravages.

Perhaps that is enough about pandemics, plagues and poxes, though I could of course numb you into insensibility by discussing still other deadly and persisting diseases, such as cholera, likewise still very much with us, as we all will remember from its outbreak in Haiti in 2010 following the horrendous earthquake there. Eventually, some 800,000 people contracted the disease and 10,000 died. But I don't need to belabor the point that, as John Irving made clear in his novel of a few years back, *The World According to Garp*, the world is not safe. And it certainly has been and will continue to be plagued by disease (no pun intended). There is no immunity from life on this planet.

So, finally, what are we to make of all this and what does this history, brief and selective as it had to be (a blog after all is not a book), have to teach us as we navigate our way through COVID-19, the pandemic of our own lifetime? Well, here are just some of my own personal reflections on the matter.

First, these diseases began with the domestication of animals and with people living in cities. I didn't have to read Yuval Harari's *Sapiens* to learn that our hominid ancestors made a big mistake when they climbed down from their trees to the savannas of Africa and became bipedal primates (our back problems stem from that decision) and then, to compound their folly, as humans to invent agriculture ten thousand years ago from which all the subsequent calamities and misfortunes of civilization derive. But of course there is no going back. History does not follow a progressive track, but it does not go in reverse. We are stuck with it, and stuck with disease. And to be fair, civilization has brought us some wonderful things, such as the invention of the electric toothbrush. It's not all been bad.

As for our current virus, one good thing about it is that has temporarily slowed the climate crisis express train before it hurdles over the cliff. It's done wonders to stymie the production of carbon dioxide and methane into the atmosphere. But can we learn from this experience before it is too late? Time will tell.

But what I have mainly endeavored to show in this little essay is that as disruptive to our daily lives as COVID-19 has been—and granting it could end up killing hundreds of thousands of people and sickening millions more—in light of what our forbearers throughout history have had to endure, it hardly compares with the horrors of the plagues, pandemics and poxes of the past. For most of us, fortunately, we are chiefly being inconvenienced and forced to undergo isolation for a few months. I don't mean to discount all the suffering that our health professionals and others have had to undergo to deal with this virus. Many will have given their lives to protect the rest of us, and we will always have cause to give enduring thanks to them. They have been the frontline soldiers on this war. But in the end the great preponderance of humanity will emerge sobered by the experience but intact. We will survive. The world will start again. The economy will take a while to recover, but we will make it.

But apart from the lessons from history, the question is, what will you have made of it? What will you have learned from having gone through this? And for those of you who survive this temporary ordeal, how will you choose to live once this is over and you can finally rejoin the world? What kind of world would you want to see blossom then?

Coping with COVID
in the Age of Ken

A Blog for Easter

I don't ZOOM. Hell, at 84 and with a severe case of spinal stenosis, I can barely walk these days. An outing for me—or perhaps I should say, an inning—involves my roaming, although usually with a sudden sense of urgency, from my office to my bathroom, where, needless to say, bathing is not my objective. These days, frankly, it is not even possible any longer. The last time I tried to bathe, I noticed that though I could descend into the tub, I could no longer arise. This led to a certainly perplexity, which was followed by a piercing cry for help I later discovered had emanated from my own throat. Fortunately, a neighbor to whom I had presciently given a key to my house heard my piteous wail of distress and rescued me from my watery predicament. Of course, I tried to conceal my privates and prevent them from becoming public, but was told in no uncertain but still in unnecessarily harsh terms, I thought, that given what I was fruitlessly attempting to hide wasn't worth the trouble. It was even intimated that a whole hand would not be necessary; a mere thumb would do.

But I digress. Last I looked I was discussing my failure at ZOOMing. Actually, failure is a bit too severe a term since I never even tried to ZOOM my way through the virus. After all, though I don't think my mug is unsightly (even if I no longer seem to score high on the ogle meter), why should I think my friends would like to waste their eyes looking at the decrepit old wreck that I've

159

become? Since many have not seen me for a long time—and then there are quite a few of my "friends" from here and abroad I have made without their ever having met me in person—I prefer that they remember or imagine me as I was during my prime rather than in my currently definitely sub-prime years. Visually, then, "I vant to be alone." Let me exist simply in the form of words on a screen that conceals my face. Even old men have their vanity.

But all this *jejune folderol* is really beside the point, which despite what it may seem, I actually have one in mind. It's about not just how I am coping with the virus (I will get to that), but what thoughts living under the COVID cloud have occasioned in me.

For one thing, the pandemic has expanded time while it has also shrunk my horizon. And I'm sure what's true for me has been true for many. I mean, consider: Before the pandemic hit with its mandatory requirements for self-isolation, most people were busy with their lives out in the world. People, like all primates, are not only social animals but we are busy creatures and when we are busy, time flies. But now that we are immured in our houses or apartments, time has slowed to a crawl. Figuratively speaking, we have time on our hands now. What to do with all that time?

Of course, most people—I do not include myself here—are creative. My son, for example, tells me he is now trying to master the art of making baguettes. But since he is not French, good luck, Dave! At least it keeps him occupied. And apparently many people have found this a propitious time to reorganize their kitchens (even I did that) or their closets (forget it). More creative types have been busy sending out sheets of surplus toilet paper full of humor, anecdotes, poetry and feel good stories. And then our inboxes are now groaning under the weight of podcasts, videos, essays, blogs (guilty!) in sufficient daily quantities to result, if we are not careful, with our eyes becoming permanently yoked to our screens. A writer friend of mine, who also works with clients on their own books, informs me her business is now booming because the pandemic has freed up so much time that everyone is writing a book or threatening to (not guilty!). The pandemic may be bad for our health, but it is apparently doing wonders for our creativity.

On the other hand, it is, as I have claimed, also narrowing our horizon. What I mean is that, once you stop watching TV (which I recommend), you wind up watching yourself, as it were. The outside world, from which we have been cut off, reduces to our own little world, to ourselves, to our petty concerns and trials. As if we weren't already self-involved as it was, but now narcissism is having a field day. *L'etat, c'est moi.*

I certainly notice this in my own case, which is why I referenced "the age of Ken" in the title to this blog. But since I am also "of an age," that phrase has a double meaning. As I have already mentioned, surely to the point of tedium to some of my readers, I am not only old but decrepit and infirm. Virtually every morning when I awaken, I realize I have made an error. Why should I continue to live in a body that is clearly long past its expiration date? I am apparently doomed because I have a high bilirubin count, which seems to be associated with longevity. My dad died at 41, and I have always regretted his early death and have mourned and missed him for most of my long life. Now I think he was one of the lucky ones since he was spared the torments of old age. I joke with my girlfriend, Lauren, who is currently spending time taking care of me and without whom I am convinced I would soon perish, that I am fighting my own pandemic, old age, against which there is no cure. But the pandemic that the world is facing is just causing me to become preoccupied with my own troubles.

Who cares, Ken? They are trivial in the scheme of things. You think billions of people who have already lived and died or who are still living, haven't experienced what you are, and far worse? What you are going through is simply par for the course if the course happens to extend far beyond the 19th hole.

But that, you see, is the point I have been driving toward, despite these jocular asides. Because of the pandemic, it's easy, even if you are not old but in the spring of your life and not its winter, to turn to your own pursuits and problems—and to forget the world in which you are living now. And what is that world? Well, a good part of it is that a lot of people—many hundreds of thousands, if not millions—have become sick, and many of these have already died. And although the eventual totals may prove to be fewer than the alarming figures that were originally forecast, many more will become ill or die. Not just their lives but the lives of their families will be upended and in some cases ruined beyond restoration. Death leaves a hole in families that can never be filled.

And what about all the health care workers who have been forced both by duty and compassion to attend the sick and dying, risking and in many cases losing their own lives in order to help to save others, or even if not succumbing themselves, becoming infected and sick? How many such people throughout the world have had to deal with these energy-draining duties, day after day, sacrificing themselves, if necessary, for the sake of others?

And what about all the people—millions, just in our own country—who now find themselves out of work? They don't have time to organize their closets. Many of them are wondering where to get their next meal or how they are ever going to manage without financial ruin. Not to get too political—but at my age, what do I care what people think?—but this country in my opinion already had been in deep decay, with so much poverty, so many homeless people, so much suicide, so many addicted to and dying from opioids, and so on—long before the pandemic struck. And now this on top of everything else? It is almost unbearable to think about the sheer quantity of suffering that people have had to endure in recent years, now compounded manifold because of the pandemic. How do such people cope with this?

Added to this are just the more ordinary burdens that many people, especially families with children or elderly loved ones at home (or worrying about their elderly relatives in nursing homes or old age residences), have been forced to shoulder—how hard their lives must be. Parents going nuts with their kids underfoot all day, trying to keep them entertained or getting them to do their online learning from school, trying to figure out meals, desperate to find time to rest, wondering how long this will go on?

But I don't need to go on, do I? I trust I've made my point.

In our understandable concern for ourselves, let us not forget the wider world of which we are an inseparable part. Truly, we are all connected, we are indeed one, we are part of the whole, and our collective identity as humanity itself and what it is going through now must never be allowed, not just to be forgotten, but felt! Let us remember who we really are beyond the porous boundaries of our own egos and physical bodies. We are all those who are suffering and dying as well as those who are striving to make this a better world when at last the COVID cloud will lift, the sun will shine again on our lives, and we can finally wipe away our tears.

Doctor Fauci and the Pandemic

You've seen his face. You've heard his raspy voice. But what do you know about the man himself?

I confess I didn't know much about him at all until I read a recent twelve-page profile of him in *The New Yorker* entitled "How Anthony Fauci Became America's Doctor" (April 20, 2020) by one of its veteran staff writers, Michael Specter, who often writes on medical subjects. Specter was a perfect choice for this piece since he has known Fauci beginning in the mid-1980s and has followed his career closely ever since. Virtually everything that follows, with the exception of a few personal asides and my concluding remarks, is drawn from Specter's article. My hope is that my little blog will stimulate you to look up and read Specter's profile, but for those of you who don't read The New Yorker or don't know much about Fauci from other sources, I can at least provide something of a thumbnail sketch of this remarkable man.

So who is Anthony S. Fauci, the country's leading and now very prominent expert on infectious diseases? Since I mean to introduce you to the man before briefly discussing his career and especially his role the corona pandemic, let's begin at the beginning when Fauci was a kid growing up in Brooklyn in the early 1940s.

Perhaps significantly, he made his debut into this world on Christmas eve of 1940, when his parents were living in an area of Brooklyn called Bensonhurst. Oddly enough, a few years later, I spent a summer there myself just before the end of WW II when I was nine years old. I still remember a kid yelling after me, "Hey, California, you wanna play stickball?" Tony might have been living in the same neighborhood then, but even if so, stickball was not to be his game; he would be keen for hoops.

Tony's parents were Catholics, and he would wind up having a thorough and very superior Catholic education, but as a kid he was also busy making deliveries on his Schwinn bicycle for his father, a pharmacist, and playing basketball. But he had an interest in baseball, too, as Brooklyn was then still the home of the Dodgers, affectionately known as "dem bums." Oddly enough, however, Tony was a Yankee fan, and those were the days to be one since as of 1947, they were almost always World Champions for the next sixteen years. Reflecting on those years, he told Specter, "You probably are unaware, but half the kids in Brooklyn were Yankee fans. We spent our days arguing who was better: Duke Snider versus Mickey Mantle; Roy Campanella versus Yogi Berra; Pee Wee Reese versus Phil Rizzuto and on and on. Those were the days, my friend."

They were indeed. I was an ardent Yankee fan myself in those years, after seeing my first big league game at Yankee Stadium in 1945, and grew up worshiping those Yankee idols during that team's glory years. But that's the last thing Tony and I had in common when we were both kids, so let's get back to him and his story.

In 1954, he began attending Regis, a very elite private Jesuit high school on the Upper East Side. It was quite a hike from Brooklyn to 84th and Madison and Fauci estimates that he had spent the equivalent of seventy days of his teen-age life on the various subways and buses he took to get to and from school.

But he loved it there and quickly showed himself to be a very gifted student. And in those days, especially at schools where the teaching regimen was rigorous, the curriculum was very demanding. "We took four years of Greek, four years of Latin, three years of French, ancient history, theology," he told Specter who also observes that at Regis, "he developed an ability to set out an argument and to bolster it with evidence—good preparation, it turned out, for testifying before Congress."

Let me now simply quote a couple of paragraphs from Specter's profile that will make it clear how Tony was obliged to give up a career in basketball and to become a doctor instead. This will also help you to see how the boy developed into the man we know today.

At the time, though, Fauci had no interest in becoming a doctor. "I was captain of the Regis High School basketball team," he once told me. "I thought this was what I wanted to do with myself. But, being a realist, I very quickly found out that a five-seven, really fast, good-shooting point guard will never be as good as a really fast, good-shooting seven-footer. I decided to change the direction of my career."

At school, Fauci's accomplished peers were headed to careers in medicine, engineering, and the law. At home, he was steeped in the humanities: "Virtually all my relatives on my mother's side—her father, her brother, and her sister's children—are artists." His mother helped tip the balance. "She never really pressured me in any way, but I think I subtly picked up the vibrations that she wanted very much for me to be a physician," Fauci said. "There was this tension—would it be humanities and classics, or would it be science? As I analyzed that, it seemed to me that being a physician was the perfect melding of both of those aspirations."

Fauci wanted to attend an Ivy League school, but his Jesuit teachers wouldn't permit it! He would have to choose a Catholic institution, and his choice was to go to Holy Cross in Worchester, Massachusetts. But as he did at Regis, Fauci was to thrive there. He enrolled in a program called Bachelor of Arts—Greek Classics—Premed. "It was really kind of bizarre," he recalled. "We did a lot of classics, Greek, Latin, Romance languages... We took many credits of philosophy, everything from epistemology to philosophical psychology, logic, etc. But we took enough biology and physics and science to get you into medical school."

Fauci was now bound for medical school at Cornell, but in those years he had to spend summers working construction jobs. And here again, I can't resist quoting another delightful anecdote from Specter's article:

> One year, he found himself assigned to a crew that was building a new library at Cornell Medical College, on the Upper East Side. "On lunch break, when the crew were eating their hero sandwiches and making catcalls to nurses, I snuck into the auditorium to take a peek," Fauci recalled in 1998, at the medical school's centennial celebration. "I got goose bumps as I entered, looked around the empty room, and imagined what it would be like to attend this extraordinary institution. After a few minutes at the doorway, a guard came and politely told me to leave, since my dirty boots were soiling the floor. I looked at him and said proudly that I would be attending this institution a year from now. He laughed and said, 'Right, kid, and next year I am going to be Police Commissioner.'"

Fauci graduated first in his class in 1966, which of course was during America's involvement in the Vietnam War. At that time, every new physician had to select some form of military service. Public Health Service was one of the options, and Fauci went for that. The dye was cast.

Fauci in the five decades since as the country's leading infectious disease expert has gone on to have a storied career, garnering more laurels than a dozen Olympic champions, and Specter's profile provides many such accolades. You will need to read Specter's article to follow the course of Fauci's career, but he provides a very full account of Fauci's involvement with the AIDS crisis, which came to his attention in 1981 and consumed much of his time for the following decade. Did you know he made fundamental contributions to the understanding and treatment of AIDS? I didn't. That part of his story is fascinating. He went from being a stickler for rigorous testing to becoming an advocate and activist for people suffering from AIDS. "I went to the gay bathhouses and spoke to them. I went to San Francisco, to the Castro District, and I discussed the problems they were having, the degree of suffering that was going on in the community, the need for them to get involved in clinical trials, since there were no other possibilities for them to get access to drugs. And I earned their confidence."

Larry Kramer, one of the most important AIDS activists, had spent years vilifying Fauci, but after Fauci confessed his errors and joined the cause they became friends. Each of them came to value the other's contributions to medicine greatly, so much so that Kramer ultimately gave Fauci his highest accolade, calling him, "the only true and great hero" among government officials in the AIDS crisis.

I wish I had time to review Fauci's career, but this is a blog, not a real essay, so I must move things along. But if what I have written so far has made you curious to learn more about this extraordinary man, who, pushing eighty, still works 18 hours a day, and who has been the one indispensable figure in helping us understand the current pandemic, I can only urge you again to consult Specter's article or other sources of information about Fauci. For now, before we turn to his role in the COVID crisis, let it suffice for me to quote just two brief appraisals of Fauci's importance.

David Baltimore, a Nobel laureate and a pioneer of molecular biology, told Specter, "Tony is unique, in that he has such credibility with politicians that he's been able to insert hard facts into the conversation. That has been wonderful for our country and the world." According to David Relman, a microbiologist at Stanford University who for years has advised the government on biological threats, "Tony has essentially become the embodiment of the biomedical and public-health research enterprise in the United States.

Nobody is a more tireless champion of the truth and the facts. I am not entirely sure what we would do without him."

The public seems to agree with these assessments, too. According to a recent poll, 78% of Americans approve of Fauci's handling of the pandemic while only 7% disapprove. Contrast that with Trump's ratings where 65%, according to the latest poll I've seen, disapprove of the President's performance during this crisis.

Indeed, rather like Ruth Bader Ginsberg, Fauci has seemingly become in a very short time, something of a cultural icon, as Spectator amusingly recounts:

> These days, nearly everyone has heard of Fauci. Pandemic-memorabilia entrepreneurs have put his face on bottle openers, coffee mugs, and bumper stickers: "In Dr. Fauci we trust." The National Bobblehead Hall of Fame and Museum has produced a seven-inch likeness of him, partly to raise money to produce protective gear for medical workers. There's a Facebook group called Dr. Fauci Speaks, We Listen, and another called Dr. Fauci Memes for Social Distance Teens. A petition has circulated to nominate him as People's "sexiest man alive."

But let's get serious now and turn our attention back to the pandemic. As we have been made well aware now, we should have seen this coming. Virtually every reputable epidemiologist and virologist anticipated one or more as a certainty, not an if, but a when. Fauci, too, had warned that we should have been prepared for one, certainly much better prepared than we were, as he has admitted.

We have been preparing for the wrong war. "We spend many billions of dollars every year on missile-defense systems," Seth Berkley, a medical epidemiologist who leads the Global Vaccine Alliance," told Spector. "And yet we will not spend pennies on the dollar to prepare for a catastrophe that is far more likely to affect us all."

The Nobel Prize-winning molecular biologist Joshua Lederberg, another expert on infectious diseases, wrote years ago that "We live in evolutionary competition with microbes—bacteria and viruses. There is no guarantee that we will be the survivors." We just haven't been paying attention to the invisible threat to humanity's future, but we have been forced by circumstances to wake up, and to pay urgent heed to what Fauci and other experts have been telling us for years.

Fauci himself has long advocated the development of a universal influenza vaccine, which would provide lasting defense against all strains. "Similar to tetanus, a universal flu vaccine probably would be given every ten years," he said. "And, if you get one that is really universal, you can vaccinate just about everyone in the world." But such a vaccine would cost hundreds of millions of dollars to develop and test. Still, we now spend many billions on defense, which really means war preparedness and serving the interests of arms manufacturers and the military. How much will Congress be willing to appropriate to defend us from our real enemy?

Spector himself is not optimistic.

Even Fauci's current value as a scientific adviser has been limited by the President's contempt for expertise. Trump's coronavirus kitchen cabinet consists of people like his son-in-law, Jared Kushner, who has no medical knowledge or experience managing crises—yet has been appointed to direct the response to the biggest medical emergency since the influenza pandemic of 1918. Trump has also turned for advice to Dr. Mehmet Oz, who for years has endorsed worthless treatments and used his television show to promote notorious quacks. Trump even seems to think that his trade adviser, Peter Navarro, should debate Fauci about the value of specific drugs. When Navarro, who has a doctoral degree in economics, was asked about his medical qualifications, he said, "I have a Ph.D. And I understand how to read statistical studies, whether it's in medicine, the law, economics, or whatever."

The President, clearly, is more focused on "re-opening the economy" and bolstering his chances for re-election than in following the advice of his public health experts like Fauci whom he seemingly only grudgingly listens to and is doing his best to sideline. And that's where we seem to stand now, trying to contain a virus in a kind of ad hoc half-assed way that we were woefully unprepared for and that the President seems to want to wish away by a kind of magical incantation.

But if after all this, if we will have failed to learn that we must make a massive investment in public health in order to be much better prepared for the next pandemic than we were for this one, the voices of experts like Dr. Fauci will again be voices in the wilderness. We cannot afford to let that happen.

The Long Game

As you will know if you've been an assiduous reader of my previous blogs or, more likely, just an occasional casual visitor to them, I don't spend much time these days watching the news on TV about the virus. Life is dismal enough without being reminded of how much people in the U.S. and around the world are suffering and how many have already died, not that our President ever seems to spend any time mourning them, but then, as we know, he was apparently born without a gene for empathy. Bill Clinton, he ain't. Never mind, that's not what this blog is about.

What I was going to say is that last night I made an exception and watched *The News Hour* on PBS. One of the guests on the program was an infectious disease specialist named Michael Osterholm from the University of Minnesota where, it being neither here nor there, I went to graduate school back in the antediluvian epoch. My memories of Minneapolis in those years were of nine months of brutally cold winters followed by ten minutes of spring, but then this isn't what this blog is about either. To begin with, it's about what I learned from listening to Dr. Osterholm.

This will be one of those good news/bad news tales. Let's start with the bad news. If you're reading this, you have an excellent chance—perhaps as much as a 2/3rd probability—of being infected with the corona virus. The good news, according to Dr. Osterholm, is that you have an 80% chance of winding up only mildly or moderately sick for a few weeks or maybe not even being aware that you've been infected. In that case, you will be laid up for a short time but then you will fully recover and that will be that. Even if you are in the remaining 20%, there's a 50-50 chance that you will not have to be hospitalized and could be successfully treated by your own doctor. And the best news of all—perhaps only .5 to 1 percent of people who come down with the illness will die. All in all, I'd say that is pretty reassuring news, assuming that Dr. Osterholm's predictions are accurate, but then, who knows? Still, I think we should take heart from these projections, don't you?

Of course, as Dr. Osterholm made clear, nobody knows what the hell will happen over the coming months or years. At this point, it's all guesswork, even if it may be educated guesswork. But Dr. Osterholm went on to tell us some things that were fairly sobering, if they prove to be true.

We don't know whether this virus will act the way the influenza virus behaves, but if it does, we can expect that it will recur and probably more than once over the next year or more. In that case, there will be periods of waves and troughs. We may have a few months when it will abate to a significant degree, but then, perhaps in the late summer or early fall, it may strike again and this time, it could be even worse than it's been. Dr. Osterholm, using a baseball analogy, said where we are now just in the second inning. It will be a long game. Get used to it. If he and other experts are right about this, we are going to be plagued with this virus for quite a while. Nobody knows how long.

And even if COVID-19 does not prove to be as lethal a virus as many had feared, it could still end up ending the lives of many thousands of people. Dr. Osterholm estimates that ultimately it could kill as many as 800,000 people in the U.S. As of this writing, about 50,000 Americans have died from it. That's obviously not a small number, but it's only a small fraction of those we can expect to perish, again assuming we can trust this projection. We just don't know, but we have been warned.

Mulling all this over afterward, I naturally thought about all the people who would die. Most of them would be old folks like me. After all, I'm in my mid-eighties now, and though, so far as I know, I don't have any serious illness or "underlying condition" that makes me particularly vulnerable, my odds of surviving aren't good. After all, I am already suffering from an incurable disease— aging. If the virus doesn't get me, my decaying telomeres will. But my own life and death is of no particular consequence in the scheme of things—even if it is to me—especially when viewed against the enormous level of suffering that billions of people now living are experiencing and will have to continue to endure.

But then I had another thought. Not about myself, but about other old farts like me. I know you will think me callous but it was a big "So what?" So what if many old people were to die from this virus? I mean, a lot of these people would die, anyway, wouldn't they, of so called "natural causes." Or if they were living, might well wish they weren't. After all, if you've already lived into your eighties, as I have, you will have learned that the promised "golden years" are a crock of you-know-what.

For years, I have joked about my own version of "a modest proposal." My idea was that people would live under a definite death sentence. If they survived until they had reached their three score and ten, they would be given a pill that would painlessly ease them into death. This, it seems to me, would have many advantages. First of all, it would save billions of dollars since an enormous amount of money has to be spent in the last years of people's lives on providing them health care and hospitalization. Second, it would free up a great deal of money for younger people since no more Social Security payments or pensions would be nec- essary after a person reached seventy. Third, most people's pro- ductive years are over by the time they reach seventy; the rest is mostly just waiting to die and years of illness, decrepitude and senility in store. Is this any way to run a navy? Do you really want to spend your "senior years" shuffling to the shuffleboard area on yet another cruise with elderly folks like yourself or making a sorry spectacle of yourself with your potbelly and ridiculous-looking Bermuda shorts tottering around on some Floridian gulf course? Or worse yet, did you ever dream when young of spending your last years languishing in a nursing home among the demented and utterly forlorn, the truly wretched of the earth? (If you have ever spent time visiting an ancient loved one in one of these places, you will know what I mean.)

Honestly, when you consider all this, wouldn't it really make sense to spare old people this kind of fate? After all, we weren't meant to live to such great ages. Evolutionarily, we were designed to live only so long as to procreate, pass along our genes, and then get off the stage. Dying in one's forties would normally allow us to accomplish all these things. Now more and more of us just hang around, are burdens to our family, and merely take up space while exhausting limited financial resources. What is the point?

Hell, if I had died when I was seventy, both the world and I would have been better off. I wouldn't have had to suffer the deliberating effects of my spinal stenosis. My hearing would still have been good, my vision, good enough; I still would have been able to hike, to travel, make love, and enjoy life to the fullest. I wouldn't have to spend days as I do now when I sometimes walk about the house like a wraith, exhausted and weary beyond belief, trapped in a seemingly interminable *bardo of ennui* hovering between life and death. Instead of often feeling like cashing in my chips, I would have still been in my chips.

Besides, one thing my years of research on near-death experiences has taught me is that death is nothing to be feared, but is to be looked forward to. Dying may be hard, but death is easy.

When I was first researching NDEs forty years ago, I collected testimonies from NDErs about the effects of their experience on their fear of death. Here's a small sampling of what they told me:

"I had been terrified of death before, it [the NDE] left me with a total lack of fear of death."

"Well, I certainly have no fear of death."

"I'm not afraid of death at all."

"I have no fear of death. I don't to this day."

"If this is what death is like, then I'm not afraid to go... I have absolutely no fear at all."

"I have no fear of death."

"I'm not afraid of dying. I'm really not afraid and I used to be scared to death."

I collected many such quotes from this research (but there is no point in endlessly listing them here) and all other NDE researchers have reported the same findings.

All this, to be sure, doesn't fully address all aspects of our fears about death. Quite apart from the fear of death, what about the fear of dying?

Of course, NDEs don't do anything to diminish that. It's understandable to fear dying. If, as Bette Davis famously reminded us years ago, old age isn't for sissies, dying is surely not for the craven. Let's not kid ourselves; no one looks forward to dying (except those in extreme pain or those who are simply weary of life). And who knows what dying will be like for us? Who can say whether when the time comes, we will die "in character?" Elisabeth Kübler-Ross, the great expert on death, apparently had a very difficult time dying and was very angry. Who knows whether Ken Ring, the guy who spent half his life studying NDEs, won't die like Tolstoy's Ivan Illich by screaming for three days before his death? It's a crapshoot and you don't have the chance to load the dice.

And coming back to our current pandemic, the prospect of dying as a result of having extreme difficulty in breathing and effectively suffocating to death is not exactly an enticing prospect, and many of us will, alas, presumably die in this way. But on the other hand, spending one's remaining time on a ventilator is not exactly an alluring future possibility either. And even if ventilators are no longer in short supply, I can't see availing myself of one. Better to stand aside, Ken, and let some younger person take that route. They still have life to live; you've had yours. Make way, old timer.

Anyway, that's how I'm feeling about things after having pondered Dr. Osterholm's commentary. On the whole, I feel encouraged to know that even if the pandemic will be with us for some time, the great majority of people who really need to live will survive and eventually thrive and those who don't would probably have died soon enough anyway. The corona virus, bad as it is now, is not strong enough to bring about even a hint of a Malthusian solution to our over-population problem, so the world will continue on with its usual struggles and problems once this crisis has finally passed its acute phase.

It's still a long game, if not for the likes of me. I'm fine with that. Really. Now you will know why.

The World's Annus Horribilis— and Mine

Not to be born at all
Is best, far best that can befall,
Next best, when born, with least delay
To trace the backward way.
For when youth passes with its giddy train,
Troubles on troubles follow, toils on toils,
Pain, pain forever pain;
And none escapes life's coils.
—Sophocles

It's now been a year that we have all lived under the threatening COVID cloud, fearful that its pestilence would rain down on us— as indeed it has during this time. Just in the United States, half a million people at the time of this writing have died of COVID, and about 28 million Americans have been infected. And the deaths and infections will continue, even if their incidence will diminish during the coming year. This is a dark anniversary that marks a year of national mourning and unbearable heartache and suffering for so many in our country, and indeed, for the world.

And of course it has not only been the pandemic that has brought so much sorrow to us. Just to focus on the U.S., all of us remember the wave of protests that followed the shocking death of George Floyd and other Black persons killed by wanton police cruelty as the Black Lives Matter movement brought home the longstanding stink of racism that has affected and infected our country since before we were a nation. This was followed by a fractious and tumultuous election campaign that went on for months, and once the election was over, it wasn't. It was during this time that then President Trump continued his delusional claim that he had actually won (by "a lot," he said) and went on to stoke the flames of insurrection among his more rabid followers that led to their assault and invasion of our capital on January 6th of this year. And these are just a few of the lowlights that made this past year one of almost ceaseless woe, worry and sporadic mayhem and unchecked violence. An *annus horribilis*, if ever there were one.

Compared to the traumas of this past year, my own sufferings hardly deserve mentioning, though as you can anticipate, that won't stop me from disclosing some of them to you. Like many, I had a tough year, though my difficulties weren't due to COVID as such, but to the terminal disease with which I am afflicted—aging. It will kill me in the end, but in the meantime it is content to inflict Jobbian indignities to a body that has clearly outlined its expiration date. At 85, I have reached the stage of life where my telomeres are breaking off and my body is breaking down. At night, I imagine I can hear it creaking, and in the morning, I could sometimes swear that rigor mortis must have already begun. In any case, I am in a daily battle with my enemy, decrepitude.

I realize that an old man's complaints about his bodily infirmities are as trite as they are tedious. After all, everything that lives will suffer eventually; it's just my turn now. So what? Big deal....

Still, if you'll indulge me for a paragraph or two, you should know that I've had a severe case of spinal stenosis for several years now, so that I can barely walk down my block and back, and live like a virtual shut-in, shuffling around my house like a zombie at times. I have a torn right rotator cuff, too, that makes it difficult to lift my right arm. Dressing myself in the morning can sometimes take twenty minutes or more. In August, after I had done a lot of typing, I developed a cervical problem on my right shoulder that became progressively worse and before long resulted in severe pain. That went on for four months during which I could no longer write or even read books, either by hand or on my computer. All my professional work and almost all of my e-mail contact had to be shut down.

During those months, I felt I had come to the end of the line as I was no longer able to work and write. At night, the pain was often so intense, I wished I could die. I knew I would not take my own life; I just wish it would be taken from me. Decrepitude I could handle; despair was harder.

I have no talent as a poet; I am not even a lowly poetaster. All I can do is write doggerel, and since my life in those dark days was going to the dogs, anyway, I banged out the following one morning:

On Growing Old

It is a misfortune to grow old
You will learn that soon enough
Eventually if not soon
Unless you are one of the lucky ones
And get to leave before your time

It is a myth that with age comes wisdom
Quite the contrary, my friend
With age, as you will see, comes decay
The body and its parts begin to falter
And then, one by one, begin to fail

And the mind, too, will start to shred
Its rich storehouse of memories
What gives you a sense of your identity
Begins to unravel and fall apart
Forgetfulness instead will be your lot

But you remember the days when you
Could run and hike with lively tread

Those days, too, are gone. Instead
You go from striding to walking, and then
To sauntering, shuffling until you can only just sit

You recall the days, or, rather, the nights
When you could sleep straight through
And dream of siren women and foolish things
But now you piss the nights away, spending
More time in the bathroom than in bed

And what of all those romances past that
Kept your loins aflame with desire
They, too, have begun to fade from view
And the faces of your lovers likewise dim
Even their names you can't quite recall

You have lived beyond your expiration date
But your body has failed to expire
So you remain immured inside your
Body's fortress, a prisoner of its
Capricious will, waiting for release

Yet each day brings you closer to death
Which means a time without a future
But each day you must live lashes you
To that unwanted future—when will it end?
Like the Sphinx, it remains stonily silent

So you wait, powerless to control your fate
Though that doesn't mean that
You don't think about how to end it
The nights are long, but the stars still shine
And people love you—you live for them

Eventually, I found some relief from an epidural injection, but it wasn't until I had a second one in January that was a special targeted epidural that I was finally free of shoulder pain and could write again. I'm "in remission" now since I was told that, with luck, I could expect it to last about three months. I could then have another injection, but because of having to get vaccinated, that will have to be postponed. So I can write without (much) pain now, but who knows for how long? And even tonight, I can feel some discomfort. Nevertheless, I'm grateful beyond words to have my life, such as it is, back now.

However—and this is the last thing in my litany of woes—two days after my second epidural, I had a sudden series of diarrhea episodes, followed by constipation, and back and forth it has gone, with stomach distention and lots of crap (literally) you don't want to know about. During this time, I have lost seven pounds and have tried everything to get it under control. It's been six weeks now, and the end is not in sight. Oh well, what the effing hell—it's always something! You have to laugh.

I guess I could say that I've lost everything but my hair and my sense of humor, and I hope to hold onto both until the end. And these days, I am actually feeling more cheerful than I have in a long time. This may have been a grim, and indeed, a ghastly year, but we must all find ways not to succumb to the gnawing fear that the COVID cloud will never lift. It will, and most of us to live to see that day. Meanwhile, I recommend that we pursue the kind of distractions that give us pleasure.

For example, some of you may remember that I am an ardent tennis fan, and particularly a proud Fedhead—a follower of the great Roger Federer. But you may know that not only has this year been a dismal one for us sports fans, especially for those of us for whom life has become a spectator sport, yet it has been worse for Federer himself. He has not played in a year owing to two knee surgeries, and at 39 his career is pretty much history. Hard as this year has been for me personally, to live without being able to watch Federer play was a thought that I could hardly bear to contemplate.

Still, I have found that there is still pleasure to be had by watching the Australian Open this month, even without Federer. Maybe Naomi Osaka, who just won her fourth grand slam title, will be become my new tennis raison d'etre. Maybe there's tennis life post-Federer after all.

I'm still writing doggerel about the trials of aging, but now with a lighter touch. I try not to take myself too seriously. I enjoy what I can, and the hell with the rest. I'm lucky to be here, and my body ain't me, is it?

When You're Old

Everything hurts
And nothing works
When you wake
You only ache
As for sleep
There's nothing deep
Too many bathroom trips
Just to see how your penis drips
And when you dream
You hear Munch's scream
At night, you feel the chills
By day, you try to avoid more spills
Even when you go to talk
What comes out is just a squawk
Your hearing is going, too
Your vision? Think Mr. Magoo
You are no longer bold
Just do as you're told
And that, my friends,
Is what it's like
When you grow old!

Finally, harking back to Sophocles' lament about the sorrows of aging, the late George Carlin had a brilliant solution, which I think someone should bring to the attention of our Creator. Let George have the last word:

I want to live life backward
You start out dead and get that out of the way
Then you wake up in a nursing home feeling better every day
Then you get kicked out for being too healthy
Enjoy your retirement and collect your pension
Then when you start your work, you get a gold watch on the first day
You work for 40 years until you are too young to work
You get ready for high school: drink alcohol, party, and you are generally promiscuous
Then you go to primary school, you become a kid, you play, and you have no responsibilities
Then you become a baby, and then...
You finish off as an orgasm.
I rest my case.

Troubles

Introduction

In the aftermath of COVID, although at this writing we are still in what seems to be an interminable and ever-changing aftermath, I wrote some blogs on some of the more troubling developments in American culture, particularly about the silent epidemic of loneliness and the longing that some people have to quit this world prematurely in hopes of a better one. Here are three of those essays.

The Last Dance

Half a lifetime ago—I was in the summer of my life then—I was running the newly formed International Association for Near-Death Studies (IANDS) at the University of Connecticut. It was at that time that I became acquainted with a then noted anthropologist named Virginia Hine who was one of the first persons to become a member of this organization. We hit it off immediately and soon became good, even loving, friends.

I had actually heard of Ginny before she joined IANDS. I had read one of her articles on altered states of consciousness, which had impressed me, and a bit later, her book, *Last Letter to the Pebble People*, which dealt with the death of her beloved husband, Aldie, of cancer a few years earlier.

Over the years, our letters grew warm and loving despite the fact that we were never able to meet. She mostly divided her time between her home in Florida and her organization, Rites of Passage, in California. Whenever I traveled to Florida, she seemed to be in California, and vice versa. Once, when she came to Connecticut, I was away myself. We came to joke about our mismatched schedules. The closest we ever came to meeting face to face was a single telephone call. I remember that she had a beautiful voice.

When one day I received a letter from Ginny informing me that she had decided to choose the manner and time of her death, and that the time was coming quite soon, I was stunned. I had not known or suspected her plans. I remember thinking, "Now we will never meet!"

I thought a good deal about that letter of hers before replying to it. I could see that she had considered the matter extremely carefully and that she had discussed her plans thoroughly with her friends and family. She had secured some Seconal, which she knew would allow her to die peacefully, which according to her family, as I was to learn later, had indeed proved to be the case.

She did not need nor did she ask for any advice from me. I certainly did not attempt to dissuade her—it was her choice, and I respected that. I knew she had been ill with cancer and in pain. In the end, I could only send her my love and prayers for a gentle passage into death. I also didn't think that it made sense to regard Ginny's death as a suicide. Instead, I viewed it as an example of a well planned and rational chosen death.

I had occasion to think of Ginny recently as a result of reading a new book by a journalist named Katie Englehart entitled *The Inevitable: Dispatches on the Right to Die*. It is full of cases like that of Ginny's. These days, many people are choosing to die the way Ginny did, and an increasing number of them are doing so by finding ways to circumvent the law.

Frankly, if you will indulge a brief confessional aside, now that I'm in the deep winter of my life, I have to admit that in recent years, I've thought quite a bit about the fact that I definitely do not want to wind up, decrepit and demented, in one of those warehouses for the those slated for death that we euphemistically call "nursing homes." No sirree, that's not for me! After all, would anyone, given the choice, opt to spend their last years in such a depressing environment surrounded by scores of wheelchair-bound human wrecks just "waiting to die," to use the title of one of my recent immortal books?

I have a couple of friends who share my concern about these end of life matters, and we have had a number of conversations over the years about how best to dispatch ourselves. A few years ago, for example, we all read and discussed Derek Humphry's 1991 best seller, *Final Exit*, which describes various ways to kill yourself (the book has sold over two million copies in twelve languages). I did not find any of the methods Humphry offers particularly appealing nor did my friends, but one of them has since made plans to lay in a supply of drugs that she feels would do the job for her. The three of us don't exactly have a "pact" with each other about how to prepare for a self-administered exit, should one become necessary, but we have certainly explored a number of options.

Englehart, however, has encountered people who have made such a pact. In fact her book begins with such an example. She had interviewed a New Yorker whom she calls Betty who had made such a pact with her two best friends. "We have a pact," Betty told Englehart. "The first one who gets Alzheimer's gets the Nembutal."

Although Betty herself was in good health in her seventies, she had been around a number of even older people, including one man in his nineties, and was distressed to see them in deep pain and just "hanging around," to use her phrase. But worst was having to witness her husband die.

> Her own husband had died quickly enough. Seventy-five years old. Cancer. Still, he suffered. Sometimes he cried. In his final days, Betty imagined taking firm hold of a pillow and smothering him, partly because she thought that's what he would have wanted, but also because she couldn't bear to see him that way. In the end, he grew so agitated that the doctors gave him enough painkillers to knock him out. He spent three days in a morphine-induced languor and then died. Betty and her friends agreed that they would never let themselves get to that place and also they would never rely on a physician to help them, because who knew where the bounds of a doctor's mercy lay?

(Incidentally, Betty's account here reminded me of Michael Haneke's marvelous and moving 2012 film, "Amour," in which an elderly husband eventually has to suffocate his demented wife with a pillow because he was unable to bear her suffering any longer.)

Betty wound up going to Mexico where she had learned she could buy in pet stores a lethal poison that is used to euthanize dogs. She was able to score enough for her and her friends. The story of her escapade is actually quite amusing and was not without risk, but you'll have to read the book for that. However, the point is that in New York, physician-assisted death is still illegal. If you wanted to orchestrate your own death, it had to be a DIY endeavor.

Actually, in the book, Englehart doesn't spend much time talking about people like Betty. Instead, she focuses on those who have serious, debilitating and often very painful illnesses, and who are often desperate to die, but who do not qualify for physician-assisted death even in the states where it is legal. She also spends a great deal of time interviewing doctors, nurses, researchers, authors, advocates for and opponents of the right-to-die movement. In each of her six chapters, she focuses on one personal story: two about doctors who specialize in helping people to die and four case studies of people who wanted to die because of unbearable suffering they were forced to endure. One because she had lived too long and nothing worked anymore; one who was suffering from multiple sclerosis; another who had progressive dementia; and a fourth who was mad.

Engelhart is herself not an advocate for the rights of the dying; she is a reporter who simply narrates these stories and who tries to listen to them without judgment but with compassion. She is open to a variety of perspectives. Self-administered death, like abortion, is a controversial subject. But when you read the heartbreaking stories of those who do not "qualify" to die because they do not satisfy the eligibility requirements, such as having been certified as being "within six weeks of dying" or for other reasons, it's impossible not to feel sympathy for those who find themselves having to operate outside the law in order to effectuate their own deaths. It's like reading what pregnant women had to go through or still do where abortion is illegal. *The Inevitable* is one long horror story. But it is also the story of some very courageous physicians who have risked everything in order to help such people.

One of themes that runs through Englehart's book—it almost becomes a cliché or a tired trope—is how many people yearning to die because of their needless suffering often mention that we euthanize our dogs and cats in a loving way. One man, at a conference on death with dignity, sported a t-shirt saying, "I want to die like a dog." Does it make sense that we can compassionately end the suffering of our beloved pets but can't extend the same mercy to ourselves? After all, we didn't really need Darwin to tell us that we are animals, too.

Recently I was reading an article about all the horses who died a couple of years ago at the track at Santa Anita—37 of them in 2019, causing a scandal. It made me remember the old film, "They Shoot Horses, Don't They?" (although that film wasn't about horses). But we don't permit horses who have no hope of recovering from a painful injury to survive. We act to end their suffering as soon as possible. What sense does it make not to grant the same privilege to people who are suffering from incurable conditions or simply from enduring, intractable pain?

I mean, why should such people suffer needlessly? If those of us who believe in abortion rights hold that women, not doctors and certainly not politicians, should have dominion over their own bodies, why shouldn't we have dominion over our own lives? Don't our bodies belong to us?

This same question was raised in another old film I saw some years ago, which was entitled, "Whose Life Is it, Anyway?" In the film, the main character, played by Richard Dreyfuss, is a sculptor who becomes paralyzed from the neck down as a result of an automobile accident. Since his life depends on the use of his hands (his whole life is sculpting, he avers), he finds there is no point in living, and he chooses to refuse treatment in order to die. The drama of the film centers on the reactions to his choice on the part of his friends and the medical staff and hinges on the question whether the medical and legal institutions in which he was enmeshed will respect or prevent his choice to die.

This film also brings to the fore a central thorny issue of

Englehart's book—whether dying is a matter for medicine to decide or whether it should be regarded as human right. One of the doctors who has been active for a long time in the right-to-die movement, a man named Philip Nitschke, the author of the book, *The Peaceful Pill Handbook*, is a staunch defender of the latter position. This is how he frames the issue:

> The medical model is where we see this as a service that you provide to the sick. If a person gets sick enough, and all the doctors agree, the person who is very sick and keen to die gets lawful help to die. The rights model, which I'm strongly in favor of, says this has got nothing to do with sickness. The idea is: having a peaceful death is a human right. And as a right it's not something you have to ask permission for. In other words, it's something you have simply because you're a person of this planet. The rights model, of course, means that doctors don't necessarily have to be involved ... The right of a rational adult to a peaceful death, at the time of one's own choosing, is fundamental.

This perspective, still very controversial and the subject of heated, often rancorous, debate, is nevertheless seemingly gaining strength and more adherents in America. After all, it's well known that the right to die movement is already strong in such countries as the Netherlands, Belgium and Switzerland, and even physician-assisted death, as limited and hedged in by complex legal and medical regulations as it is, is now permitted in a number of states. If you were to read Englehart's book—and I strongly recommend it to anyone with an interest in these matters—you would quickly learn about all the latest techniques doctors and engineers have devised to ease people into death, the books available on the subject, the organizations devoted to the right-to-die movement, and so forth.

But there is still another reason to think that in the coming years this movement will continue to grow stronger, and that has to do with demographics. The elderly are now the fastest growing segment in America. In 2010, there were about 40 million Americans 65 or older. By 2030, it is projected that one in five Americans will have reached that age. If so, that means we will soon be saddled with a population that is increasingly afflicted with dementia or otherwise seriously physically compromised. And since a quarter of all Medicare spending goes to people in the last year of their lives, there will be an even greater financial strain on our social networks, such as Medicare, Medicaid and Social Security.

What this portends, to put it crudely, is that in the future, many old and infirm people will be virtually begging to die, their younger relatives will be motivated to help them to do so (since their economic well being is threatened by having so much of our national wealth having to be diverted to care for the elderly) and organizations like the AARP and other organizations that lobby for the old will have to become advocates for the right-to-die movement. You can see the writing on the wall. The demographics make it plain. We can no longer afford (literally) to let death take its course. We must find ways to ease the burdens of life on the old by helping them to die with dignity and lessen the financial burdens on the young so that they can live without themselves suffering unduly. Medical technology has indeed enabled people to live longer than ever, but it has also served to prolong their years of pain and debility, ending with their complete dependence on others. Does this make sense? Is it humane?

Before concluding this blog, there is one more issue I need to deal with that has been with us from the very beginning. It was implicit in the story I told at the outset about Virginia Hine's death and was explicitly brought out in the film I mentioned, "Whose Life Is It, Anyway?" And that is the question having to do with the S-word. Should such deaths be regarded as suicides? And if so, what can people expect to experience when they die in this way? This is a question that can be addressed, even if not definitively answered, by the research on near-death experiences for people who nearly die, but don't, as a result of a suicide attempt. In fact, whether one prefers to call deaths like Ginny's "chosen deaths," or regards them as a form of rational suicide, we still want to know what will such people experience when they cross the threshold into the house of death.

But first, let's look at some statistics concerning suicide in America, especially for the elderly. Older adults make up 12% of the US population, but account for 18% of all suicide deaths. This is an alarming statistic, as the elderly are the fastest growing segment of the population, making the issue of later-life suicide a major public health priority. Moreover, in 2018, seniors ages 85 and older had the second-highest suicide rate in the nation. From what I have already written, I think you will understand why. Finally, estimates suggest that for every reported death by suicide, an additional 29 attempts are made.

Now turning to what we know about what people experience when they make an unsuccessful suicide attempt, the data both from my research and that of my longtime friend and colleague, the psychiatrist Bruce Greyson, are in agreement. Although many people who come close to death in this way remember nothing (that is true as well for other modes of near-death onset, such as a cardiac arrest), those who do tend to report the same kind of classic, radiant NDE as do people who nearly die from injuries or cardiac conditions. Greyson has found that about 25% of his suicide cases report such NDEs. My findings were similar. I concluded therefore that there is nothing unique about NDEs triggered by a failed suicide attempt.

Furthermore, most of those who do experience an NDE are not tempted to try suicide again, and, indeed, often conclude that suicide would solve nothing—even if they had succeeded, they seem to feel that they would have to deal with the same issues that prompted their attempt in the first place. But most importantly, they typically don't feel that they would be punished, much less "sent to hell," because of trying to kill themselves. As with NDEs that occur in other ways, they are not judged, but usually experience compassionate understanding and unconditional love during the time they hover between life and death.

However, most of my cases, and I suspect this is also true for Greyson's, involve people who are relatively young and who normally have attempted suicide because of personal problems, such as alcoholism, drug addiction, financial troubles or a failed love affair. These we may call collectively "despair-based" suicide attempts. But for the elderly, the motivations tend to be different in many cases. For them, there is often a feeling that their lives are complete, that they are suffering needlessly for no good reason, and that they simply "want to go home." For such people, suicide is more of a considered rational decision, not one governed by an impulsive act stemming from an acute condition of despair and despondency. At least, this is the sense one gets from reading the many cases to be found in Englehart's book.

The trouble is, so far as I know, we don't have much if any data on what is experienced by elderly people who take this route toward death, in large part, of course, because they succeed in taking their lives. So here I can only speculate.

First, from all the research I've done on NDEs, I know that someone who nearly dies in whatever way is not judged. Instead, they tend to be greeted by a warm loving light. They feel that they are home, where they belong and where, in some eternal sense, they have always been. As one man I know well put it, "It was eternity. It's like I was always there and would always be there, and that my existence on earth was just a brief instant."

Since I've mentioned several films in this blog, I can't help thinking of a famous film actor from another era, Charles Boyer. He often played the part of a sophisticated lover. These days, he is probably best remembered for his role in "Gaslight" in which he starred with Ingrid Bergman.

I mention him here because I remember reading some years ago that he so loved his wife that when she died, he was so distraught that could not bear to live without her. Two days after her death, he committed suicide by taking Seconal.

I was very touched when I learned that. Personally, I just cannot persuade myself that Charles Boyer, when he took that last dance into the Light, would have been made to suffer for his actions. No, that's just inconceivable to me.

Likewise for my friend, Ginny, who also chose to die so that she could again be with her beloved husband, Aldie.

It is my profound hope and prayer for all those who, having lived a full life and who no longer choose to live in pain, that they, too, will find surcease in the Light. That would only be just, don't you think?

The Silent Epidemic of Our Times

I recently read a very touching story about a woman named Virginia, who is 92 years old, and her cat, Jennie. She adores her cat who is almost always nearby. She likes to look at Jennie's green eyes. She likes that Jennie is with her in the morning when Virginia wakes up. And sometimes when Virginia feels sad, she just sits in her soft armchair while Jennie rests on Virginia's stomach. She nuzzles, purrs, stretches and just does her cat-like things.

Talking to an interviewer, Virginia said, "I can't believe that this has meant as much as it has to me." When she dies, she thought she might bring Jennie with her.

Jennie is a robot.

I came across this vignette in a recent article in *The New Yorker* that was written by Katie Englehart, the author of the book, *The Inevitable*, which I featured in my previous blog. In the article, she was addressing a problem that two English researchers, writing in *The Lancet*, had characterized in the following way:

> Imagine a condition that makes a person irritable, depressed, and self-centered, and is associated with a 26% increase in the risk of premature mortality. Imagine too that in industrialised countries around a third of people are affected by this condition, with one person in 12 affected severely, and that these proportions are increasing. Income, education, sex, and ethnicity are not protective, and the condition is

contagious. The effects of the condition are not attributable to some peculiarity of the character of a subset of individuals, they are a result of the condition affecting ordinary people.

The condition to which these authors are referring, as you might have guessed, is loneliness. And, as we also now know, this condition is particularly acute among the elderly, which is why caregivers have been interested to see whether providing them with robot pets will help to alleviate their loneliness. In fact, as a number of researchers and scholars have recently pointed out, the pervasiveness of loneliness among the old in America has now reached what the Surgeon General, Vivek Murthy, was frank to call an "epidemic." But in contrast to the pandemic we have all been through for the last year and half, this has mostly been a silent epidemic. The plight of the elderly, despite suffering unduly from the pandemic and dying in much greater numbers than younger people, did not receive the kind of sustained attention that we gave to families having to cope with children underfoot or workers who had lost their jobs.

This is understandable, of course. As a society, we no longer venerate the old, assuming we once did; all too often, we simply abandon, forget or ignore them. To be sure, individual family members usually continue to care for their elderly loved ones when they can. And we have all heard horrific stories of the contagion of COVID and resultant deaths that plagued our nursing and other old age homes during the first year of the pandemic. But as a society, we no longer provide the kind of social welfare net that permits most older people to continue to live out their lives in relative comfort in the company of other family members.

There was a time, of course, when, even in America, many people lived in extended families, either in the same house or nearby in the same neighborhood. In those days, when grandma became old and frail and could no longer hear well, she would still be cared for, and could still enjoy the loving company of her family. These days, however, grandma is usually shipped off to a nursing home to live among decrepit and often demented strangers, who cry out piteously during the night and during the day often sit, vacantly, strapped into their wheelchairs. This happened to my mother, too, when she had become old (I was living in Connecticut then while she, who had never flown, had to remain in California). During those years, I would continue to visit her as often as I could arrange to come out to California, but every time I had to leave her in her bed alone and without friends or other family, I felt a wracking guilt.

But even when older people can continue to live in their own homes, they are often left alone, and when that happens, they can suffer from acute loneliness and feelings of abandonment. And more and more of our elderly do live alone now—more than ever—as a result of the modern way of family life which has seen the rise of isolated nuclear family settings at the expense of extended family networks. Statistics show that nowadays almost 30% of Americans over the age of 65 live by themselves, most of them women. And during the period when COVID raged, this isolation, as we all know, was even more of a torment to the old and to their families who could no longer see and comfort them. How many of these elderly died, alone and afraid, without a hand to hold? One can only shudder when one imagines people dying in this way. How many tears have been shed by their helpless family members? Perhaps you were such a person or knew others who had to endure such emotional and traumatic distress.

Even before COVID struck, however, the deleterious effects of isolation among the old were evident to researchers. Let me take just a moment to acquaint you with the range and severity of some of these effects.

To begin with, 43% of the elderly in America complain about being lonely. According to Englehart, loneliness can "prompt a heightened inflammatory response, which can increase a person's risk for a vast range of pathologies, including dementia, depression, high blood pressure, and stroke." To amplify this point, consider the following statistics that come from a book dealing with the effects of social isolation in older adults:

- Social isolation has been associated with a significantly increased risk of premature mortality from all causes.
- Social isolation has been associated with an approximately 50 percent increased risk of developing dementia.
- Loneliness among heart failure patients has been associated with a nearly four times increased risk of death, 68 percent increased risk of hospitalization, and 57 percent increased risk of emergency department visits.
- Poor social relationships (characterized by social isolation or loneliness) have been associated with a 29 percent increased risk of incident coronary heart disease and a 32 percent increased risk of stroke.

Of course, old age in itself is hard enough to endure for most of us oldsters, quite apart from the dangers, physical and emotional, of isolation, which I have just briefly adumbrated. The so-called "golden years" are really just the olden years when sentiment is absent and the reality of life as one ages is bereft of any illusory euphemism. Growing old is scary enough when one contemplates the prospect and then the reality of increasing decrepitude, loneliness, illness and then, finally, dying and death. If you have the misfortune of living long enough, you may even find yourself not only alone but without anyone any longer knowing who you are and what you have been in your life. This is probably the most terrifying kind of existential isolation.

I remember when I was in my early eighties and was writing some (mostly) humorous essays about my own vicissitudes of aging that I eventually collected into a little book I puckishly called *Waiting to Die*, I had one of those moments of anticipatory existential fright. This is what I wrote at the time:

One day long ago I had a shocking realization. I received

a new credit card whose expiration date was November, 2023, when I would be almost 87 years old. Surely, I thought, I would expire long before that. But, then, a horrible thought occurred to me: What if I don't?! What if I live to 86? Honestly, before seeing that card, I had never imagined such a thing. No, no! Will I still be walking on this road toward death, still waiting to die, for years to come? What a ghastly thought.

I realized I'm not afraid to die; I'm now afraid of living too long!

A few years ago, the well-known physician, Ezekiel Emmanuel (you have probably seen him often interviewed on television where he became a frequent commentator on the pandemic), wrote a now famous piece in *The Atlantic*, which he provocatively entitled, "Why I Hope to Die at 75." In it, he reflected my own thinking, but took the time to lay out his reasons. This is how his article began:

That's how long I want to live: 75 years.

This preference drives my daughters crazy. It drives my brothers crazy. My loving friends think I am crazy. They think that I can't mean what I say; that I haven't thought clearly about this, because there is so much in the world to see and do. To convince me of my errors, they enumerate the myriad people I know who are over 75 and doing quite well. They are certain that as I get closer to 75, I will push the desired age back to 80, then 85, maybe even 90. I am sure of my position. Doubtless, death is a loss. It deprives us of experiences and milestones, of time spent with our spouse and children. In short, it deprives us of all the things we value.

But here is a simple truth that many of us seem to resist: living too long is also a loss. It renders many of us, if not disabled, then faltering and declining, a state that may not be worse than death but is nonetheless deprived. It robs us of our creativity and ability to contribute to work, society, the world. It transforms how people experience us, relate to us, and, most important, remember us. We are no longer remembered as vibrant and engaged but as feeble, ineffectual, even pathetic.

Exactly. Which is why I argued in my previous blog that people should have the right to terminate their own lives. Emmanuel would not choose to do that, but many people who no longer wish to live doubtless would if they could do so peacefully. Who, when young, dreams of getting old? Instead, we pretend it won't happen to us. I never really thought it would happen to me either. But one day, after I had turned 81, I realized that my time had come.

Right now, even though I live alone (and have for many years—it's easier for us introverts), I am lucky to have a loving girlfriend, now nearly 80 herself, who is able to spend some time with me as well as a caretaker who can assist me when I need someone to go grocery shopping or do errands for me. But my three children all live far from me, and I would never want to burden them with my care if one day I should find myself alone in this world. But who knows—it may be that I will eventually be one of those people I have been writing about—on my own, sick and feeling forlorn, lost in my dotage, just waiting to die. Knowing what I have learned about the effects of isolation, I am not keen on spending my last days like this, even if I should have a robot cat to keep me company.

Of course, old age needn't be a drag or a seemingly unending series of tribulations and sorrows. It's important to keep things in balance after all. As Emmanuel implies, old age can also be rewarding and full of pleasures, including sex. I have an old girlfriend, now well into her 80s, who frequently writes me about her deeply satisfying sex life with her husband. And there are certainly people in their nineties who are happy still to be alive and able to enjoy life.

Since this blog has been grim and uncharacteristically sober (at least for me), suppose we take a moment for a little levity to lighten the mood. One thing that I've been struck by is how many comics live to a great age and seem to leave this world laughing, at least figuratively speaking. To take one example, I can choose one of my favorite comics from an earlier era, George Burns, whom you may remember as God since late in life he became famous (again) for playing God in a film with John Denver. I mention him and comics generally because, as I have previously argued in some of my blogs, humor is often the best defense against the trials of aging and the prospect of death.

George Burns died at 100, and like other centenarians, he was asked to explain the secret of his longevity. He was inclined to attribute his success to smoking cigars daily. But there were other factors as well that contributed to his aging well until the end, as witness this obituary:

George Burns died at age 100 on March 9, 1996. Mr. Burns spent his lifetime in show business and created millions of laughs. It is reported that Mr. Burns was buried with three cigars in his pocket, had on his toupee, his ring and watch, which was a gift from his wife, and in the pocket of his suit were "his keys and his wallet with ten 100-dollar bills, a five, and three ones, so wherever he went to play bridge he'd have enough money."

Several years ago, he was asked by an interviewer if he ever considered retiring. "Retire to what?" an amused Mr. Burns asked. "I play bridge for two hours a day to get away from work. Why the hell would I want to retire to play bridge 24 hours a day?" George Burns played bridge every day of his life. He loved bridge. But at 3 o'clock, he could be in the middle of a hand, he'd stand up (and say) "Thank you gentlemen," and go home to take a nap. He used to say: "Bridge is a game that separates the men from the boys. It also separates husbands and wives."

Burns was perhaps one of the best bridge players in Hollywood. Well, if not the best, the funniest.

I loved George Burns, and his raspy voice—from all those cigars, no doubt. He knew how to enjoy himself and when to rest. He also did yoga. We oldsters can all take a lesson from George Burns. Keep laughing and don't allow yourself to languish—that's the ticket.

Still, George was the rare exception. Most people suffer when they get very old and often yearn to be free of the burden of living. Nevertheless, even though life is hard for the old and is in end universally fatal, as long as we are still here, we old-timers have to make the best of it. What will help us get through our battles with loneliness if robotic animals aren't enough?

We are social creatures, and older people, who were so cruelly deprived of that kind of vital contact during the pandemic, are particularly vulnerable to the lack of face-to-face interaction. They can starve psychologically without it, but they can rebound and even thrive again with it. We must find ways to address the social deficit of the aged in order to forestall, if not completely defeat, the insidious dangers of loneliness.

And social workers and other caregivers have not been slow to realize this. Here's just one example of this kind of intervention:

> The good news is that friendships reduce the risk of mortality or developing certain diseases and can speed recovery in those who fall ill. Moreover, simply reaching out to lonely people can jump-start the process of getting them to engage with neighbors and peers, according to Robin Caruso of CareMore Health, which operates in 8 states and the District of Columbia with a focus on Medicare patients. Her "Togetherness" initiative aims to combat "an epidemic of loneliness" among seniors through weekly phone calls, home visits and community programs.

What can you do? It's obvious: Visit the old. So what if they just natter and chatter—they matter! Now that the COVID cloud is finally beginning to lift, don't go out solely for your own pleasure. Do you have a loved one or someone you know who is living alone or in a nursing home? If so, visit them. Even better, bring them a pet, a real pet, not a robot, if they don't have one. And don't just visit once. Come back. Help to assuage their loneliness. You'll be doing a mitzvah. You will be old one day yourself. Sew some good karma while you can. It will come back to you.

Englehart found that many older people whom she visited were reluctant to see her leave. They relished the time with her; they wanted her to come back. As she writes about Virginia:

> It was the same with almost every robot owner I met. "I haven't had anybody to talk to for a while, so chatter, chatter, chatter," Virginia said, when I first called. Near the end of my visit to her home, she insisted that I take a doughnut for the road and told me to come back sometime. She thought she would probably be around, though she also wondered if she would die in the big empty house: "Maybe this is the year."

> "Your bags are packed, right?" her daughter-in-law said, laughing.

> "Gotta go sometime," Virginia said. When she died, she thought she might bring Jennie with her. She liked the idea of being buried with the cat in her arms.

All the Lonely People

All the lonely people
Where do they all come from?
All the lonely people
Where do they all belong?
—The Beatles

The whole conviction of my life
Now rests upon the belief that
Loneliness,
Far from being a rare and
Curious phenomenon,
Peculiar to myself and to a few other
Solitary men,
Is the central and inevitable fact
Of human existence.
—Thomas Wolfe

I have to begin with a confession: I am a literary thief. That epigraph from Thomas Wolfe doesn't come from my reading the books of this short-lived author (actually, does anyone still read Wolfe's once famous novels?—never mind). No, I stole it from another author and then had the effrontery to compound my sins by re-arranging it as a poem. And whom did I filch this quote from? No less than the current Surgeon General of the United States, Vivek H. Murthy.

You've probably seen him on television. Although he is not as familiar a presence on your screens as Tony Fauci or Rochelle Walensky, the current head of the CDC, lately I have seen him any number of times and also just heard him interviewed on NPR's *Science Friday* program. Every time I watch him, I have been struck, not just by his uncommon articulateness, but by a certain sweetness in his character. He radiates a calm imperturbability and kindliness, even a sort of gentleness. He doesn't bloviate like some politicians do; he doesn't talk like a politician at all. He seems to speak to his interviewer in a sincere, authentic manner. You feel as if you can trust this man to tell the unvarnished truth.

So when I heard that he had written a book on loneliness, a topic that I had addressed in my previous blog, I decided to purchase it. Both because I was still interested in that topic, but also because I had become interested in Murthy himself. I wanted to learn more about the man. Among other things I had heard him say, almost as an aside, in one of his recent interviews that he had already lost ten of his family members to COVID! My heart really went out to him when I heard him say that in his matter-of-fact way.

When I started to read his book, which is called *Together*, I discovered something terrible. It couldn't have been published at a worse time; it was already out of date. Vivek (as I prefer to call him) had actually finished writing the text of his book just as COVID hit. All he could do was to allude to the onset of COVID in his preface (which although it comes first is normally the last thing an author writes). But COVID changes everything and both qualifies and, to some extent, vitiates, some of Murthy's principal findings and conclusions. Just to take one example, as you can already tell from his title, Vivek is big on togetherness, which is the social glue that binds to good health and mitigates loneliness. But as we have learned over the last eighteen months, enforced and involuntary "togetherness" can easily strain relationships in a family and seems to be implicated as the chief cause in the rise of domestic violence during the pandemic. In short, "togetherness" in itself is no panacea for what ails us during this time when we are already suffering acutely from the pangs of loneliness.

I learned something else about Vivek from reading his book. *Surgeons General* — and this is Vivek's second tour of duty in this role (he also served as Obama's Surgeon General from 2014 to 2017)—are normally referred to as "the nation's doctor." This appellation doesn't quite capture Vivek's view of his mission. If you were to read his book, you would quickly see that he is more like the nation's psychotherapist. He is very psychologically-minded and sensitive to our human dramas to preserve our mental health, not just to avoid disease. In fact, the "disease" he is most concerned with in his book is the plague of loneliness, which also makes us sick in any number of ways.

And one last thing about Vivek before we take up what he has to say about loneliness and how to assuage it: He himself has had to deal with many bouts of loneliness in his own personal and professional life. He writes as someone who is upfront about his emotional vulnerabilities and insecurities. This is not your usual Surgeon General. He is someone who truly cares about human suffering and has a well of deep compassion for the struggles we all face in coping with life's challenges.

In my previous blog, I was mainly concerned with the problem of loneliness in the elderly, but one of the things I first learned from Vivek's book is how pervasive it is in our society as a whole, and how pernicious its effects can be.

Various surveys show that about one-quarter to one-third of Americans feel lonely. For example, a study carried out by AARP and validated by UCLA found that one-third people over the age of 45 are lonely.

And what do people do when confronted with loneliness, which has only been accentuated by the pandemic? Vivek: "Many people use drugs, alcohol, food and sex to numb the emotional pain of loneliness."

And there are many other deleterious effects of loneliness as well. Several studies have shown that loneliness is associated with a greater risk of heart disease and strokes, high blood pressure, depression, anxiety and dementia. Self-described lonely people also sleep more poorly, have more immune weakness (which makes them particularly vulnerable to COVID) and are more likely to suffer from impaired judgment and impulsivity. Finally, not surprisingly, they die at younger ages than people who are not lonely. In sum, loneliness makes us sick and kills us prematurely.

And loneliness does not only result in earlier "natural" deaths, but also leads to a higher risk of suicide. Moreover, we know that COVID has led to a spike in suicides. And that in general suicides have increased by one-third in the U.S. over the last twenty years or so. Loneliness, then, especially during COVID, makes suicide more of a danger.

Vivek doesn't stray too often into the fraught and bitterly divided world of contemporary American political life, but it's clear that in recent years the degree of polarization, vituperation and outright violence has reached alarming levels. And one casualty of these trends, which has not been emphasized as much as it should be, is the corresponding decrease in empathy.

According to the research of Robert Putnam, the author of the book, *Bowling Alone*, this reflects the decline of various social networks that began in the latter third of the 20th century. During this period, religious attendance declined as did membership in community organizations—even the frequency with which people invite others to visit in one's homes has decreased. And all this seems again to point to an erosion of empathy in the United States. Just to take one example, one study revealed that empathy scores among college students had dropped a whopping 40% between 1979 and 2009, with most of that decrease occurring in the 21st century. We just don't seem to care as much about other people these days, and the rise of loneliness and people living on their own certainly are contributing factors to this fraying of the bonds of social connections in our time.

Well, you get the picture—loneliness is an insidious and

worrisome factor and trend in American life. According to Vivek, it also underlies various common forms of personal and social pathologies such as drug and alcohol addiction, crime, and violence, both domestic and outside the home. Even Bill Wilson, the co-founder of Alcoholics Anonymous, wrote that "Almost without exception alcoholics are tortured by loneliness."

This of course suggests that "the cure for loneliness" is meaningful human connection. Without it, we suffer. Deprived of it as infants, we do not develop normal bonding with others. Deprived of it as adults, we get sick or commit various forms of anti-social activity. All this should be obvious by now. We hardly need a modern Aristotle to tell us that we are "social animals." Aside from the occasional recluse or hermit, we all need the company and love of others. But when we look at how our society has developed in recent years, we can easily discern how much we have unknowingly sabotaged our communal social life for the allure of privatistic concerns.

I sometimes joke that human beings in the course of their evolution have made three disastrous wrong turns.

The first was the invention of agriculture. Yes, really. If you don't believe me, take a look at Yuval Noah Harari's bestselling book of a few years ago, *Sapiens*.

The second is much more recent. It's the rise of the isolated nuclear family in America and the corresponding decline in extended family networks. I discussed this in my previous blog, so don't need to dwell on that here. However, Vivek also mentions this and comments that in countries in southern Europe, such as Italy and Greece, where extended family units are still more intact than in America, the problems of loneliness are less acute. After all, for thousands of years people lived in tribal or communal settings and humans could simply not survive on their own; ostracism meant death. But now? Vivek writes: "I think many of us feel pushed by modern society to be more independent, even as, deep down, we crave the inner connectedness that our ancestors depended on."

The third fateful error was the invention of the Internet and, in due course, the advent of social media and cell phones. I am not kidding, although of course I do not deny all the obvious advantages that the development of the Internet has brought us. After all, who can live these days or would want to without Google and Amazon? But still, we have certainly become more aware of the dark side of the Internet with its power to surveil and spy on us, to track our every move on our iPhones, to hack into our personal, business and government networks, to carry out cyber warfare, and so on into the frightening night. Any technology is neutral in itself, but any technology can also be used for malign purposes. Years ago, in a popular novel by John Irving called *The World According to Garp*, the main lesson was "the world is not safe." Do you feel as safe now as you did before the Internet took over our lives?

But what does all this have to do with loneliness? Plenty, as you will soon see, if you don't already. Vivek's thesis in his book—and he provides countless, often inspiring examples of this—is that the way to cure or reduce the adverse effects of loneliness is to foster various means of renewed social connection. We hunger for social companionship; without it, we atrophy or sink into apathy and isolation. We need to connect.

But what kind of connections are readily available these days and with what or whom?

In these discussions, sooner or later someone is bound to bring up that famous line from E.M. Forster's novel, *Howard's End*: "Only connect." (Another confession: I never read the book; I only saw the film.) Actually, Forster wasn't really referring to connecting with other people, but that is how the phrase is commonly understood now. And how do we connect nowadays?

Facebook of course comes immediately to mind. Mark Zuckerberg has become the apostle of the virtues of connection. Of course, he is not talking about face-to-face encounters. He is offering Facebook as the medium. Let us connect virtually. We don't actually have to go out to see people (especially during the pandemic when social contact is so risky). Not when they are just a click away. And that exactly is the rub.

Jill Lepore is a staff writer for *The New Yorker* and a Harvard-based historian. I recently came across one of her articles, which turned out to be an excoriating indictment of Facebook and all the many ills it has unleashed from its own electronic Pandora's box. She also has seen just how much it has actually contributed to what she calls, as I did in my previous blog, our current epidemic of loneliness. Here's an excerpt:

"Our mission is to give people the power to build community and bring the world closer together" is a statement to be found in Facebook's Terms of Service; everyone who uses Facebook implicitly consents to this mission. During the years of the company's ascent, the world has witnessed a loneliness epidemic, the growth of political extremism and political violence, widening political polarization, the rise of authoritarianism, the decline of democracy, a catastrophic crisis in journalism, and an unprecedented rise in propaganda, fake news, and misinformation. By no means is Facebook responsible for these calamities, but evidence implicates the company as a contributor to each of them. In July, President Biden said that misinformation about covid-19 on Facebook "is killing people."

Collecting data and selling ads does not build community, and it turns out that bringing people closer together, at least in the way Facebook does it, makes it easier for them to hurt one another. Facebook wouldn't be so successful if people didn't love using it, sharing family photographs, joining groups, reading curated news, and even running small businesses. But studies have consistently shown that the more time people spend on Facebook the worse their mental health becomes; Facebooking is also correlated with increased sedentariness, a diminishment of meaningful face-to-face relationships, and a decline in real-world social activities. Efforts to call Zuckerberg and Sandberg to account and get the company to stop doing harm have nearly all ended in failure.

Vivek, too, spends considerable time warning against the adverse effects of digital technology, especially its addictive qualities, which can lead to excessive use. He cites several such studies, such as one carried out at the University of Pittsburg in 2017 that showed high levels of social media use was harmful and contributed to loneliness. Here, heavy users were twice as likely to feel lonely compared to those whose use was low. Another similar study found that heavy users were more likely to be depressed. Vivek sums up his conclusion as follows:

> As we learn more about these various dimensions of technology, it is increasingly clear that technology holds mixed blessings for us. Social media can help people find meaningful connections, especially when they come from communities that have traditionally been isolated or marginalized. But in the wrong circumstances, it can exacerbate loneliness by amplifying comparison, enabling bullying, and substituting lower—for higher-quality relationships.

Some years ago, on one of my visits to The Netherlands, I visited the famous Rijks Museum where you can see a number of Rembrandt's works, including his colossal and celebrated "The Night Watch" from the Golden Age of Dutch painting.

Recently, someone sent me a photo of six Dutch kids sitting on a bench before this magnificent painting. It shows all of them staring at their cell phones and ignoring the painting altogether.

Need I say more?

I would actually love to write more about Vivek's book because I have really said very little about all the wonderful examples he gives of how people have found ways—or at least did before the pandemic hit—to overcome loneliness and find meaningful personal involvement with others. If you were to read his book, which I encourage you to do, you will find many moving and inspiring stories in it of people he has personally interviewed who have triumphed over their own loneliness and gone on to lead very fulfilling lives. He spends a good part of the last part of his book discussing innovative ways to cultivate loving connections among students. What a shame that with schools closed for so long during this seemingly endless COVID pandemic (just when we seemed to have turned the corner, we find that we have smashed into a wall called the Delta variant) that all of these worthwhile endeavors have had to be abandoned at least for now. One hopes that they can be revived once the COVID cloud finally lifts.

But to end this blog, I think it only fitting to return to Vivek himself since I wound up having only more admiration and respect and—I would even dare to say—love for this man than I had prior to encountering him in his book.

Vivek, who is in his mid-forties, is married with two small children, and toward the end of his book, he writes a letter not just for his own children, but one that expresses his hopes for all children in future generations. Here are a few excerpts that will give you a sense of the man:

> Dear Ones,
>
> May you inhabit a world that puts people at the center, where everyone feels they belong. Where compassion is universal and kindness exchanged with whole-hearted generosity for all.
>
> The most important thing we wish for you is a life filled with love—love that is given and received with a full heart. Love is at the heart of loving a connected life. Chose love, we tell you. Always.
>
> You are precious precisely because you have the ability to give and receive love. That is your magic.
>
> The greatest gifts you'll ever receive will come through

relationships. The most meaningful connections may last for a few moments or for a lifetime. But each will be a reminder that we were meant to be a part of one another's lives, to lift one another up, to reach heights together greater than any of us could reach on our own.

The Women in My Life

Introduction

The great Polish-American pianist, Artur Rubinstein, was my kind of man. He had a great zest for life, lived until the age of 95, and played marvelously until his late 80s, even though by then he was nearly blind. He was especially famous for two things: his performances of Chopin and his love of women. He once said, "I am 90% interested in women."

Me, too.

In this section, I will recount a few of my relationships with women whom I have loved and who sometimes loved me, but not always and not necessarily in the way you might expect.

The Rose That Failed to Bloom: Memories of My Mother—Part I

Rose at the Beginning

Today, June 30, 2021, is the twentieth anniversary of my mother's death. I have spent a lot of time this month remembering her and her sad life. My mother, née Rose Friedman, was a rose that never bloomed. By her mid-thirties she had started to wither, and before many years more had passed, she had died long before her death.

Apart from my daughter, Kathryn, I imagine no one but me ever even thinks about her these days, and I am the only person still living who knew her intimately from the time she was a young woman until her death.

Friendless and all but abandoned except by me at the time of her death, her passing hardly caused a ripple even within my small family. We did have a little gathering at my house two months afterward, which I had intended to be at least an informal memorial of sorts for her, but even that affair quickly turned to other family stories, particularly revelations about my father and grandfather, thanks to my Uncle George, then in his nineties, who relished his role as the genial raconteur of family gossip.

So my mother had died, but was not really missed or mourned, other than by me, and even then, I can't say that I did much to keep the flame of her memory burning for long. I did visit her grave twice in the first year or two after her death, but I haven't been back since. Thus did my mother pass into oblivion, as we all will, of course, but before I do—I am now on the far side of 85—I want to take the time to relate something of her story and tell you how it was that this once beautiful woman lost her way and why she failed to bloom. This is my love offering to her before it is too late.

~

My mother was the last of five siblings to be born, but her immediate older sister, Mary, soon forged a very strong bond with my mother which would endure for the whole of their lives. Mary was the elder by two years and always served as Rose's protector, advocate and advisor. Mary was the strong and competent member of the pair, Rose, the shyer, less confident and more troubled.

My mother grew up to be a beauty—the only one of the Friedman children (there were two boys and two other girls) who had exceptional good looks. So much so that as a teenager she had entered and won at least one beauty contest that I know of.

I don't know how much, if at all, she dated during this period of her life, but I know she was much sought after. Eventually she met a man who, according to what I was told, she fell passionately in love with. Rose's father was apparently a rather tyrannical man, and I know my mother was eager to get out from under his thumb as soon as she had finished high school. She felt that the man she was in love with could be the means, and she was eager to marry him. But fate had other ideas; he turned out to be a homosexual. My mother was desolated when she discovered this. As far as I know, this man, whose name I never learned, was the only man she ever loved.

But Rose did have other suitors, and one man in particular had begun to court her ardently. His name was Phil Kurman, and he was an artist. At that time, he made his living playing the piano in clubs, but he had aspirations to become a painter. Phil apparently had a great deal of charm, was intelligent and articulate, and although he was not particularly good looking, with a somewhat long nose, he was far from unprepossessing. He also was buoyed by a great deal of self-confidence, and from what I was later to learn from Mary, he was wild about my mother.

It was at this point that my mother made the first of her fateful errors. She consented to marry Phil—on the rebound. He would now be her ticket out of her own household and her father's control over her life. She was already twenty-two, both of her older sisters had already married, and Rose would not be left behind.

In the mid-1930s, my mother's family moved to California, and to begin with, my mother and her new husband lived with Mary and her husband, George, in San Francisco, where, toward the end of 1935, I joined them. Although for reasons I will soon explain, I don't think I was a desired child, but all the same after I arrived my mother seemed happy to have me.

The reason I believe that, at least on my mother's part, I was an unwelcome baby is that I know by the time I was born, my mother was convinced her marriage had been a mistake, and now with a child to raise, she was stuck. She did not love my father, and as I was later to learn, she had never loved him and never would. Phil, however, had certainly loved her, and at first had loved her passionately. But to no avail. And no one in the family seems to have taken a liking to him either. He apparently was full of himself, tended to brag about his talents and, from what I later gathered from Mary, he was generally found to be an obnoxious character. Again, according to Mary (my mother would never talk to me about Phil and later destroyed all of his paintings and almost all the photographs of him), Rose—who by that time preferred to be called "Ro"—had become "turned off" by Phil and refused to have sex with him any longer. Phil, naturally, was forced to turn elsewhere for physical affection, as he did. According to George, who knew my father well, after a while Phil was "in and out" of the marriage even before he departed permanently during World War II. Probably my mother was relieved to see him leave. From now on, it would be just my mother and me.

Ro and I soon formed a close emotional bond. My mother clearly had changed her mind about me. Actually, I think she did shortly after my birth because I was a happy baby, easy to care for, with blond curly hair, and from an early age I loved to sing (my mother told me that I would sing along to jingles on the radio even before I could talk). In effect, I believe I was the compensation to my mother for the unhappiness in her marriage. All her love went to me and not to her husband.

Nevertheless, my mother was not a physically demonstrative woman (I can't recall whether she ever hugged me as a child or even in later life), but I never doubted her love for me. I remember how she used to say goodnight to me when I was young, perhaps seven or eight. I can still recall the purple and black checkered comforter on my bed. Before I went to sleep, my mother would steal into my room. She wouldn't kiss me, but she would look playfully into my eyes and then softly press her check against mine.

During the war years, we were living in Oakland, still with Mary and George, and, as of 1940, their son, Cliff. During those years, I became very close to my mother emotionally, even though my main caretaker was my aunt Mary, since my mother had, even then, psychological problems, mainly, so far as I later was able to discern, having to do with her feelings of inadequacy, anxiety and depression. Once, when I was about eight, I believe, I discovered a book in her nightstand by a psychiatrist named Cowles whose title I still remember, *Don't Be Afraid!* That said a lot about my mother's fragile psyche of which I had already become aware.

As a naïve child, of course, I was not familiar with psychological concepts; I did not realize then that my mother was a depressive. Mostly, I remember her tendency to sleep late and often resting, but she did confide in me about her problems, and I know I listened sympathetically to them. I realize now I was the only person she then had to whom she could express her love unreservedly, but the fact is, I felt very loved by my whole family, and cherished. My own nature was sunny and seemingly uncomplicated.

Nevertheless, my mother was mostly a recessive character in

our household. She did not cook or bake; she left that to Mary. The only foods I can ever remember her preparing for me were an occasional artichoke or peanut butter and jelly sandwiches. She didn't work, never held a job and couldn't drive. I do know that she would occasionally take me shopping with her in downtown Oakland and that she liked to sunbathe. I later learned that she was a reader, but did she ever read to me? Not that I recall. In a way, she was a kind of a recluse in the house she shared with her sister and her husband, almost like a guest. She was there, but absent at the same time.

Suddenly, during the spring of 1945, as the war in Europe was drawing to a close, I learned that we—my entire family—would be moving to Brooklyn, New York, for the summer. I had actually been taken to New York once before, in 1941, for a short time, but living there for an entire summer would be another matter altogether, especially now that I was nine years old. Ostensibly, the reason was that George's mother, who was widowed by then, was in ill-health and George needed to be there to help take care of her. Only years later did I come to learn that there was another reason for us to travel there at that time.

Unbeknownst to me, my father was about to be discharged and had arranged to have a surreptitious meeting with my mother in July of that year—at least it was a meeting that was kept secret from me. It was only from Mary many years later that I learned about it and more about what my father had been up to during the war. From what my mother had disclosed to her sister at that time, Phil had apparently been something of an "operator," rather like the character Milo in Joseph Heller's classic novel, *Catch-22*. He was, my mother said, always "making deals," and seemingly had managed to enjoy his time while in Europe as millions were dying—and where at the time, with the war there over, millions of survivors and refugees were starving and fighting among themselves.

Therefore, my mother must have listened with complete stupefaction to the shocking proposal my father had come to New York to make to her. He had so loved being in Europe, he told her, that he wanted to return after the war to make his home and his living there— and he wanted my mother and me to join him as soon as possible!

Of course, I have no idea how my mother actually responded to this preposterous proposition, but I like to imagine it was something along the lines of—"You want me to take my only begotten son and myself to Europe while it is still on fire and people are starving and in rags there? Are you completely daft, Phil?"

In any event, my mother, for once, made a definitive decision for herself. She would of course have none of it. That didn't stop my father, whose penchant for Bohemian adventurism had obviously only been enhanced by whatever opportunistic contacts he had made during the war. Born in Europe, he was returning home and would take up the life of an itinerant artist there. Thus it was, even without my knowing it then, that my father left me for the second time, this time for good. My mother and I went back to California shortly afterward.

While we were on the train heading home, the Japanese surrendered, and since the train was already crammed full of servicemen, the hoopla and celebrating made it a very memorable trip. My mother, still beautiful and no longer tethered to her European-bound husband, was now in fact being wooed by several servicemen. One of them, a sailor named George (who, I remember, told me that he weighed 236 pounds) tried to charm my mother by teaching me how to play pinochle. Unfortunately, George succeeded only in charming me.

After we returned to Oakland, Mary was forced to confront my mother with a problem that she would have to take steps to solve, and soon. As I was to learn years later, during the war years George had been providing all of my mother's financial support. But now that it was clear that Phil would not be returning, George had put his foot down—Ro had to find some other means to support herself, either by working or finding someone to marry after her divorce became final. Accordingly, since many veterans were now returning home, Mary advised Ro to go to the service clubs that were then so popular and see if she could find someone suitable to marry her. My mother was still a "looker," and dressed well.

It did not take my mother long to find a number of men who were attracted to her (though it helped that she lied about her age).

A few months later, I would take another train trip with my mother, this time to Reno where she would obtain a "quickie divorce." My mother was about to make her second fateful mistake.

The Rose That Failed to Bloom:
Memories of My Mother—Part II

The Withering of the Rose

He had still been a sailor when he met my mother, but he took to her right away, and she, desperate for the security of a stable relationship after my father's long absence and years of unfaithfulness, succumbed to this young, vigorous and enthusiastic he-man. Indeed, Ray Ring was a muscled, tattooed bull of a man, still in his mid-twenties and full of life. To me, however, it was as if an alien creature had suddenly burst into our house with a kind of demonic energy and taken over the lives of my mother and me. I had, without any warning, acquired a stepfather and lost my own father forever at the same time.

Before Ray's entrance into our lives, my mother and I had continued to live with my aunt, uncle and cousin in a fairly roomy house in Oakland where I had in fact grown up. However, as soon as my mother and stepfather were married in July of 1946—I was now ten—the three of us moved into a very tiny down-at-the-heels dwelling in a dilapidated court in the same general area where I had grown up near Mills College. Another life was beginning for all of us, and the deep bond that had grown up between my mother and me during the war years was sundered at this time by this strange intruder, my stepfather, who was so unlike all the other members of my own family.

Meanwhile, I could see that something was happening to my mother. She had gradually become more withdrawn and seemingly troubled. Of course, my suspicions immediately centered on my stepfather, and eventually, when he was out of the house, my mother started confiding in me again, telling me of her unhappiness with him. Although she was not specific, she intimated that her sex life with Ray was deeply unsatisfying. She just wasn't attracted to him; indeed, in some ways, she seemed repelled, even frightened, by his physical ardor. She had made a mistake in marrying him, she said, but she could see no way out now. From what my mother indicated to me, however, although she was always oblique about this too, I knew she had—even then—other suitors and that one of them, a furrier, wanted her to leave her marriage so that they could be together. Naturally, by this time, I encouraged my mother to do exactly that. I wasn't any more happy than she was in this new family constellation, and I urged her to find a way to break free. But she never had the courage to do it, and this is when I began to lose respect for my mother. She would only complain, but she would never take any action. She was defeated, a captive in a marriage that she thought would save her, but had only confined her to a prison run by a benevolent but completely controlling warden. It was at that point that my mother started her descent into mental illness, which was her only escape.

Something, then, was beginning to happen to my mother, although at that time, when I was completing high school and beginning my college studies, I was too preoccupied with my own life to pay that much attention to that of my mother. I had also moved away to Berkeley during those years, so I also did not have as much contact with my mother as before. She was left alone now with her husband, another controlling man in her life, as her father had been, but from Ray there would be no way out.

I knew of course that my mother suffered from anxiety, that she was riddled by unnamed and untamable fears and was deeply unhappy in her marriage. And, naturally, all this depressed her, so that she was tempted to withdraw from life as much as possible.

Stuck at home and unable to drive, she seemed to have no friends at all. Mary was her only companion and confidant, even more important now than ever since my relationship with her was no longer as close and intimate as it had been.

However, when my parents moved out to Berkeley themselves—my stepfather had arranged to manage the apartment complex where they lived—I was at least able to visit my mother frequently. We often played Scrabble together—as a reader she was good with words. A longtime subscriber to *The New Yorker*, she introduced me to the magazine when I was thirteen (I have been reading it ever since). And she did have a sly sense of humor. I think at that time, I was just about her only distraction from the tedium and stress of her marriage.

My mother never was interested to talk to a therapist, and I don't think Ray would have countenanced it, anyway. Instead, I recall that she frequently saw a Dr. Goodman about her ills, and it was because of him that she began to take Valium daily, something I never learned until years afterward. At that time, Valium was a frequently prescribed tranquillizer, and it was not then known that it could become addictive and, in some cases, could even lead to a Valium-induced psychosis.

That was the fate that was to befall my mother, but by degrees over the ensuing years.

By now, I was already a young professor at the University of Connecticut, so the only contact I had with my mother was through an occasional letter (and birthday card) and during my visits back to California. At first, I didn't notice anything particularly alarming about my mother during my visits. There was one thing, however, that struck me. As I've said, she was not a demonstrative woman, but I noticed on these occasions that as soon as she saw me, she would invariably tear up.

After a while, though, her behavior had become distinctly peculiar and a source of some concern. At that time, she and Ray were living in a condo in a gated community in San Leandro, but for some reason they never wanted me to visit them there. They would insist that we meet at Mary and George's house in Oakland. That was fine with me because I particularly enjoyed spending time with Mary, long my favorite relative as I was her favorite nephew. But a typical visit with my parents would take this form: After about fifteen minutes, my mother would become agitated and say something like, "Ray, we really have to go now," and so they would with a hurried goodbye. It left us all puzzled and perplexed, figuratively scratching our heads. Well, that was my mother, that's just how she was these days, it seemed. But the signs were there and some years later I was to learn the devastating secret about why my parents never wanted me to visit them at their home.

So in those years, I was never able to meet with my mother privately, but, as I said, she would at least occasionally write to me. Sometimes it was to relate a violent quarrel that she had had with Ray who was choleric, impulsive, and was able easily to intimidate my mother and cause her to cower. He was never physically abusive toward her, but he ruled her with an iron will. But many of her letters were about money matters, particularly after Ray, in a characteristically rash episode, had taken all of their money (including some that had belonged to Ro, and without her permission) and invested it in a "get rich scheme" that predictably had gone bust, with the result that they were suddenly far worse off financially than ever. (George to the rescue again.)

This had created both a family and financial crisis, and my mother wrote me several anguished letters about it, and her seething anger at Ray for what he had done—not only acting foolishly without consulting her, but also because he had committed an act of theft. She was understandably bitter.

After that, she often wrote me about certain bank accounts of hers (apparently they had been replenished to a degree at Mary's insistence through George's grudging largesse) that she wanted me to be sure to know about in case she died. She had always been a secretive woman, and she was determined to keep these accounts hidden from Ray. He would never learn about them.

But, meanwhile, with my mother's continuing use of Valium,

her behavior was becoming more erratic, as Ray himself told me once when he had come to the airport to pick me up. This in itself was unusual, as I had spent very little time alone with him, nor did I care to, during my years away in Connecticut. But this time he wanted to talk to me; he was also beginning to be concerned about Ro's behavior. I knew he wouldn't want her to see a therapist; he seemed to think only her doctor and drugs could help her. But he confessed that he was at a loss as to what to do, and I doubted that he would be open to any advice that I might offer. I actually think he mainly wanted to talk to me just to unburden himself.

What made this such a memorable encounter, however, was when he told me something I had never known. He said, pretty much in these words, as I recall, "You know, Ken, in all these years your mother has never once told me that she loved me, never once!" How I then felt for my stepfather who, for all his flaws and failings, did so deeply love my mother, despite everything. How he must have suffered from this knowledge, and how much courage it must have taken for him to disclose this to me. Still, afterward, I could not help reflecting that my mother, in her two marriages, had never loved either husband; she had passed her life in two loveless unfulfilling marriages, and now seemed to be spiraling out of control in a vertiginous descent into increasing despair and mental disintegration.

Unfortunately, the worst—far worse—was still to come.

The Rose That Failed to Bloom:
Memories of My Mother—Part III

Rose at the End

This final episode coincides with the exact 75th anniversary of my mother's marriage to my stepfather, Ray. It was on that date, July 14, 1946, that she made the second fateful error of her life that would lead in time to her ultimate disintegration, which you will now read about in the blog to follow.

In December, 1991, as I was preparing to take a trip to Venezuela with my then current lover, Maude, I received an urgent call from California. My stepfather had just been discovered to have an advanced and fatal form of cancer and had already been hospitalized. Because my mother was by then old and demented, and because I was her only child, there was no other choice but to cancel my holiday plans with Maude and leave for California as soon as I could purchase my tickets for the flight.

A day after Christmas, I was on my way to the Bay Area to help take care of my mother but chiefly to do whatever my stepfather needed. At that point, it was mainly a matter of filial duty; in the end, it turned out to be a journey of love.

What follows is an edited version of the diary I kept of that visit.

When I first arrive, I cannot find my mother.

I drive to my mother's fortress—she lives in a gated community in San Leandro. It is impenetrable from the outside.

She does not respond to my voice message.

There has been no word from my mother by 9 a.m., and I am about to discover why not.

When I was still in Connecticut, in a plangent voice, she had averred that she no longer wanted to live, that she did not know how to live without Ray. As you now know, my mother had for years been an unknowing addict to Valium and had suffered terribly as a result of having been made to withdraw from it "cold turkey." Had she perhaps taken an overdose of her tranquillizers? Would I find her unconscious or even dead when I was finally able to enter her home? Or might she have simply wandered away, in a disoriented demented daze of grief, unable to stay in her house and too confused to be able to call anyone for help?

Fortunately, George had a set of keys to her gate and to the house, so I am able to get in at last. I pause for a moment at the door, trying to compose myself for any eventuality.

When I unlock the door, I smell the stench immediately, and then hear my mother's raspy voice call out, "Ken? Oh, I was frightened that it might be someone else."

She is wearing only a rumpled blouse and her underwear. Her lank hair has gone completely gray, and her lips are twisted into a grimace of pain. She shuffles down the narrow hallway and approaches me warily, like a wounded animal.

Embracing her gently, I begin to take in the dimensions of the noisome squalor that has been my mother's home for so long. (I had not visited my parents at their home—had not been permitted to—for some ten years. Now, in an instant, I knew why.)

The hall mirror I am facing does not reflect me—or anything. It is caked with grime from top to bottom. There is a large and still spongy wet strain on the carpet beneath me upon which heaps of towels have been laid in an only partially successful effort to sop up the water. The nearby bathroom is unusable, the toilet blackened with scum and smelling like the shit it was stuffed with. Clothes are strewn everywhere, helter-skelter, and great masses of wadded up tissues are scattered all over.

Entering the kitchen, I find the linoleum floor ruined and covered with a sticky film of encrusted dirt. A carton filled with empty Sprite cans sits on one counter next to a large but empty refrigerator, which I soon determine is no longer working. ("It's on the blink, Ken," my mother helpfully explains.) But in the middle of the kitchen is a small working refrigerator at least. However, when I peer inside, I find it full of spoiled food, empty milk cartons and some still barely eligible food, mostly dairy products on which my mother apparently has managed to subsist. All around on the counters is discarded debris—dirty dishes, soiled paper cups, half-empty plastic pill bottles left uncapped, piles of unopened mail—the material detritus of years of fitful neglect. On the floor are assorted grocery bags of still undiscarded garbage.

My mother has turned into a bag lady who lives in a garbage dump of her own making.

Looking through the kitchen toward the living room, my eyes spot a large round table stacked high with letters, bills, business cards and whatnot—another mountain of chaotic papers and documents that appear to represent my father's desk and working area. To its left is what used to be the living room with a couch and chairs littered with old newspapers, clothing and the apparently ubiquitous wadded-up tissues. There are some books still lying on the coffee table—I notice one about the history of the Holocaust and other serious books, along with broken candy dishes and a pile of mildewing clothes. (I make a bad pun to myself—"awful offal.") An enormous television screen—it must be nearly three feet square—stares blankly at me.

When I enter my mother's bedroom, I find it in darkness—she likes to keep the lights off, she tells me, and I can soon discern why once I flip them on. On her double bed on which she is now lying, her head on a pillow, are two crumpled blankets, seemingly almost twisted into knots. To her left are masses of used up tissues. Her nightstand also has reams of tissues splayed about as well as many notes that have been scribbled nearly illegibly onto the backs of envelopes. On her dresser is an assortment of objects covered with dust and seemingly unused, including two non-functioning electric clocks. There is still another clock sitting on an ironing board facing the bed that is otherwise covered with my mother's clothing deposits, more of which are scattered around the floor.

It was as if I have walked into a seemingly abandoned Gothic house, only to find it occupied by a demented elderly recluse. The interior of the house seems to reflect the state of its lone resident's disordered brain. In fact, all that is missing is the fecal matter on the walls (though I may have missed that). It seems to be a nut house gone wild in which I find my mother lost in the wilderness of her own mind.

And sadly but hardly surprisingly in view of what has greeted me when I entered, I soon see that my mother is indeed demented. Although she is still capable of lucidity at times, when her attention is elsewhere she soon lapses into protracted utterances of imprecations, curses and self-blame, muttering that she isn't crazy but in general talking like one of those street crazies that one encounters so often in New York. I have the spooky feeling of listening to my mother's thought stream in audible form, and it is nothing other than a farrago of a rant.

She also begins to undress herself in the presence of others, as I later discover. She takes off her slacks and stands around in her underwear, and then begins to unbutton her sweater, exposing her bra. She changes her clothes very often, all in a few moments, while out of my sight. And then she shuffles around, muttering to herself, her voice rising in occasional shouts of anger while lost in her own confusion. My feeling is that every resentment she has had to suppress when living with my father is able to come out now that he is no longer there to inspire her fear.

Then she comes out of her fog, becomes sensible and coherent again and speaks rationally. However, she denies—vehemently—that she talks to herself. She is just thinking, she says. And she is right—that is exactly what she is doing. She just doesn't realize that she is vocalizing her thoughts and that I can hear them.

At this point, still not knowing in what condition I will find my stepfather, I now have deep concern about what will become of my mother after Ray's death. She doesn't even know (nor did I then) whether Ray owned the house or, if not, to whom the rent was paid. She is living, not unreasonably, in fear that she will soon be evicted. She does not know or cannot tell me how much money Ray has in the bank, where his checkbook is, much less what bills need to be paid. She is a fount of ignorance on all such practical matters, and I can only hope that Ray will still be able to answer those questions for me.

Standing before my mother in this state, she seems like a lost and confused child without her father-husband, and all I can do is to try to reassure her that I will take care of things, of her, and not to worry. I tell her that she certainly will not be evicted, but that I need her help in order to start helping her.

First, I make out a list, with her help, of questions I need to ask Ray. I find out the name of her bank and call it to explain the situation. Since my father has been heavily involved in veterans affairs, I am able to get in touch with some of his vet buddies who are glad to offer their assistance. I erase the answering machine with Ray's outgoing message and substitute one of my own. Then I show my mother how to use the answering machine of which she is not only ignorant but seemingly afraid. ("All machines are inherently aggressive," said Carlyle.) And then reassuring her that I will be back in the afternoon, I leave for the hospital wondering what more horrors may lie in store for me there....

Before leaving, I tell my mother that she will probably be moving to The Jewish Home for the Aged, and try to inform her as much as I need to about Ray's plans for her. I have to reassure her again and again of his concern for her welfare and of his unwavering love, even as he is approaching his own death.

My mother is still in a confused and disoriented state, but she appears to be able to absorb most of this information. (Nevertheless, she later calls me for further reassurance, saying she is still confused about what is to happen to her.) Ro finds it difficult to keep from reverting to longstanding fears, which have plagued her entire life, it seems. She may also now have a memory deficit so that things have to be explained to her over and over....

It takes me fully five minutes just to clean the mirror in the vestibule until I can finally begin to see the glass. Coat after coat of Windex is necessary in order to scrape away the grime and encrustations of years—who knows how many?—of neglect. The next two hours are spent picking up litter from the carpet in the hall and adjoining corridors—hair curlers, pink plastic pins in abundance, perhaps a hundred pennies, and countless wads of tissues—and then sweeping clean the little cabinet underneath the mirror on which stands a small dirty vase containing a single pathetic plastic red rose. (An apt metaphor, I can't help thinking.) After all this, I can finally vacuum the carpet itself. Two hours—and just a small corner of the house has been liberated from its debris...

When I arrive back at my mother's house about 2 p.m., I am distressed not to find her at home. But I soon discover her outside, a little old lady wearing a black beret, dressed in brown (at least she has clothes on!). She is slowly padding up the sidewalk toward the house whose front door, by the way, she has left open.

I endeavor to do a wash. My mother, however, is difficult to deal with in this matter. She attempts to round up her dirty clothes—God knows this must be a difficult task for her in her disoriented state of mind—but soon loses track of her objective and wanders off, muttering.

I hear her loud, angry quasi-whisper: "Geez, that's crazy! He's going to think that's crazy. I'm not crazy." She repeats these statements or similar ones frequently, but when I approach her, she immediately ceases—as if I have found her engaged in some indiscretion. When I try to confront her gently about this, she denies talking to herself and becomes defensive.

Then, when my back is turned, she starts again to undress herself down to her underwear, and when I reproach her, she claims that she is just changing her clothes, something that she does often, she says.

So goes the way of the wash, which finally, small thanks to her, gets done.

Once I get all the clothes into the washing machine, we have a little talk during which she is entirely, so far as I can tell, present. I tell her that she has to see Ray—that it is very important to him, and why. She appears to understand and agrees to do so without resistance. I try to explain to her that she will be moving and in general how things will be from now on, and again she appears to grasp the gist of what I tell her. Throughout, I have to reassure her about her finances, that no matter what, she will be taken care of.

After that talk, I start on the kitchen beginning with cleaning the counters and the sink. Then I take on the encrusted appliances, such as the electric can opener, the toaster and orange squeezer. Meanwhile, my mother resumes her aimless parade around the house, muttering fiercely as soon as she is out of my sight and trying to appear normal when she passes through the kitchen on her rounds to nowhere.

However, despite my remonstrating with her, she has by now unbuttoned a bit of her sweater while elsewhere in the house—a little gesture of defiance, a small assertion of her control over at least her body, which is all she retains dominion over these days.

I clean, she wanders about vacantly. So passes the afternoon.

How ironic, then, that Ray who is loved by so many of his veteran friends only really cares about receiving love from the one person who has always withheld it—my mother. They have been married for 45 years and, as I have mentioned, never once in all that time has my mother ever explicitly said that she loved him. My stepfather, on the other hand, claims that not a day has passed when he hasn't avowed his love for my mother. Probably an exaggeration, but still, I suspect, a substantially true statement. I don't think I have ever known a man who has for so long and so passionately loved a woman with so little to show for it—45 years of a tormented unrequited love. What could be sadder—and for both—but my sympathies lie largely with my stepfather. Indeed, in my final days there, I have had a kind of healing with Ray and have come truly to love him. We have had some extremely tender and loving moments together as he approaches the end of his life. I wonder whether my mother will make one last gesture and go to see him before he dies so he can tell her once more how much he loves her, and perhaps finally hear the words from her that he has waited in vain to be spoken all these years.

Meanwhile, she continues to pad around the house like a zombie. Out of my sight she mumbles harsh curses and sometimes shouts angry phrases. Seeing me, she stops and attempts to act normal. She is always "changing her clothes," i.e., undressing. I try again to reassure her that she will be taken care of, but I'm not sure how much sinks into that softened brain of hers.

Truthfully, I am finding Ro to be a bother and a nuisance, and my patience sometimes wears thin. Of course, I don't want anything bad to happen to her, but I'm aware that all my feelings of love and care are going to my stepfather while toward my mother, I am all duty. How different it was for most of my life when I only cared about my mother while ignoring my stepfather. Life is full of ironies—and unexpected reverses of affection.

She never does go to see Ray. She balks, refuses to go.

After Ray's death, my mother was a basket case. My then girl-friend Lucienne and I drove her down to Los Angeles so that she might stay with an older sister. That didn't work out, so I had to fly out there again and drive her back to the Bay Area where I was finally able to place her in a "board and care" home in Berkeley where residents are still ambulatory. At least they would look after her there. (I could not afford to place her in The Jewish Home for the Aged, as my stepfather had wanted, because she was now indigent. The house did have a lien on it and was lost.)

Some of my women friends sometimes joke that they fear that when they become old, they will turn into bag ladies. Unfortunately, that's what became of my mother. She would wander off, with permission, on the local streets and poke her nose into garbage bins. But she could do some surprising things, too. Once when I was visiting her, the staff told me that they—and the other residents—really enjoyed hearing my mother play the piano. I never even knew that my mother played the piano!

Sometimes Lucienne and I would fly out there in order to see my mother and take her out to a local restaurant, Edy's, that she had liked to frequent when she was younger and lived in Berkeley. She was impossible and would eat nothing.

Eventually, she developed "contractures" and could no longer walk. At that point, she had to be moved to a nursing home in Berkeley, which was her final home. She shared a room with three other women, all but one demented, though by that time my mother had recovered most of her faculties. She always recognized me and was able to carry on coherent conversations.

During her first years there, I was still living and teaching at the University of Connecticut, and though I explored the possibility of flying my mother out there so she could live near me, for various reasons this was impossible. (Indeed my mother had never flown in her life, and never would.) So I could only visit her whenever I could arrange to get out to California, about a half dozen times a year.

But in 1996, I moved back to the Bay Area and once I arrived, I saw her regularly, usually once a week. When the weather was clement I would push her around the neighborhood in her wheelchair and try to keep up a certain level of chatter. She complained that I talked too much.

Otherwise, we would sometimes sit out in the backyard at a table and play cards (usually gin). Or sometimes I would read to her. She was particularly fond of stories by Chekhov. I read quite a bit to her. She seemed to like that better than to listen to me natter on.

By then, although her mind had pretty much recovered, she was becoming hard of hearing and had developed glaucoma as well. But she was largely uncomplaining unlike her son who frets whenever he has a pimple. I'm sure my mother never read

Montaigne, but she was a model stoic all the same. I hated to leave her, seeing her in her bed, surrounded by women who would be crying out in lunatic fashion, unable to move and uninterested to listen to the radio I had bought for her or to watch TV. She didn't even like to be touched.

Once, when I thought she might not have long to live, I spent five minutes or so telling her about my work on near-death experiences. Finally, I asked her, "So, mom, what do you expect will happen when you die?"

She narrowed her eyes and replied in a flat voice: "Nothing. I expect to be dead."

On another occasion when we were outside, as I was pushing her wheelchair along, I asked her to name some things that had really made her happy in her life. She took a while to answer.

"You," she said.

She lived until she was almost 89 and died on June 30, 2001. She is buried next to her beloved sister, and my aunt, Mary. Never separated in life, now forever together in death.

School Days

I was twenty-two when I left Berkeley to attend graduate school at the University of Minnesota. That year—it was 1958—I had graduated from Berkeley, with a Phi Beta Kappa feather in my cap, and a Bachelor's degree figuratively in my hand, and I was keen to go.

I had never been to the Midwest. I had scarcely ever been anywhere. Aside from spending two summers in Brooklyn before the age of 10, I had spent virtually my entire life in California. So the rest of the country was truly a terra incognita for me. I had hardly even ever encountered snow.

So Minneapolis was a shock. Graduate school was hard enough at first. Although I had received a $10,000 scholarship and had been accepted into a very prestigious social psychology program, my graduate school confreres all seemed brilliant and far more sophisticated than I was. Compared to them, I felt myself to be a hick. This did not do wonders for my self-esteem. I would go home to my little rooming house and plunge both into despair and Tolstoy's *War and Peace*. I did not think I would survive the first quarter and wondered what would become of me.

But I also soon felt that I could not and would not survive the weather either. I did not have a car and had to walk about a mile to the building on campus where the Department of Social Relations was located, which is where I shared a large room with my fellow graduate students (and they were all fellows, too).

My route took me to the Mississippi River, which I had to cross (albeit with the help of a bridge) every morning, and by the time early winter had come, my jaw would be nearly frozen by the time I had reached the other side. And I am not exaggerating. I had never experienced such penetrating, bone-chilling cold. Even if I could manage to survive the rigors of graduate school, I was becoming convinced I would never be able to survive the rigors of a brutal Minnesota winter.

But soon I was rescued—or at least distracted—from my misery through the friendship of two graduate students in my program who had somehow taken a shine to me. Or maybe they just felt sorry for me. In any case, they became true friends and proved to be my salvation.

One was Bernie Saffran, a Jew from Brooklyn (who had the accent to prove it), who, although he was somewhat younger than me, took me under his wing, the way an older and wiser brother would. He educated me and tried to bring me up to speed by telling me what I should read (forget Tolstoy and start reading E. L. Doctorow and Henry's Roth's recently discovered novel, *Call It Sleep*). An economics major and destined to become an outstanding professor of economics at Swarthmore College, Bernie—whom I invariably addressed as Bernard while he called me Kenneth— also introduced me to such then esoteric terms as "stochastic," which has remained in my active vocabulary ever since, as well as making me aware of the critical difference between early and late Marx (Karl, not Groucho, of course, as I had grown up with the latter).

Noting that I loved classical music, Bernie soon told me about a special deal for graduate students concerning the Minnesota Symphony Orchestra, which, I learned, actually held its concerts on campus. "You can get seven concerts for seven dollars," Bernie told me, and then told me how. I might be freezing during the day, but at least on some nights on the cheap I would be sitting in comfort listening to Antal Dorati conduct the orchestra.

My other friend and also a friend of Bernie's was a Catholic sociologist from Milwaukee who had graduated from Marquette. Bernie was loud, boisterous and ugly. Frank was quiet with a wry sense of humor and very good looking. Definitely second fiddle to Bernie, who was our leader, but Frank—whom Bernie would insist on calling Francis—proved to be a stalwart buddy, too, and the three of us quickly became an almost inseparable trio.

I soon learned from Bernie that there was a certain house in Dinkytown—the area around and to the north of campus—where we could obtain good delicious meals for the veritable song. Can you believe that their advertisement read "All you can eat for $10 a week"? And that included all three meals a day as well as a big breakfast on Sunday! So once Bernie had alerted me to this culinary godsend, I naturally became a steady patron and took almost all of my meals there. Bernie was always finding "deals." He knew the ropes. In a way, he was both an intellectual and a street smart operator, the way you'd expect a gifted Jewish kid from Brooklyn to be. Frank and I were glad to follow where Bernie led.

Those evenings at that dining establishment—the equivalent of the Café Momus for us famished graduate students, eager to escape the winter cold—were memorable occasions, full of fun, laughter and sparkling conversation. Bernie, a slob whose food only occasionally found his mouth, which he felt was mainly an organ for talking, would entertain us with ribald tales of his years growing up in Brooklyn, and then suddenly launch into the virtues of the mad poet Hölderlin, and somehow connect the two. Frank and I were content to listen to the Bard of Brooklyn while covertly eyeing the female graduate students who, if they noticed us at all, probably looked away with disdain.

Frank, whose table manners were as impeccable as Bernie's were atrocious, and who tended to be quiet in contrast to Bernie's volubility, seemed already to be "sweet" (as we said in those days) on a graduate student with the memorable name of T. Anne Cleary who was destined to play a pivotal role in my own life, though not a romantic one. Anne was apparently some kind of wizard in statistics but was enrolled in the School of Child Development. I don't think Frank ever got to "first base" (as we also used to say then) with Anne, but then as a good Catholic, Frank was not a lascivious sort of fellow. In any case, we all did eventually strike up a friendship of sorts with Anne, one consequence of which I will have occasion to describe shortly.

However, I have to interrupt my story to tell you of the tragic way Anne's life was to end three decades later. I had not stayed in touch with her after graduate school. But recently I learned that she had had become a distinguished professor and beloved academic administrator at the University of Iowa. I was horrified to discover that it was there, in 1991, that she was shot and killed by a deranged student. I was both shocked and devastated at this dreadful news and thought about it for days afterward.

It's hard, after that kind of interruption, to return to my reminiscences of my first months in graduate school, but I must continue with my story nevertheless.

Although I enjoyed the camaraderie of my friends—we were having our share of high jinks by then, especially at night—and friendships with other graduate students I was meeting, there was still one problem. I was still living far from campus, still without a car, and still freezing my tuckus off on my long trek to campus. And, if anything, the winter was getting even colder and snowier. I wasn't sure how much longer I could endure living this way. I remember thinking, "Why would anyone choose to live in such a godforsaken hell hole where you risk frostbite if you're outside for more than ten minutes?" Of course, I'm exaggerating, but you get the idea.

And in light of what I have just told you about Anne, it is almost creepy to bring her back into my story in the early winter of 1959, because it was Anne who was then to bring about the most important event in my life as a graduate student in Minnesota. She had also, inadvertently to be sure, found a way to keep me from freezing to death when I had to make my way to the university in the morning in sub-zero temperatures.

I first noticed her sitting across from me in the library, and I remember the exact date, too—March 11, 1959. A small dark-haired girl with a studious expression on her face, which was also small with a somewhat pointed chin. She was no beauty, but there was something quietly appealing about her, and I found myself surreptitiously looking at her from time to time.

Concentrating on her book, she took no notice of me. I was oblivious to her.

Sometime afterward I happened to be visiting Anne at the School of Child Development where I saw this girl again. And it turned out that she was a good friend of Anne's so she introduced me. The girl's name was Elizabeth, and she was a second-year graduate student in that School.

I don't remember exactly what happened after that, but I must have asked Elizabeth to have coffee with me (in those days, I drank coffee). Anyway, I soon got to know a bit about her, and I remember one of the first things she told me was the she had recently lost ninety pounds! She had once weighed 215 pounds but was now a svelte 125. Wow, that impressed me. But the most important thing I learned about her almost at the outset was—she had a car!

Kismet! Salvation!

We soon found that we seemed to have a lot in common although our backgrounds were very different. She had grown up in St. Paul, the only girl (she had two brothers) in an Irish Catholic family (though her mother was a Protestant). She was wicked smart, laughed easily and was fun to be with.

And she had a car.

It seemed both wise and prudent to cultivate a friendship with her, a close friendship. Close enough to earn car-riding privileges. Before long, indeed, she was picking me in the morning and driving me to school. And to other places, too, of course. Soon I wasn't spending nearly so much time having dinners with Bernie and Frank. I was out on the town with Elizabeth.

Six months to the day I first saw her, we were married. At twenty-three, I had acquired a wife—and a car. It was September 11th.

～

I was happier by the time the snow started to melt in Minneapolis, and although spring—which I was later to learn lasted about ten minutes before the oppressive heat and humidity, prefiguring the proverbial "long, hot summer," took over—was still a month or so away, it was already a new season in my life. Having a girlfriend now in Elizabeth was certainly a major reason for my newfound cheerfulness, but not the only one.

By then, I had also been able to effect a transfer from the original program into which I had been accepted, which had brought about a kind of existential crisis for me, to one that was much more congenial to my talents and interests. This had led me into the then burgeoning field of experimental social psychology where I could study under the direct supervision of two of the leading men in the field. One of them, Harold H. Kelley, I had actually met at Cal, where he was then a visiting professor. Since I had graduated in January, I had to wait until September before I could begin my graduate studies. In the interim, Kelley had hired me as his research assistant, and came to take a personal interest in me. As kind as he was gifted, he induced me to change my mind about where to pursue my studies (by then I had already been accepted by several top universities) and follow him back to the University of Minnesota where he was already a full professor. When the university made me one of those Godfather offers I couldn't refuse, I was compelled to decline those I had received in order to saddle up and head to the north country.

As it turned out, when I had to confess to Kelley that I was having a hard time at many levels coping with the demands and trying exigencies of life as a graduate student in Minnesota, he suggested I would surely do much better studying directly under him and another distinguished social psychologist, Stanley Schachter, and he proved to be so right. Kelley saved my ass, and I will never forget his solicitude for me. In the years since, I have often wondered what would have become of me had it not been for Kelley's wise and decisive intervention during that critical period of my life.

The best thing was, I could still retain my place at the Lab for Social Relations and continue to hang with and get to know my fellow grad students there. Soon enough, I was a regular part of our fun and games, too, which consisted at that time of intense cribbage matches and bridge games during lunch. And of course, I continued to see and have my adventures with Bernie and Frank as well.

But, naturally, the hugely consequential change in my life involved my relationship with Elizabeth whom I was now seeing frequently. As I soon discovered, Elizabeth was a very bright and dedicated graduate student, specializing in child development. It was clear that her professional interests were paramount in her life, and, at the time, mine were also. So at that level, we were very compatible.

Although we enjoyed each other's company and relished our shared intellectual and professional interests, it was clear that Elizabeth, who was a virgin when I met her, was socially and sexually something of a disappointment. She was not a sexually-oriented woman and there was nothing sensuous about her body or manner. I suppose, if I wanted to be unkind, and I don't, some would have described her as a bit of a "cold fish." She laughed easily enough, but her laugh had a somewhat metallic, harsh quality that was off-putting. Somehow, although she was now a small woman without any outward physical deformities, inwardly she still seemed to be that shy, awkward and socially somewhat inept fat girl she had been for so many years before I had met her.

It will not surprise you, therefore, to learn that our sexual life, certainly at first, was far from satisfactory or even enjoyable. But the fault did not by any means lie entirely with Elizabeth's inexperience. I, too, had had limited sexual encounters before coming to Minnesota, and I'm sure I was a distinctly fumbling, bumbling lover at first. This was really relatively new territory for both of us and we were having a hard time finding our way. Eventually, as all couples do, we managed to figure out "how to do it," but our sexual life was never what I'm sure both of us hoped it would be.

It was dutiful, but it lacked passion. Passion wasn't in Elizabeth's make-up either. Her strength and gifts were in her mind; her body seemed to be more or less a forgotten afterthought. This would prove to be an insuperable stumbling block a few years later, but at the time of course neither of us could know or anticipate the anguish it would cause us.

Still, apart from those issues, we seemed outwardly and were in fact a happy enough couple. True, Elizabeth seemed to lack any real interest in or talent for any of the domestic arts, but since we did not live together, at least to begin with, that wasn't a real problem. Since we both were relatively well off as graduate students due to our respective scholarships, our solution was simple: we ate out a lot! And we enjoyed doing so since it gave us plenty of time to chat about our work and our other interests, and provided ample opportunity to get to know each other better.

Since I was Jewish and Elizabeth had never spent time with any Jews, I took it upon myself to introduce her to what I jokingly called "Jewish cuisine"—the Jewish deli. At that time, there was an area of Minneapolis called St. Louis Park that was a Jewish neighborhood, so we often went to a deli there. Elizabeth came to like the food well enough, which pleased me, but we were both offended yet also amused when the wealthy Jews from the local temple paraded in. I'm afraid that they embodied the usual stereotypes—fat men with their "stogies," and heavily made up women draped in glitzy jewelry in fur coats. Well, we liked the food, anyway, and each other.

In due course, Elizabeth felt it was time for me "to meet the family." They still lived in St. Paul, where Elizabeth had grown up. Her father, Tom, was Irish and very affable. But he was a hemophiliac and had suffered a lot because of that condition. Her mother—I'm fairly sure her name was Mabel, but I have honestly forgotten—was a rather fat woman with, I remember, very large arms, worthy of a football tackle. I should perhaps have drawn the obvious conclusion about how Elizabeth herself would turn out as she aged but I don't believe it even occurred to me at the time. Her older brother Tom, who was slender like his dad, and her younger brother Mike, who was a bit pudgy like his mom, were both cordial to me, though I must have seemed like an alien to them. I had the impression at the time that they were just glad that Elizabeth was at least dating someone now—anyone!

I also recall that afterward we went to see a ball game in St. Paul and that we had seats in the stands right in back of home plate. I remember that night because of something ghastly that happened to me, which still causes me pain to think about. Someone hit a foul ball in back of the protective netting and it was coming right to me. Mittless but undaunted, I reached up to catch it so I could impress Elizabeth, and, naturally, being the klutz I am, I muffed it and promptly turned fifty shades of red.

Fortunately, I was good at something else that really did impress Elizabeth—my skills as a bridge player. In those days, bridge was still a popular avocation, and as I had grown up with a card-playing family, I took naturally to bridge and was a regular in our games at the lab. Elizabeth showed a real interest in the game and she quickly became a proficient bridge player, too. In fact, I have to admit that in time she became an even better player than I was, but the two of us made a good team. At that time, I had become friendly with another grad student named Karl Hakmiller, and his wife, Marie, who were avid bridge players themselves. So in those days, we often went to the Hakmillers' house and played many a rubber.

Eventually, bridge became quite an addiction for both Elizabeth and me, and we each liked to read and discuss various books on bridge, bidding systems and the like. This also boosted my esteem rating with my lab mates since we were then accustomed to read and discuss the daily bridge column in *The New York Times*. For bridge geeks like us, our heroes were not sports stars, but champion bridge players whose skills we admired and whose exploits in bridge tournaments we followed closely.

But bridge is or can be a dangerous game. One time, Elizabeth and I stayed up all night playing bridge with a couple of other grad students (not the Hakmillers) and once it had become light, we decided to drive out to a beach at one of Minnesota's ten thousand lakes. We narrowly avoided what surely would have been a fatal accident that would have nipped our nascent bridge careers in the bud. Needless to say, that cured us of all-night bridge marathons.

By now, the spring quarter was soon ending and the heat of summer before the summer was already upon us. Since neither Elizabeth nor I had any special duties during the summer, I suggested that maybe it was time for her to meet my family. They still lived in California, of course, but since Elizabeth had never been there, she readily agreed.

We had saved enough money to be able to fly out there, but for one reason or another, we kept having to postpone our trip until the very beginning of September.

My folks—my stepfather, Ray, and my mom, Ro (short for Rose)—were then in their forties and lived in Berkeley where they managed the apartment building in which they lived. They received Elizabeth warmly, and of course my mother delighted in showing Elizabeth all my childhood treasures—my artless drawings of fighter planes during World War II, my postcards, full of spelling errors, that I had sent home during my summers with my grandfather in the Gold Rush country of California (they afforded many a laugh), photos of me as a kid, etc. At any rate, by the time our visit was drawing to a close she had learned quite a bit about me and had become very fond of my parents. Elizabeth and I had grown closer, too.

A few days before we were due to return to Minnesota, I had an idea.

"Let's get married," I said.

Elizabeth looked stricken.

My parents whooped it up. They were all for it.

Elizabeth remained doubtful and conflicted, but three against one soon led to the decision in favor of the majority.

But how to get married in a hurry? My dad took charge and found a justice of the peace named (fittingly enough) Kelley, who agreed to perform the ceremony the next day.

Elizabeth broke out with a terrible case of hives. At the ceremony, her face was still a study in unsightly red blotches.

Elizabeth's maiden name was McLaughlin. Justice of the Peace Kelley beamed. "This is my first all-Irish wedding," he proudly told us. We didn't have the heart to tell him. Well, two out of three, anyway.

Elizabeth and I spent our honeymoon on a Greyhound Bus back to Minnesota.

We didn't have enough money to fly home. In fact, after buying our tickets, we hardly had any. My father in a fit of uncharacteristic generosity laid a twenty-dollar bill on me, accompanied by a bag containing a dozen bagels. Our wedding present.

Elizabeth and I, somewhat numb but excited, took our seats. It was a scene out of "The Graduate" at the end with Ben and Elaine on the bus, wondering what they had just done.

When we reached Nevada for our first rest stop, I decided to see if could increase our remaining cash by playing the slots. Mistake.

It was just bagels all the way home.

Married now without a *sou* to call our own.

Women, Past and Present

My Encounter with Whittaker Chambers, Once Removed

Not long ago, while reading a recent issue of *The New Yorker* over dinner, I happened to come across an article by George Packer about the lives of some famous men who had once been Communists or held other ardent politically-committed leftist positions but had eventually become disillusioned and ultimately came to adopt almost antipodal political points of view. One of these men was Whittaker Chambers, the author of one of the greatest American autobiographies of the 20th century, *Witness*, which Packer likens to Augustine's *Confessions* since it is a searing confessional tale of redemption through faith after a life of political sinfulness.

Chambers of course became famous, or rather, notorious, in the middle of the 20th century for his role in the Communist witch-hunting era in American life when he was able to testify and prove that Alger Hiss, a highly placed bureaucrat in the Roosevelt administration, had been, with Chambers, a Communist agent. Chambers' participation in these hearings made him the most well-known figure of his day and helped to make the reputation of a then young Republican politician, Richard Nixon.

But all that is a matter of history. I have a different tale to tell, and that one takes us back to the beginning of Chambers' book. It begins with a foreword in the form of his letter to his children. In it, as Packer also recalls, there is a very moving passage where

Chambers writes that one day while watching his very young daughter eating porridge in her high chair, he was suddenly struck by the delicate perfection of her ear, which prompted the thought— heretical to an atheistic Communist—that it could only have been created "by an immense design." This was perhaps, as Chambers allows, the first crack in the wall of his belief system.

Many years later, I was to caress that ear, and how I came to do so is the story I mean to tell here.

In 1963, I was a young professor at the University of Connecticut, and in the fall semester of that year, I was teaching a large graduate seminar in social psychology. Over the course of the semester, I was struck by a very quiet woman in the class who said little—she seemed shy—but who seemed to be very and uncommonly bright as I could tell from the papers she submitted. She was not beautiful by any means, though she was attractive with her long dark hair, but there was something about her manner that appealed to me strongly. Since my marriage at the time was crumbling, I took a certain interest in her and decided to look into her graduate records. She turned out to be a couple of years older than I, and she was indeed highly intelligent. I remember that she had scored at the 100th percentile on the Miller Analogies Test, which was then used as one of the criteria in terms of which prospective graduate students were evaluated. Her name was Ellen.

After the course was over, I found a way to establish personal contact with her. I quickly discovered that she was divorced, but was the mother of three children and was living in a rather large house in a nearby town. Somewhat to my dismay, I also learned that she had a boyfriend named Steven A., who had also been a student in my seminar. In fact, it was through Steve, with whom I had already became friendly and who remained a friend of mine for years afterward, that I had learned a bit about Ellen before I ever had a chance to visit her at her home.

I could see that she was very attached to Steve, and under the circumstances, I could hardly hope to have any kind of intimate relationship with Ellen. But we did become friends—I would visit both her and Steve at Ellen's home—and during those visits I was able to get to know Ellen quite well, up to a point.

She was indeed quiet, but deeply intelligent, sensitive and thoughtful. She had a very marked spiritual nature, and after it became obvious to her, without my having to say anything about it, that I had become very smitten with her (indeed I felt I had fallen in love with her), she gently steered the boat of my burgeoning but futile passion into spiritual waters toward the books that people were reading in those days (in the middle 60s), particularly the then popular books of Hermann Hesse. I remember she urged me to read such books as *Demian, Siddhartha* and *Steppenwolf.* Looking back on that time now, after a period fifty years, I can see that it was Ellen who first planted the seeds of my spiritual life into my psyche.

But Ellen was always somewhat vague and evasive about talking about her own life and particularly her family background. I knew that her mother was alive, that she had an older brother John, and that her late father, whom she never named, had had some kind of career as a writer or editor, I wasn't sure which. But one day, she alluded to the fact that he had worked for a well-known national magazine.

The next day, by some process of intuition I have never been able to grasp or explain, I suddenly was sure I knew who Ellen's father had been. I remember racing over to the university library and hunting up a copy of *Witness.* (I had never read the book, but I had heard of it.) Sure enough, in that foreword, I quickly saw that Chambers had mentioned the names of his children—Ellen and John. I already knew Ellen had a brother named John. Bingo!!

I then drove down to Ellen's house and burst in almost without knocking.

"I know you who are," I cried.

Ellen looked shocked, aghast.

"I mean, I know who your father was—Whittaker Chambers!"

Ellen became highly upset and couldn't speak for a few moments.

"You must never tell anyone," she told me solemnly.

I then learned about her secret life and why she had had to keep her identity a secret. Her father had often had cause to fear for his life and the life of his family, and Ellen was still scarred by the life of trauma and secrecy that she had been forced to live for some years growing up, and then, after her father's notoriety, of being caught in the limelight of the attention and opprobrium her father had received, hounded by reporters and others that had made the life of the Chambers family a nightmare. After her father's death, she had done everything to conceal her identify. Her surname was that of her ex-husband.

I swore I would tell no one, and for many years, I didn't.

As a result, however, I was able to forge a new kind of intimacy with Ellen in our friendship. I learned a lot about her earlier life and even met her mother. Because I shared in her secret life now, my love and admiration for her only grew, but there was never any physical intimacy between us. She didn't really love me, anyway, and was still living, on and off, with Steve. But we were close, in our fashion.

Ellen eventually graduated with her doctorate in clinical psychology and moved with her children to Vermont in order to practice psychotherapy there. We lost touch with each other.

Fast forward forty years.

I was now living in the San Francisco Bay Area. Somehow or other—I no longer remember how—I discovered that Ellen was now living in San Francisco. I was thrilled to discover she was still alive and living here. I tracked down her number and called her.

She was suspicious and wanted to know why I wanted to see her. I was astonished since it was only out of friendship, like finding a lost love, though, as I say, we were never lovers, and the love was always one-sided. But she was reassured and agreed to meet me at a restaurant in San Francisco.

She was old now—in her early 70s—and had developed the early stages of Parkinson's Disease. She had practiced therapy for a long time, but was winding down her practice. She had also been and was still an artist (she had a studio, which I visited more than once) but she made her living mainly in real estate. And she drove a truck! Well, she had grown up on a farm; I guess I shouldn't have been surprised.

I would drive into San Francisco fairly often to see her. Although I visited her in her home a couple of times, we mostly met in a non-descript pizza house in the north of the city, which was convenient for both of us. She would often bring a scrapbook or an old photograph album, and would tell me more stories about her family as well as about her present personal life. She had never again married, but she had had some lovers, though the last one had gone from her life by the time I met her. She was still close to her daughter, Pamela, whom I had met when she was a little girl, and when I met her as an adult, I could see how like the young Ellen she was. I could have easily fallen in love with her, too, though I was now an old man myself.

Ellen and I grew closer; a kind of love developed between us. Sitting together in the booth of the pizza house, she would playfully bump her shoulder against mine and laugh. Her hands would shake. She would grow quiet and inward.

I felt sad to see my friend decaying before my eyes.

She couldn't do e-mail but I would write to her when I couldn't arrange to see her. I still felt the same way about her as I did when I was that young professor. She was still dear to me.

Eventually, her Parkinson's became worse and she decided she needed to leave San Francisco with her daughter, and to move back to the family farm, which her brother, John, had maintained all these years. She was going back to die where she had grown up.

We stayed in touch by phone for a while, but after a time, I heard no more from her. I later learned that she did in fact die on her family's farm. Reading about Whittaker Chambers tonight reminded me of her, of course.

I found his book in my library and took a look at it once more. To my surprise, I found a card in it with a painting by Ellen of red roses against a yellow background. When I turned it over, I found a note in Ellen's hand. In red ink, she had written: "5/27/64 Ken, This should make things more understandable. Ellen."

~

The Queen and the Kike

In August, 1995, I was speaking at a conference in Hartford, Connecticut. After my talk, a dark-haired woman waited until others had left and then asked if we could talk about the research I had discussed. We adjourned to an outdoor picnic table and had a very animated discussion for forty-five minutes or so during which we found that we shared a number of professional interests. Afterward, I attended a talk she gave, and found that I was very drawn to her luminous intelligence and, to be candid, her beauty, which oddly enough, I hadn't noticed during our conversation.

After she returned to her home in Philadelphia, we began corresponding by e-mail, which was just coming into vogue. Indeed, she told me that she was "an e-mail virgin," and I joked that I was honored to be the first to visit her inbox.

Over the next couple of months, after exchanging many messages, which began with professional matters but soon turned personal, we found that we had fallen wildly in love.

There was only one problem. The woman I had fallen in love with was married! Shit!

Nevertheless, we resolved to meet in New York as soon as possible in order to see whether this was "the real thing" or just an epistolary romance.

November 5, 1995. Exactly three months to the day when we had first sat across from each other at that picnic table in Hartford, J. and I arranged to meet again. This time we chose a more romantic locale for our assignation: The Plaza Hotel. I remember that, despite all my excitement, fears and distractions of the past few days, I was feeling quite calm by the time I arrived at the Plaza. Somehow, inwardly, I felt assured that our meeting would be a success, and that it would confirm for both of us that what we had come to feel for each other was not mere fantasy or projection but was based on something solid, even if the form our relationship was yet to be determined.

I arrived first and waited for her, reading a book, standing with my back to one of the walls of the small ornately-decorated ante-chamber that leads directly to the Plaza lobby. It was, as usual, swarming with people, many of them ornately decorated themselves, who were pouring into and exiting from the hotel. I looked up from time to time, but only saw strangers hurrying by, none of them approaching me.

Suddenly, there she was—before I had seen her from a distance, she was standing directly in front of me as though she had been dropped there. She was shorter than I remembered, and her face was only vaguely familiar, but I did recognize her after all (it helped that she had told me what kind of a dress she would be wearing). I noticed that, over her dress, was some kind of fur wrap, which I thought was brave of her.

We didn't stay at the Plaza. Instead, we began walking down toward the part of town where J. had formerly lived—around 23rd Street. I remember several things from that long walk. Mostly I "interviewed" her, asking a long string of questions. (These were not premeditated—I hadn't really thought much about what I would say to her—they just seemed natural at the time.) I spent a long time asking her to tell me more about her family, and then inquired about her life in the business world that had brought her to New York in the first place. After that, it was an easy segue to what factors had led her to leave that world in order to pursue a new career as a scholar. Through our lengthy and somewhat meandering walk that day—it was early afternoon by then—the focus was entirely on her. During it, apart from listening to J., I noticed two curious aspects of her demeanor. One, she never looked at me directly. Second, her wrap kept slipping from her shoulder, and periodically I would have to gently return it to its proper perch. It was the only time I touched her.

Finally, as we were both getting hungry, we stopped at a

non-descript restaurant. I don't remember it exactly, but I think it was an ordinary Italian eatery of some kind. We sat in a booth (J. would have to look at me now, I thought). She ordered a Caesar salad, heavy on the anchovies. When I heard that, I couldn't help remarking that I myself could not abide anchovies. She gave me a look. I ordered some kind of a tofu dish, which caused J. to roll her eyes with dismay. And when she observed my table manners, or perhaps I should say my lack of them, she could barely conceal her disdain and was forced to avert her eyes. I could see that she must have thought she was sharing a meal with the rudest sort of peasant.

Of course, when two potential lovers get together, it is natural that they would try to explore what they had in common. Clearly, it didn't seem to be our taste in food. J.'s, it became obvious, was very refined and she was very knowledgeable about a great variety of relatively exotic foods and interested in their preparation. I was the equivalent of a steak-and-potatoes man, though I didn't eat meat—I ate tofu, as all real men do, I told her, as indeed she had just seen with her own eyes. J. looked appalled but held her tongue.

I started in, finally taking the floor, to declare some of my own interests. For one thing, I told her I loved classical music. She had a tin ear, she said. Well, there's always Cole Porter, I countered. "Who's he?" she asked (and she meant it; she truly didn't know the name). She loved Old English; I had heard of it, I said. I was fond of Woody Allen; "I can't stand him," said J. And so it went. She was an 18th century person and identified with the French aristocracy during the ancien regime, with Louis XIV being her king of kings. I had no use for the 18th century, but only for the 19th after the overthrow of the aristocracy. My leanings were always toward the oppressed and with the artists of that period; we would have been on opposite sides of the barricades had we lived in France in revolutionary times. As far as America was concerned, J. was deeply wedded to the South and its genteel antebellum traditions—for her, living on a plantation, with an abundance of slaves and servants, was her natural milieu. I, by contrast, was a deracinated Jew (and Yankee) whose forebears were trying to avoid being enslaved while J's were overseeing their own. What I called the "Civil War," she called—reprovingly—"The War of Northern Aggression."

I tried a different, less freighted, tack. "What about avocations," I asked. "I played a lot of cards, especially bridge, when I was younger, how about you?" J. looked at me, almost as though I had committed a gaffe of some kind. And then tartly informed me that she wasn't competitive, never played cards or any board games at all, for that matter. "Sports?," I asked, without conviction, after confessing that I was an ardent Red Sox fan. "No interest in sports at all, I'm afraid. If you ever dragged me to a baseball game, I would have my nose buried in a book the whole time."

After about five minutes of this futility, I remember we exchanged a look that said, in effect, "this is hopeless—we have nothing in common!" Not just that, but we often seemed to be an antipodes as well. I do recall a sinking feeling inside of me that perhaps an epistolary love affair was all that we would ever have, and maybe even that would now lose its luster since we were discovering the gulf—nay, abyss—that seemed to separate us with regard to our tastes, interests and values.

But, still, we had come to meet each other and to talk, so we soldiered on. After the debacle in that restaurant, we walked for a while further and eventually, in part to avoid the cold, we stopped in at a coffee shop for some further refreshments. During this time, I was sharing more of my personal stories with J. and, despite our divergent worldviews, she seemed to listen to them with interest, even absorption. I felt somewhat heartened, but still unsure where all this was going to take us. We had not broached any matters having to do with the future our own relationship.

Finally, since it had now grown dark, we decided to have a drink, before parting for the evening, at the Grand Hyatt Hotel, next to Grand Central Station. We found a small table and each of us sat with our drinks, talking about our pending arrangements for the evening and where to meet the next day. At one point, I was sitting with my hands before me on the table, holding them together in an inverted-V formation, when suddenly J. took them in hers—it was the first time she had even touched me—and blurted out these exact words: "I can never leave you!"

I was stunned, and I think J. was, too. I looked at her. She obviously was dead serious. It was as if when she clasped my hands in hers, she was giving herself totally to me, committing herself to me, though these thoughts only came afterward. After our whole day together—by then we had talked for more than 8 hours straight—everything was summed up and completed in that one impulsive gesture.

We would have to talk about this later—it was too much for the time we had left. We both had to call the people we were staying with to advise them we would be arriving soon. I paid our bill and we got up to leave the table, with J. leading the way. I saw something then that I had not observed before when J. had been walking beside me or sitting opposite me. She had a regal air—she walked like a queen. It was just a glimpse but it afforded an immediate, and, as it turned out, an accurate realization of J.'s archetypal nature. She really was royalty, and I could see it in her carriage.

We adjourned to a corridor where there were both phones and restrooms, and we made use of each. I was standing to one side, after making my call, when J., having completed hers, came up to me. She raised to her face toward mine, as if to kiss me, and I bent down to meet her lips. I kissed her gently, partially because I was self-conscious since finely dressed women and elegant gentlemen were swirling around us, and, I'm sure, staring at us. J. continued to kiss me, more passionately now.

I could hardly believe what was happening. Here, this woman of such obvious decorum and self-proclaimed "good breeding" had totally surrendered to her feelings and was acting heedless of our surroundings. I had to think fast.

"Come with me," I said, and, taking her by the hand, led her around the corner. I had no idea where I was going.

Suddenly, providentially, I spotted an alcove with—of all

things—a screen. We ducked behind it, and then starting kissing passionately, like hormone-driven adolescents. I felt I needed to keep my head while J. was apparently losing hers. Before things had gone much further, I said, "J., really, we can't do this here. We have to stop." With reluctance she agreed, and we gathered ourselves before returning to the hotel corridor.

We parted shortly afterward, each of us taking a cab to our respective destinations, after agreeing to meet back at the Hyatt the next day for breakfast....

That was the beginning. She kept her word. She has never left me, even after we ceased to be lovers after ten years. The Queen and the Kike.

~

The Girl of My Dreams

My girlfriend Lauren and I met online in March, 2015, just as she was about to leave her home in Piedmont, California in order to join her son, Rob, a flight surgeon in the Navy, in Florida where he was to get his "wings." Lauren is, like me, an e-mail junkie, and in the first month of our correspondence, before we had met, we exchanged no fewer than 200 messages, some quite lengthy. I had obviously met my match and the epistolary girl of my dreams. We fell in love writing to each other, but of course we didn't even know each other—we were only words on a screen. All she knew about me by then was that I had apparently been married a dozen times and had had innumerable affairs. I feared this one would turn out to be an affair to dismember.

Lauren is a therapist and like all therapists she had been seeing one for years. Of course, it's a game all therapists play—a racket, in my jaundiced opinion, but never mind. In any case, I imagined the dialogue that would take place when Lauren finally got back home and had a chance to have her next appointment with her therapist.

I call her E. here, which stands for Eliza, my pet name for

her, as I often play the insufferable Henry Higgins when we are together....

T. Let's see if I can get this straight, Eliza. Are you telling me that you've fallen in love with an old man—pushing 80—that you've never met and have only corresponded with for the last couple of weeks or so?

E. I know it sounds mad....

T. (interrupting). And that he's a Jewish retired professor who has apparently made a career of studying arrant nonsense like near-death experiences and other such pap?

E. Well, I haven't had a chance to look into any of that yet.

T. You mean you only have his word for all this? You haven't even Googled him?

E. I really haven't had time. I've been so busy.

T. Not so busy that you apparently, according to what you told me over the phone, couldn't be writing to him night and day, dozens of e-mail notes and letters, isn't that true?

E. Well, yes, but....

T. (Interrupting again). And didn't you tell me that this old coot has, according to what he's told you, had innumerable lovers and at least four, maybe five, wives already?

E. He's admitted that. He seems pretty honest....

T. Ha! Eliza, don't be naïve. He sounds like an amatory serial killer to me. What in hell are you thinking? That you'll be number 25?

T. (continuing, as Eliza has fallen mute). And didn't you tell me that this guy is, to put it gently, visually challenged and possibly now suffering from some kind of neurological impairment? Are you so addled and besotted that you have forgotten what you went through all those years with Michael?

E. Well, don't I at least deserve a few years of happiness before I die? This man really loves me. I know it and I trust what he says.

T. You know what they say about love, Eliza—that it's blind. Didn't you admit to me that in a loose and unwise moment—maybe when you had drunk too much—that you had indicated to him that you were well-off financially?

E. Well, yes, but....

T. That you even unwisely, for God knows what reason, told him about the diamond mines in your family?

E. I just blurted it out. I know I probably shouldn't have mentioned it.

T. Good Lord, Eliza. How do you know that this Ken is not like some character out of a Henry James novel and is just after your money? What do you know about his financial circumstances?

E. It's never come up. Besides....

T. (Interrupting again). Have you even talked to anyone who knows this man? Anyone who can vouch for him? What about those ex-wives of his? I bet they could give you an earful.

E. (crying). Please—you just don't know him. If you could read what he writes to me.

T. Really, Eliza, anyone can write anything. And a seductive guy like him could easily tell you exactly what you want to hear. For Chrissake, you haven't even met the guy—not that that would answer most of these questions—and you're already almost ready to shack up with him?

E. Don't put it that way. It's so vulgar.

T. I think I've said enough for now. Please think about what I've said and please don't do anything rash. If you decide to explore this, despite all the warning signs and cautions I've mentioned, don't make any decisions without first consulting me, all right? Do you agree?

E. (Reluctantly) All right.

T. I'll see you next time. Better make it in a week before you run off to Mexico with your inamorato.

~

Well, Lauren never ran off with me to Mexico, but she did take up with me after all despite her reasonable doubts about my amatory history and character. And I can say honestly and truly, I have never been happier with any relationship I have ever had. Lauren is a blessing to me in every way, and guess what, she is not only a superlative cook, a veritable Eloise around the house, but she is literate, charming, fun to be with (in bed and outside of it), and eminently educable. (I have been conducing a remediable film course for her for the past five years since that is one lamentable lacuna in her background.) And you what else? She loves to laugh. She writes very amusing e-mail, too. She is a master of drollery and le aperçu juste. Occasionally, she even appreciates my sense of humor, though I do sometimes have the feeling she is laughing at me and just humoring me about my quirky sense of humor. Anything to make the girl of my dreams happy.

And I'll tell you something else. Five of so years before I met Lauren, when I was unhappy with my last relationship, I made out a list of what I desire in a woman. Here's what I wrote at the time.

What I Want (and Don't) in a Relationship

1. Shared intellectual interests—in music, literature, art, film, politics, history, Palestine, near-death experiences, spirituality, sports, etc.
    a. Especially going to classical music concerts, opera, the movies, and eating out.
    b. And is physically active and basically in good health.
2. Appreciation for my writing and need to write.
3. Someone who is fun to be with—light, funny, romantic.
    a. Someone whose company I delight in and with whom I can have lively and intellectually rewarding conversation.
    b. And to whom I am sexually attracted.
    c. And has a good, preferably quirky, sense of humor.
4. Passion.
5. Someone who is monogamous, loyal, trustworthy, fundamentally honest and true-blue.
6. Someone who can drive at night.
7. Someone who can cook.
8. Someone who appreciates how much my friendships,

especially my friendships with women, mean to me and who is not jealous of them.

9. Someone who respects my need to be alone at times.
   a. And who would be OK with my retaining my own place to live.
10. Someone who has her own creative life, her own circle of friends and is basically independent.
11. Someone who can tolerate my eccentric ways and bodily preoccupations.
12. Someone who, if necessary, could be a good caretaker and who, if the situation calls for it, could be nurturant.
13. Someone who likes or at least can get along with my friends and family.
14. Someone who can be happy with mostly intra-California and domestic traveling—which is not to say that some traveling abroad wouldn't be possible, my health permitting.
15. Someone who is basically self-supporting.

And guess what again? Lauren satisfies every one of these criteria. That's why I say she's my dream girl. I dreamed her up, and now I have the girl of my dreams.

April Fool

In early April, 1993, I received a curious letter. It was from someone I had never heard of, though the writer appeared to live in my town, Storrs, Connecticut, where I taught at the university, judging from the return address post office box on the envelope. On reading the letter, which was short and to the point, I became convinced that, despite its seeming to be a kind of fan letter, it was actually a hoax perpetrated by one of my prank-loving friends. Intrigued, I brought the letter home that day to show to Sonja, my girlfriend at the time.

Dated (revealingly enough, I thought) April 1, it read:

Dear Ken Ring,
Well, I have decided, I have to write to you. For a long time I have been wanting to do so. I have discovered you here, so close, but I could never make myself write to you. I could not tell you that your book moved me because it was not the book that did. And I couldn't say you did because I didn't really know you! However, I did. I did know you and not because I know of your life. (I have, by chance, known of you and of things about you). But today I woke up and I thought of you as if I had known you for ages. This is why I am writing finally; because I know you, I know I can write to you. And because we cannot ignore an old friend. Who are you really? And who is the man who writes your books? Tell me about you, if you will.

(I was on the verge of telling you all about me. But I
hesitated one second too long and I found myself without
the courage to do so.)
As ever,

PS: Yes, there is a lot to be said about my name....

Her letter was signed with a single letter—the letter "T"—but
her postscript drew my attention even more forcibly to her unusual
name. Gazing at it for just a moment, I saw that her first and last
name made a perfect anagram for the name of my favorite pen, a
brand I had been using for some years—Pilot Razor. In fact, my
fondness for this kind of pen was so well known to my friends that
Sonja had made a practice of buying them for me at Christmas in
sets of ten or so, and then plying my Christmas stocking with them.
Thanks to her, I never ran out of them or had to concern myself
with buying my own.

Furthermore, a fellow who used to be a housemate of mine and
who had worked for me on my research on near-death experiences
when I was just starting out in this field—and who was also an
inveterate practical joker—shared my proclivity for this brand of
pen and was long familiar with my own addiction to it. From the
coyness of this letter, and the way in which the writer had called
attention to her name (though I was by now convinced that the
"her" was actually a "him"), I was certain this letter was written
by my friend. It was in short a tease and a lure to suck me into
writing my usual reply to a fan letter. Except this time, I would
be replying to a fictitious person and eventually be exposed as a
credulous fool. Here, the April 1 date was another obvious clue
pointing to my friend's shenanigans and his aim.

Well, he had been a little too obvious for me, and I wasn't
falling for it.

Proud of my clever sleuthing, I explained all this to Sonja. She remained a bit skeptical; she still thought it might be on the level. However, I already knew how I was going to reply, and a few days later, I sent this note to my whimsical correspondent, making sure also to date it April 1.

Dear T. [though I spelled out her name, deliberately mis-spelling it, however],
Your letter was certainly to the point, if you catch my meaning [the full name of my favorite pen was Pilot Razor Point], and was razor-sharp in its frankness. The only thing that really surprised me, after not hearing from you for so long, was that you didn't pen your letter to me.

No matter, I am prepared to tell all about myself, even though you already seem to know many things about me. However, since I can't take the time to reveal all this infor-mation in a single letter, I will begin with just an item or two that few of my friends are aware of.

First, though, I have a question for you: Does the expression, "Detroit Tigers," by any chance, have any special meaning for you? [My friend was an ardent fan of this team.]

Now, to my promised disclosures. Although my name sounds Anglo-Saxon, I am actually descended from an old French family whose roots I have been able to trace to 11th century Marseille. The only indication of my Gallic ancestry, however, is in the nickname my parents gave me as a child. They called me their "petit Pinot," and so I'll sign myself to you.
As always,
Pinot (AKA Ken Ring)

I sent my smug little riposte off with pleasure, confident that I had flushed out my friend and wondering only whether he would reply with a jocular confession of his own. A little over a week later, I had my answer.

April 16, 1993

Dear Ken Ring,

For many reasons your letter surprised me. But let me first tell you what happened after I wrote to you.

I knew you would have received my letter on Friday because I mailed it on Thursday. To my own surprise, that entire weekend I found myself thinking very often about the letter and your reading it. Also to my surprise, I found myself fearing that you wouldn't reply, but I knew you would. But I didn't expect to read what I read.

You said that you had not heard from me for so long. If it wasn't for some other parts of your letter, this would have astonished me beyond measure! Every time I look at your letter part of me wants to read it to mean that you also know me, in the same way I meant it in my letter to you. But other portions of your letter cast a shadow on that and it gives me the desire to ask you to clarify what you mean. However, I will not, and I will tell you later why. I will just leave it at that—that for some reason you think that I am someone else perhaps: you say that I normally handwrite my letters to you, you misspelled my name (on purpose?) and put quotation marks around it on the envelope (or perhaps this is an example of what I meant when I told you that there was a lot to be said about my name; you don't know how much I have heard about it, to the point of having had the desire to change it). I also found it interesting that your letter was dated April 1, as mine was. I wonder if perhaps when you were reading my letter you wrote the same date by mistake? And last, although I don't know why you asked, I want to reply to your question, no, the expression you wrote doesn't have any special meaning for me.

Now, why I don't want to dwell too much on this subject. My writing to you came after a very long time of soul searching and of trying to understand so many things about my life and about life. It was an important moment for me, an important moment of decision, which, I thought, would bring me something also as important. I don't want to close the door of that dialogue which I know we can have (because I know how you write and somewhat who you are from what you write) to let unimportant little things take over. This is too important for me. Maybe one day you will tell me what you meant and perhaps I will see that they are not unimportant nor little. But for now, I just want to continue to write to you, I want you to know me, even though I still (and even more now, after your letter) waver at this thought. I want us to exchange what I know we can.

You spoke of your French heritage. I cannot make myself call you by your nickname, you have been Ken Ring for a long time for me now, but thank you for sharing it with me. I don't have any, believe it or not, but people often mispronounce my name. I can tell you of my heritage too, if you are interested. It is different, I suppose, than most Americans, but I am sure you know people from everywhere. For a great part of my life I lived in a beautiful very small city by a lake in South America, where the only exciting things that happened outwardly were the great festivals with flute players and colorful dresses that the men and women wore as they danced joyfully on the streets, while the moon shone magically on the lake. These memories often return to me in such vivid colors and feelings that sometimes I think I am there again, looking at all of it as a painting of an unforgettable scene. So much of what was there was so much purer than anything I have encountered in my life ever since.

There is so much more I can say about that place and the people that live there and their wonderful stories. There is also much I want to say about many other things. Yet, I hesitate because I fear I will never hear from you again, although you replied to my letter. Will you trust me? Please do. I don't know who my letter might have reminded you of or what hesitation you might have had when you wrote your letter, but I hope they are gone now. I find solace in your book so often, and it helps me. Thank you. And thank you for answering my letter. How are you these days? Is there anything that crosses your mind this moment, or that has crossed your desk or your eyes lately that you would want to share with me?

As ever,

T.

Of course, I was disconcerted by this reply, and puzzled by it too. I had been so sure I had spotted the trickster hand of my friend in T.'s first letter, but my confidence was shaken a bit by her second letter. I wondered whether I was being had even more ingeniously. After all, my friend was a gifted writer himself (he is now a professor of English), and he was perfectly capable of pulling off such a stunt. Uncertain now of my ground, I decided I would explain myself and then issue a new challenge to my correspondent

April 21, 1993

Dear T.,

An explanation, then:

The date of your letter, April 1 = April Fool's Day (a day, as you must know, when people play practical jokes on one another). Hence, I dated my letter—also a joke, as I will shortly explain—April 1, too.

Your remarkable name is, as you must also surely be aware, a perfect anagram for "Pilot Razor," which happens to be the name of my favorite pen. Indeed, I have used this brand exclusively for years, a fact with which a fair number of my friends are well familiar. One of these friends, with whom I lived for two years, is also addicted to these pens and has a wry sense of humor. He and I also share an interest in baseball but root for different teams, his favorite being the Detroit Tigers. Finally, the full name of the pen in question is "Pilot Razor Point." With this information, you can now decode the remainder of my letter. Take for example, the opening paragraph:

"Your letter was certainly to the point, if you catch my meaning, and was razor-sharp in its frankness. The only thing that really surprised me, after not hearing from you for so long, was that you didn't pen your letter to me."

Thinking that my old friend may have sent this (i.e., your) letter to me as a joke, I naturally raised the question, "Does the expression, "Detroit Tigers," by any chance, have any special meaning for you?"

Finally, as to the paragraph about my French ancestry (also fictitious, by the way), that was all an elaborate pretext to arrive at a false nickname, "Pinot," which as you will now understand, is simply a way of completing the full anagram—"Pinot" being of course an anagram for point.

Naturally, I was a bit disconcerted when I received your second letter. I had two immediate reactions. One, my God, maybe her first letter was actually completely on the level, and not a prank after all! And, second, maybe this is turning out to be a very elaborate prank, and my leg is being pulled nearly out of its socket.

Wanting to determine which of these was true, I actually called the local post office to see whether a person with your name was listed as having your P. O. Box. That was confirmed. Hmm, I thought. Score one point for the first alternative (though the second could still be true).

I read your letter a second time. I dug out your original letter and re-read that. You are either, I thought, someone with an exquisite sense of humor or, and possibly more likely, someone who is remarkably direct, sincere, and with a capacity for immediate and deep intimacy.

This time, I thought a little more before writing you. It comes down to this: I think I must know who you are before writing to you further. Since you live in Storrs (or at least your mail box does), I invite you to come to speak to me in my office at the university. I hold office hours Monday and Tuesday from 4-5. If you prefer to call first, and, if I should not be there, you are welcome to leave a message. If you'd rather write again, that's all right, but another letter will not necessarily serve to answer my questions about you the way an in-person visit would.

In any case, your two letters have given me much to think about. Whether the laugh is on me, or whether this is no laughing matter, I won't be able to determine, I think, until you show up in person. That is the thought, you see, that crosses my mind at this moment of still lingering uncertainty.

As ever what?

Two days later, I was forced to surrender. I had been an April fool, all right, but not in the way I had ever imagined. Instead, Sonja, as usual, had been right all along.

April 23, 1993

Dear Ken,

For the second time, I was surprised beyond words when I saw your name on the envelope. So soon! But I was even more surprised when I opened the letter and read its contents. You actually called the Post Office to make sure I exist! But I understand now that you truly believed (or may still, unfortunately) that my letters are not from me but from someone who wanted to play a joke on you. Ever since I read your first letter, I have remembered once in a while the enigma of some of the things you wrote, but I have tried not to think about that. And now that you explained it, even deeper questions come to my mind. But again I find myself not wanting to detract from the "me" that has come out from reading your book and from what it has given me. I want to keep these letters and, most importantly, I want to keep myself, at least in this contact, where your book has placed me. I understand why you want to resolve what you think is a puzzle. For me it is different, of course, for I am sure who I am! But there is another aspect. And that is that it may be a temptation for me to want to know why this happened, in the bigger picture. But that can quickly and easily lead to my getting involved in an illusionary speculation about why an unexplainable string of events is connected with my letters. Although I myself am not free from illusions, this moment in my life, rather, my decision to write to you is too important for me to let it fall into the endless complications of life. This is why I cannot allow myself to fall into the usual traps I know only too well. I understand very well, however, that this doesn't help you but I wanted to take the time (and a very long paragraph!) to at least try to explain to you a little of what (me) you, of course, don't know yet.

For the same reason, I must decline your offer to meet you in person. Because I know that this will not help resolve matters for you, I feel you deserve an explanation. First of all, I wouldn't be able to meet you in your office since I am rarely around during the day and there are other complications in my life that may prevent me from doing this at this time. But even if these weren't issues, something in me is resisting this idea very much. I don't understand it myself completely, but I have a feeling of what it may be. My writing to you was a very important part of a series of events that seemed to have been perfectly planned in time and space, so to speak. And their unquestionable wisdom has clearly shown me the vital importance of letting things follow their course naturally. In other words, if you're thinking that my letter was a joke hadn't happened, you probably would not have invited me to speak to you in person. This is not the reason I would want you to want to know me. I understand, however, that you feel that another letter of mine will not necessarily serve to answer your questions about me the way an in-person visit would. All I can say now is that if my position can be acceptable to you at least for the time being, I can assure you that you will know me much more than you would if we met in person. I do ask you to believe me.

By the way, thank you very much for your lengthy explanation and for replying so soon. I am sorry that my letters have caused you to feel the way you did. And thank you for what you said about my directness and capacity for intimacy. To hear you say this is almost a contradiction in itself. My life for a while now has been so removed from this. But you, of course, as you did with your book, have not only brought this self of me out but have seen it where I myself have almost completely forgotten it. When I read what you wrote, it reminded me of my childhood and of how almost everything was filled with connections from the inside out and yes, you are so right, everything was so clear, so direct. I remember when I was once walking on the streets of Copa one night, and I was smelling the sweetness of the flowers. I was wearing a hat even though it was night because I loved that hat. It had been given to me by a tourist sometime before. She was a wonderful woman and I caught her looking at me with such tender eyes, as if recognizing me. I was filled with amazement, but also fear. But when she approached me and touched my face softly, all I felt was an indescribable love for her. She looked at me, her eyes were large and black and were shining like the moon. She came down to me and looked deeply at me again, then she left, slowly walking in the wind. I knew I would see her again and I did. That was in the morning. In the afternoon, with the scorching sun silencing everything (the sun there becomes almost unbearable at about 4 or 5 pm), she appeared again and was holding a beautiful round hat, off-white, with a border to protect my face from the sun, some little delicate flowers all over it and a ribbon of many colors dancing in the wind. She gently put the hat on my head and smiled with such delight that I felt something melting inside of me. I knew then that I would never part with that hat although I knew that I couldn't part with it. She seemed to have said something, her voice was like the lake, very deep and very soft. I don't know what she said but it didn't matter then. I never saw her again, but her face is forever etched in my memory. If I were a painter, I would paint her; in my memory of her she is wearing the hat she gave me.

But back to my walking down the street one night, it was like the wind was talking with me. I had heard a lot about the sacred islands that were near our city. You must have heard of them, the Island of the Sun and the Island of the Moon, on Titicaca Lake. My father used to take tourists to these islands on his little boat. He would wake up very early in the morning while it was still dark (the tourists had to, too, and they didn't like it, but did it anyway) to prepare the boat and they would all leave before dawn. Sometimes, he would tell me, there was a soft rain falling and he would inwardly laugh knowing that it would go away as soon as the sun would come up, but the tourists didn't know and, of course, were not happy about it. Except for that one woman, of whom he told me the story. And it was the same woman who gave me that beautiful hat. I was sure it was her. It had to be. He said she sat on the boat, apart from the others, she was quiet and seemed to be elsewhere, but at the same time was very present. At times, she would lift her head and feel the soft drops of water on her face as if she was receiving the morning dew (my father had a wonderful way of telling stories). I knew it was my lady.

I don't seem to be able to ever talk about that walk I had at night. Well, I was thinking of my father's stories then and of the immense figures of our old Indian warriors that adorned almost every place in the city and I felt a tremendous desire to visit those islands. Also a tremendous fear. (You have noticed by now, probably, that fear often accompanies some of my most significant experiences.) Yet I knew I had to tell my father that the time had come. I was still very little. He looked at me and silently nodded, I could almost read his thoughts but I couldn't understand their meaning, they were deep and had symbols and it was as if each of his thoughts was embracing me. I felt a complete protection and ... an indomitable fear. He said nothing then. But sometime later he told me to get ready as he would take me with him in the morning. He had waited until there were no tourists. Why, I came to understand only later—but I don't know how he knew that it had to be exactly that way. I just know he knew and that he planned it that way, but he never told me so. He took me to his boat. I had taken with me water, a little bag with small boiled potatoes, and my precious hat.

I jumped into the boat and immediately stepped into a different world. The fog that preceded dawn was enveloping me and I thought I started hearing a very soft melodious sound coming from everywhere. I felt the same stillness my lady had felt. It was almost as if she had done it that way for me to know how when the time came. Who was she, who so briefly yet so deeply touched my life? As we arrived at the first island, la Isla del Sol, I knew that my father would not come with me, and he didn't. We had barely spoken on the boat but he made me know that he would be waiting for me there on the boat when I was ready to leave. I turned to the island the moment my feet touched the ground and, again, I stepped into an even more different world, of which I have never spoken before to anyone. But I know I will to you one day, maybe even now, somewhat. And my father knew of this world; he was of those places himself; I know. He always seemed to have part of himself elsewhere, deeper somewhere. My heart seemed to grow out of myself and it was as if it was drawing me to a place, I could call it home but it really wasn't, except that it knew where it was going. I also knew where I was going and for a brief moment I knew everything that would happen and come to me there and I just went through the motions, only to fulfill it all. The island is very small. I ran up the hill and the sunshine flooded me (did the lady know all that would happen? The importance of the hat on that sunny day on that place that only she, my father and I seemed to understand?).

I spent the day (minutes, days?) walking around the island like any other girl would, discovering corn plants and all sorts of greenery, but the strange thing was that there didn't seem to be anybody in the island and my father was so unconcerned about what would happen to me (he probably knew the island so well). Even the one boy I saw working on the land at one point seemed to be part of a landscape separate from mine and we never acknowledged each other. One place that drew me immediately was a little house on the top and edge of one of the high places of the island. It wasn't a house. It was a round (actually it was a polygon, perhaps eight or even ten sides), one large room, with windows all around from half the height of the wall up, just enough for me to place my hands on the sills and look out to the waters of the lake. There was nothing inside, yet it was so welcoming and warm and there was so much light. I would return to that place many times in my life, although sometimes not via the boat. After a while, that day, I understood the meaning that that place had for me, and I realized that that island was a gift to me from my father. It was my own island. But I didn't know how to thank him, what could I give him that would make him know that I understood his beautiful gift and his love for me that inspired it? At that moment lying on the stony and grassy incline of the little hill, I felt I could even give him my hat and somehow, when I thought that, I felt that my lady, my father, the hat, the island, and me, were already all united forever in one indecipherable magical way. And I knew I didn't have to give him the hat. But I still wanted to, so when I took my hat off to give it to him, he turned to me and looked at me and touched my arm and he came down to me and kissed me on my head. I could feel his face in my hair and I don't know how long it lasted but when he came up again and looked at me; I knew what he would do. He took my hat and gently placed it on my head, as the lady had done. And I knew he understood everything.

Yes, you made me remember that this is possible, that this is still possible.

All the best to you. I promise I will make it up to you somehow.

As ever

T.

T.'s letter was a turning point for me, but in the sense that I couldn't turn back. Too much was happening inside of me—an explosion of the heart. Because of Sonja's jealousy of my relationships with women and her fear that I become too intimately involved with them in my communications, I also decided not to tell her about T.'s letters. And when, predictably, she asked about her, I lied, pretending I hadn't heard anything further. Instead, in the now secret chamber of a private study I had at the university, I wrote her of my own fears—and of my love for her.

April 28, 1993

Dear T.,

You realize of course that a certain kind of love is inevitable between us. Indeed, it was already there in your first letter, extended to me in your opening sentence which was like a sudden unexpected embrace in the night from a mysterious stranger. As you know, I thought you were someone else, merely pretending, and I dismissed it. Your second letter startled me and threw me into confusion. You latest letter caused me to give up my defenses and suspicions, to trust that you are not, after all, deceiving me, and to believe you are who you say you are. Once these walls of resistance collapsed, I could open to you completely, which is love.

Should I explain myself more fully? I hardly think I need to, but for me who has listened so much to the sacred stories people have felt moved to tell me, I have come to understand that to know a person in this manner is a form of love no less intimate than that between lovers. The only difference is that it is purely word-built, but it still creates a private world between two people and becomes hallowed ground. If one enters into a person (and that world) in this way with full openness to whatever comes forth, it can only be both an expression and a consequence of the love and trust that exist between them. You have evoked that response from me by what you have written.

You were right, instinctively right, in deciding not to see me in my office. There is no need. I have only one request to make of you in this respect, one assurance to ask. Since, at least for now and perhaps for the duration of our correspondence, we shall not meet, can you at least promise me this: that my letters to you will remain private? Of course, here I must and will rely on your word. I only ask that you give it to me in friendship.

My fear: that you will cause an upheaval in my

emotional and personal life. My second fear: that I may need this upheaval in order to find a solid ground for my life again. My third fear: that you will disappear from my life as suddenly as you entered it. My fourth fear: that you will not.

Whatever my fears, I know and accept you are writing for me for reasons that are important to you and which, in time, I will become aware of. I also understand that there are things you already wish to tell me and they will, too, will be revealed in time. To what extent our correspondence will become a mutual exchange, as opposed to my chiefly receiving you in whatever way you wish to share your life with me, will depend on factors I have no means to assess right now.

I know about Lake Titicaca; I have read about it and I have friends who have been there. Though I will of course leave it entirely to you what to write about, I would like to know more about your life there. It seems important, that it is a key to your character, sensibility and life. You write like a combination of Gabriel Maria Marquez and Jamaica Kincaid, which is to say beautifully, evocatively, hauntingly, and with an awareness of how easily the worlds blend into each other and everything is redolent with significance and magical portent. Are you, then, a writer yourself?

Some practical and personal considerations: We are in the last few weeks of the semester, which is a fearfully busy time for me. Once it is over, I have to prepare for a trip to Italy. My summer will be busy, too, with professional trips to Canada and Australia. My correspondence is voluminous, and my frequent extended absences make it worse. I also need to spend time on my writing. Please take all this into account in writing to me. You can be sure I will read your letters (your latest one I have already read three times over), but I may not always be able to reply.

My personal life, like yours apparently, is complicated

and demanding. If I were free of commitments, it would be easier for me to receive and respond to you, but as it is, I must balance my emotional availability to others with the obligations I have already taken upon myself. Love doesn't have limits, but, alas, I, as a person, do. That has always been the agony of my life.

Write to me when and as you will.
In friendship, then.

Thus began the most important relationship of my life. In the three years we corresponded regularly, T. became the most important person in my life. No one ever had a greater impact on me than she did. She transformed me at a radical level through her searing insights into my character and by the impeccability of her perfect, unconditional love. At one point in one of her letters to me, she said "I will give you everything." She did.

We never met. I never learned much of anything about her—why she was living in Storrs, how old she was, what she looked like, how she could know me in the way she did, why she chose to write to me, and why she loved me so.

We stopped writing to each other only after I moved back to California. We were complete. I have not heard a word from her since nor have I tried to write to her. I have no idea where she is now or what has become of her. But I know what has become of me because of her.

A few years after moving to California, I wrote a long epistolary book about T., which ran 629 pages. You have just read its antic beginning and how it so quickly became the most important and even sacred correspondence of my life.

Made in the USA
Middletown, DE
30 September 2021